The Thought War

The Thought War
Japanese Imperial Propaganda

Barak Kushner

University of Hawai'i Press
Honolulu

Library of Congress Cataloging-in-Publication Data

Kushner, Barak.
 The thought war : Japanese imperial propaganda / Barak Kushner.
  p. cm.
 Includes bibliographical references and index.
 ISBN-13: 978-0-8248-2920-9 (hardcover : alk. paper)
 ISBN-13: 978-0-8248-3208-7 (pbk : alk. paper)
 1. Japan—History—1926–1945.   2. Propaganda, Japanese.
3. Sino-Japanese Conflict, 1937–1945—Propaganda.   4. Sino-Japanese
Conflict, 1937–1945—Psychological aspects.   5. World War,
1939–1945—Propaganda.   6. World War, 1939–1945—
Psychological aspects.   I. Title.
 DS888.5.K895 2006
 940.54'88752—dc22

         2005015648

Designed by the University of Hawai'i Press production staff

Printed by The Maple-Vail Book Manufacturing Group

Contents

Acknowledgments

Any author undertaking a long project owes a heavy debt of gratitude to his family. Through health and sickness, with unwavering support even when they doubted what exactly I was doing all the time in Asia, my parents and sisters remained steadfast in championing my research and travels. Professors Rudy Binion and Steve Whitfield offered insightful comments, criticism, and compliments, urging me beyond what I thought I was capable of producing as an undergraduate at Brandeis University. Only a true martyr like Rudy would have corrected every page of my undergraduate thesis, although sometimes I think it was actually because he liked the cookies I served at the film series that went along with the research. I must also thank my long-suffering high school French teacher, Annie Sokolov. She should know that only her patience set me on the path that eventually led to this book. Even bad students can sometimes turn out okay, Annie!

Initial graduate study with Professors George Wilson and Kenneth Wells at Indiana University proved stimulating. Their generous funding allowed me to take larger steps into historical questions and use challenging sources in original languages. My fellow students Charles Andrews, John Clayton, and Margaret Key provided solace in those early "dark years." My initial time in Japan would have ended much earlier than planned had it not been for the humor and warm hospitality of the Shimizu family, especially Oshōsan and Noriko, in Yamada village in Iwate prefecture. They opened their Zen temple to me and fed me virtually every meal for a year. Magariyama Rumiko and Professor Reinier Hesselink encouraged me that foreigners actually could learn Japanese, and Reinier tendered constant counseling concerning how to accomplish research in Japan. I am eternally grateful. Alan Singerman, professor of French literature at Davidson College, probably still cannot fathom how his class on French film nurtured my interest in Japanese history, but I owe him a debt of gratitude for his unwavering assistance in the study of French. Years later he became a colleague at Davidson College and that old relationship grew into friendship.

Attending Professor Awaya Kentarō's graduate seminars at Rikkyo University on modern Japanese history and the "Friday evening seminars" turned out to be a major key to future success. In the course of time my fellow graduate students there, Nakazono Yutaka, Nagai Hitoshi, Chatani Seiichi, Yoshi-tsugu Kōsuke, and others, provided assistance, ably transforming my stilted Japanese prose into something representative of intelligible commentary. Akagawa Hiroaki's introduction to whale meat and the joys of the history of publishing in Japan brightened up many Tokyo evenings. Other scholars at the Study for Media History meetings, Professors Ariyama Teruo, Satō Masaharu, and Yamaguchi Makoto, allowed me to present my work, as did Professors Kitagawa Kenzō, Yoshimi Shunya, Akazawa Shirō, and Yoshida Yutaka, at their various study groups. I would also like to thank Inoue Yūko for providing access to the archives at Ritsumeikan University and explaining to me her own research on wartime advertising.

Princeton University provided an excellent second stage for continuing research and crafting my work as an historian. Professor Sheldon Garon improved my frantic writing, for years abroad had whittled away at my command of English grammar. Professors Ruth Rogaski and David Howell also provided sound advice in culling extraneous material and helping me to focus. Professor Martin Collcutt was generous with funding that allowed me to produce several film series for Princeton. Scholarship and funding from Federal Area Language Study (FLAS) grants, the DAIEI summer funds, Fulbright, and the Princeton history department also supported my endeavors. As a result of my attendance at Princeton I never went hungry and managed to finish speedily. Marc and Kara Abramson, Jason Webb, Ono Masako, Tony Tavares, Steven Covell and his wife Wei-wei, Conan Cary, Sujeet Mehta, the Japanese "crew from Indiana," and others made the time spent there engaging and festive.

Throughout my travels to Japan, Nishimura Sachiko, Ohara Fumiko, Timothy Finley, Maeda Ayako, Mori Akira and his wife Masako have constantly assisted me in ways too plentiful to elaborate. Through the entire project Professor Michael Baskett of University of Kansas (and of course Kuroda Dariko) has constantly challenged most of my assumptions and forced me to be more specific in my approach. Without his encyclopedic knowledge of Japanese popular culture and history I would have lost my way long ago. Lora "Manatee" Saalman has also scrutinized my work with an acumen I only wish I personally possessed. My goal of holding her intellectual interest has always provided a high standard.

A David L. Boren National Security Education Program Graduate Fellowship allowed me to take a treasured year and study Chinese in Taiwan at the excellent ICLP center in Taipei. The staff there helped me more fully digest the records of wartime Sino-Japanese relations. In Taiwan, Hu Hisao-ping, Hsiao Hui-fen, Vickey Wei, David Elstein, Peter Goodman, Jeff Moser, Cheng Shiow-jiuan, and Yamagata-san all made life and study much more pleasant. In Tokyo, fellow scholars Paul Dunscomb, Roger Brown, Paul Saulski, Okamoto Kōichi, my Fulbright advisor Professor Kitaoka Shin'ichi, Katō Atsuko (who helped me decipher handwritten police reports) all in no small way made the final production of this research and book possible. Lori Watt patiently urged me to organize my thoughts instead of just blurting them out, and I hope she will detect her influence in these pages. Fellow colleagues at Davidson College were supportive. Kristen Eshleman and her crew in instructional technology constantly provided assistance in digitizing and editing images. Professor Shelley Rigger's largesse with Freeman funds allowed me to return frequently to Asia, deliver talks, and debate my findings with scholars in China, Taiwan, and Japan. I am truly grateful. Last-minute funding from Duke University's East Asian Library Travel Grants also allowed me to recheck some sources. My editors at Hawai'i Press also deserve praise for their diligence.

After such a long list as this, it remains only to mention that I have surely forgotten many individuals over the years who explained, cajoled, patiently listened, responded to, laughed at, or corrected my work over the years. I thank them as well.

A similar version of chapter 4 appeared as "Laughter as Materiel: The Mobilization of Comedy in Japan's Fifteen-Year War," *The International History Review* 26, no. 2 (June 2004): 300–330. Reprinted with the permission of Simon Fraser University.

Propaganda for Everyone

Offstage a traditional three-piece Japanese instrumental band strikes up a tune. To a resonant drumbeat a *rakugo* performer slowly shuffles onstage, bowing as he approaches his seat cushion in the middle of the stage. It is a typical weeknight at Suehirotei, a popular *rakugo* and performance hall in the heart of Shinjuku, and the audience eagerly waits to see which comedy routine Kawayanagi Senryū will perform. Tucking his legs under himself and sitting down onstage, Senryū faces the audience, bows again, and smiles. He looks rather grandfatherly in his somber brown kimono, with his short-trimmed hair almost completely white. A few older patrons call out for him to repeat a favorite routine; he politely nods in their direction. Looking calmly at the audience, Senryū quickly breaks into a Japanese song from World War Two.

> Hello, I am sorry to have not written for a while
> I am doing better and better.
> I'm not bragging but I do want to show you . . .
> From the time I arrived here until today,
> the marks on my helmet from the bullets flying around.[1]

Senryū sings the entire popular wartime melody "Shanhai dayori" (Letter from Shanghai), whose lyrics take the form of a letter from a Japanese soldier at the battlefront near Shanghai. The jaunty words, along with the peppy, upbeat tempo, signal a military secure in its destiny.

Rakugo is at the same time a traditional and contemporary comedic performing art. Many performers, although they are dwindling in number, perform standard routines from a century ago and even before. But others have made their name performing completely new material divorced from the traditions. Anyone attending a performance of *rakugo* expects some of both kinds of routines. The audience pays one price for entry, but once in, people can stay all day and night to watch the shows. *Rakugo* also has a history of insensitivity and the desire to shock, so it is with this expectation that the audience experiences a delicious thrill when they hear wartime songs sung in the context of a comedy show.

1

Famed comedian Kawayanagi Senryū is known for his popular wartime song routine, and he performs it regularly throughout Japan. The routine is funny because it is over the top, filled with off-color humor. Ordinarily, no one today expects to hear wartime songs as part of a comedy show. The routine shocks patrons a little—just as traditional *rakugo* tried to do—and the singing itself is amusing because it seems so dated in today's Japan, both completely disassociated from wartime Japan and inappropriate. Senryū sings, gestures, makes faces, and jitters about on his cushion, recapturing the mood of the past through the irony of today's mindset.

A child during World War Two (1931–1945), Senryū now recreates the Japan of that time through the songs of the era. In his opening remarks he informs the audience that Japan easily won all its early battles so that a cheery, light mood permeated the countryside. Between 1931 and 1937, with relatively few military casualties, Japan took control of Manchuria and set up its own puppet empire, Manchukuo, so the songs from this early period exude an optimistic outlook regarding Japan's mission in Asia. As Senryū gleefully sings the vibrant tunes, contemporary audiences experience the propaganda that propelled wartime Japanese society to mobilize.

But military victories alone did not monopolize the attention of Japanese audiences at that time. The early part of Senryū's performance includes equally appealing wartime hits that trumpeted Japan's role as "the light of Asia." In 1940 Japan planned to host the Olympics and simultaneously celebrate the 2,600th year of the country's founding. A song, "2,600th Year Imperial Anniversary," became a radio favorite, marking Japan as more than a military powerhouse.

> Under our just and commanding flag
> We will create the Asia of tomorrow.
> Today we demonstrate our power and perseverance
> The imperial dynasty has reached its 2,600th year![2]

When military losses slowly began to escalate after the Imperial Japanese Army invaded China in 1937, and then became bogged down there, the airy swing tunes gave way to positive, but slightly more somber songs. Senryū's performance recreates the war's progression, so now he sings the 1942 "Final Battle for Greater East Asia Song." The lyrics explain how the home front and battlefront will be unified as one, with a "blistering and booming stride, the time for our country to rise has arrived."[3]

By the start of the Pacific War against the ABCD bloc (the Americans, British, Chinese, and Dutch), Senryū tells his audience, the early heady jingles

give way to slower songs of more melancholy reflection and to patriotic eulo-
gies. Senryū demonstrates the change with "Sinking the British Pacific Fleet"
and "God Soldiers of the Sky." By the war's end, popular music had lost the
optimism and vitality it had manifested during the previous decade, although
hopefulness quickly returned during the American occupation.

Senryū's routine demonstrates that contemporary Japanese audiences are
titilated when recalling the wartime songs and propaganda that shaped and
mobilized their wartime society.[4] When singing the songs and swinging to the
beat, Kawayanagi Senryū recognizes that his routine is part nostalgia, part
sociological analysis. Older Japanese in the audience still remember parts of
the songs and the era, while the young, jolted by their often ambivalent feelings associated with the war, laugh at the contrast between what the songs say
and what was actually happening. The fact that these wartime songs remain in
the public memory and motivate laughter (albeit often nervous) supports the
fact that Japanese wartime propaganda was actually more effective than postwar scholars thought. Wartime Japanese propaganda helped mobilize Japanese society to establish an empire in Asia, and the propaganda lived on after
Japan's military defeat. Japanese wartime propaganda is not a dead issue.

A more careful analysis of wartime Japanese propaganda is important for
two reasons. It illuminates the social psychology that helped Japan pursue its
wartime aims. Second, it demonstrates that the Japanese populace in general
were active participants and not mere followers of their government officials
and military commanders.

Old wartime propaganda continues to exert an influence on Japan today.
Over the last few years a conservative group in Japan that sponsors what it
calls "antimasochistic history" has grown more vocal in its declarations that
Japan liberated Asia prior to 1945 and ended western racist hegemony. The
well-known Japanese manga artist Kobayashi Yoshinori has drawn innumerable comics illustrating this conservative group's position. Kobayashi's prolific
output, including several volumes on World War Two and Japan's role in Taiwan, consistently tops Japanese bestseller lists and ignites public debate.[5] A
close examination of Japanese wartime propaganda reflects its "everydayness,"
which helps account for why it became a virtually unassailable part of the
social consciousness that stabilized wartime Japanese society. Such an investigation also allows us to see more clearly why contemporary Japanese conser-
vatives lament Japan's decline as a military and political power player in Asia.

An analysis of propaganda is necessary to explain not only how the Japanese waged war for so long, but also why the same propaganda could help
rebuild the country in the postwar era. A study of Japanese wartime propaganda helps to elucidate how a popular base to support the war in Asia was

formed, how it grew, and why it remained stable throughout Japan's Fifteen-Year War. Scholars have asked similar questions regarding the Nazi movement in Germany, but the Japanese case is more intriguing, for not only did Japan's propaganda war last longer, but the Japanese also never managed to establish a central authority like the Nazi's Ministry of Propaganda.[6] Unlike Nazi Germany, a fascist party never took control of the government in Japan. Individual Japanese had to make a choice to participate in the developing war in China and later against the Allies.

Propaganda is a complex concept; it should not be considered merely an irrational web of deceit and lies. One theorist eloquently notes that propaganda "supplies ersatz certainties."[7] To paraphrase several other theories, propaganda should not be thought of as persuasion, because persuasion is a dialogue based on reason that satisfies both parties. Propaganda, however, "is a deliberate attempt to shape perceptions to achieve a response that furthers a desired action."[8] More importantly, propaganda appeals to emotion, while persuasion centers on logic. Propaganda is a collection of techniques used to influence mass opinion, and it therefore affects the social psychology of a population. A group mindset is a difficult ethos to form, but once established it proves even harder to eradicate. As historian of social science Minami Hiroshi articulated, "once a group mindset has been codified, individual opinions are overwhelmed by the social pressure to conform," and propaganda plays off of these psychological strengths.[9] Propaganda is not always rational because the aim is to cause action, not reflection.

Propaganda also differs from education, although they share similarities. A strict definition of education is a system where the acquisition of knowledge is the goal and there is little speculation on how the knowledge will be used. The individual is free to employ the knowledge or ignore it. Propaganda, in contrast, seeks to impart knowledge with a specific end in mind.[10] Education is not linked to specific psychological and media techniques to disseminate knowledge, whereas propaganda is intricately tied to certain technologies. For propaganda to succeed, media and technology must be carefully calibrated to galvanize action. Advertising is related to propaganda but pursues different goals. The advertising industry's intimate relationship with capitalism and the market makes its goal the stimulation of a desire to purchase a product or service even if the individual's needs have already been satisfied. Ads employ media and technological techniques that resemble those of propaganda, and they even influence the mass society, but advertising's aim is still to gain capital, while propaganda seeks to stimulate action.[11] Propaganda and advertising are not always mutually exclusive, as we shall see, but their goals are distinct.

A series of comics illustrating Japanese victories on the Chinese mainland in the magazine *Tabi* (Travel), December 1937, p. 72.

Japan's wartime propaganda pushed the nation to mobilize during World War Two to an extent that far surpassed many of the fascist states to which Japan was frequently compared. During its Fifteen-Year War this tiny island country with a population of approximately 70 million invaded China, carved out a puppet empire in northern China, occupied and colonized vast regions of Southeast Asia, and waged a bloody war not only against China but the United States, Great Britain, and Australia. Unlike Germany and Italy, no major portion of the Japanese population or intelligentsia fled, nor were there any major domestic revolts against the military incursions of the 1930 and 1940s.[12] The Japanese suffered privations, both personal and economic, yet during the fifteen-year battle for supremacy in Asia, the people of Japan remained committed to guarding and expanding its empire.

Japan's wartime propaganda centered on one major goal: unifying the battlefront with the home front. Numerous lesser goals, such as defeating racism and "liberating Asia," fed the main objective, but all the efforts helped create a symbiotic relationship between soldiers at the front and civilians throughout the empire in support of imperial expansion. Because of this relationship between home and battlefront, Japanese propaganda cannot be viewed solely in domestic terms. Moreover, the fact that the propaganda also focused on uniting disparate geographical locations and populations into a Japanese empire means that we must examine the propaganda as a tool for integrating Japan's wartime empire. War propaganda cannot be separated from imperial propaganda. To the Japanese of the 1930s, Japan's imperial goals were not chimeras—the population believed in its mission.

The Japanese did not confine propaganda to the upper levels of the military and bureaucracy. Instead, in support of the primary goal, plans called for propaganda that either sprang from society itself or was made to appear that way. Japanese on all levels of wartime society deemed reciprocity—alliances among the civilian, military, and bureaucratic circles—to be the key to successful propaganda campaigns. Reciprocity meant that Japanese society believed they had a role in producing propaganda in coordination with the government and military. The government did not simply mandate what society's actions should be. Mirroring the Japanese military and political realms at the time, no single organ for propaganda, no ministry of propaganda, existed. A Japanese counterpart to Joseph Goebbels, Nazi minister of propaganda, never appeared. Obviously, government and civilian organizational systems existed, but no single authority reigned over the entire propaganda apparatus the way Hitler and Goebbels ruled at the top of the Nazi propaganda pyramid. Hitler felt that propaganda messages should be kept simple and feed stereotypes. Goebbels supported Hitler's directive but remained adamant that propagandists could not grow lax. Fresh propaganda was continually needed to maintain the Nazi party's roster of members and to inflame emotional attachment, even after the party grew strong.[13]

If the structure of Japanese propaganda differs from its Axis counterparts, it is perhaps even more unlike its American counterpart. Overall, in the west, the term propaganda carries a history of negative connotations. During World War Two, British diplomats assiduously tried to avoid using the term to describe their attempts to persuade America to join the war against the Nazis. Americans viewed propaganda as an antidemocratic activity that perverted the truth and distorted reality.[14] As much as the Americans avoided the use of the term "propaganda," the Japanese employed it. The pursuit of democratic ideals did not hinder Japan's engagement of propaganda for the simple reason that the Asian nation had little, if any, desire to be democratic. Moreover, historically, propaganda had deep roots in Japan.

Innumerable studies in the English language focus on Nazi and Fascist propaganda, but there is little research on wartime Japanese propaganda.[15] In the Japanese and Chinese languages research has proliferated in the last few years, but the emphasis still centers on domestic Japanese programs and glosses over how the propaganda manifested itself within the larger Japanese empire.[16] These studies elucidate Japan's situation only at a theoretical level. It is true that Japanese wartime propaganda often appeared nebulous and Zen-like with its slogans concerning "spirit" and "national polity" (*seishin* and *kokutai*). Nonetheless, its actual effect at the local level in Japan—and even some propaganda directed toward the United States and China—demonstrates that Japanese propaganda exerted a broad and powerful influence.

Japanese wartime propaganda was diffuse, arising simultaneously from sectors as diverse as advertising and comedy. Because no single Japanese propaganda authority existed, and no central institution dominated the landscape, defining wartime Japanese propaganda can seem a hopeless academic exercise. It helps, therefore, to understand that propaganda has existed in Japan for centuries, but only with the advent of modern media did appeal to an instantaneous mass audience become possible.

Imperial Roots of Japanese Propaganda

For the Japanese the most important change that came with wartime propaganda was the shift from its Confucian antecedents. The Tokugawa era (1600–1868) had promoted classical Chinese notions of leadership and morality, with the shogun's administration, the bakufu, continually educating the people regarding correct social behavior. The Meiji government (1868–1912), no longer bound by traditional social hierarchies, created a more broadly focused imperial bureaucracy, but one still bent on guiding the masses morally. Beginning in the 1900s the Japanese bureaucracy had transformed itself into a technologically astute staff that employed propaganda created by sociologists, media research analysts, and pollsters. By the early Shōwa era (1926–1989) the advent of radio, the proliferation of cinema, the arrival of wireless technology to transmit photos, airline transport, advancing print techniques and publishing tools had all increased the ways in which propaganda could manipulate the increasingly urban inhabitants of the expanding Japanese empire, including Taiwan and Korea. The ever-growing possibilities had far surpassed the government's ability to exercise complete control over propaganda. The Meiji model of government, in which elite bureaucrats educated the masses, became ineffective for a society about to go to war. In addition, unlike previous eras, wartime Japanese society made propaganda demands on its government when people saw a need for improved social control or more skillful manipulation of public opinion.

For a brief time the Japanese did not remain sequestered on the four main Japanese islands. A few decades after the Meiji Restoration the empire swelled to include Korea and Taiwan (Formosa). Japanese cultural policy in these two formal colonies differed greatly from later efforts in the expanded wartime empire, most notably with regard to local language and culture. Following the Allied victory in World War One, the Japanese received the mandate to control the Marshall islands, taking over Germany's charge. Between 1931 and 1942 the Japanese empire gradually extracted obeisance from Indochina, Burma, the Philippines, Singapore, Malaysia, Indonesia, Sakhalin, the Kurils, and numerous other islands dotting the Pacific. By the time the Japanese government solidified its Greater East Asian Co-Prosperity Sphere in 1942, Japan threatened land borders with India and Thailand and water borders with Australia and even the United States. To cover such diverse territories, Japan's propaganda could no longer remain monolingual and monolithic.[17]

As early as 1933 Japanese officials had declared that Japan aimed to liberate Asia. Although lifting the yoke of western imperialism, Japan found itself in an entirely new situation. It was now a colonial occupier promoting local and indigenous languages. Japan's older holdings, Korea and Taiwan, had faced harsh colonial strategies, which largely strove to eradicate the use of Korean and Chinese. In the new parts of the empire, however, lauding local culture was seen as a way of shedding dependence on western education and values, defined as "vile western imperialism." In these places Japan strove to "liberate" the populations, not to make Japanese out of the Burmese or Chinese. Nonetheless, as other historians have argued, and Japanese archives reveal, wartime Japanese society did retain a strict hierarchical view of Asia in racial terms, with Japan at the apex.[18]

To show that its empire differed from western imperialism, Japanese officials and propaganda professionals had to strenuously avoid their prior monolingual and monocultural policies. Wartime imperial propaganda had to reflect the variety of languages and cultures that made up the empire. The hierarchical cultural organization of the empire, with Japan at the top, persuaded the mass Japanese audience to adhere to the war project. But the broad range of symbols used in the propaganda—such as physical strength, industrial capability, political stability, modern architecture, and advanced standards of hygiene—clearly indicates the extent to which wartime propaganda extended its influence throughout the Japanese empire in realms often removed from the military and the emperor.

Wartime Japanese theorists of propaganda—Kanda Kōichi, Yoneyama Keizō, Koyama Eizō, to name a few—wrote lengthy discourses on the nature of propaganda. These professional analysts were of the opinion that propaganda created by the masses, which emanated from the bottom of society, would prove successful in the long run for two reasons. First, if propaganda appeared to come as an official order, the people would resent it as a government proclamation. Second, the propagandists had noted that people behaved like all living creatures; they thought in terms of immediate benefits and disadvantages to themselves or how specific actions or policies would affect the future. It did not matter how much the media emphasized something vague and spiritual; in the end such things would not have the power to mobilize people.[19] The people needed to be presented with concrete benefits that would arise from the imperial program.

The Japanese government also realized that effective propaganda did not grow out of explicit directives issued from its offices. Propaganda that could be counted on to mobilize had to "grasp the hearts and minds of the people," *minshin haaku*. To do so, the government and military first had to establish a relationship with the people. Ultimately, this relationship rested on the unity of battlefront to home front and the reciprocal relations of propaganda campaigns activated throughout the Japanese empire.

Even with the clear goal of uniting the home front and battlefront, propaganda theorists understood why it was sometimes better for propaganda campaigns to originate from society instead of appearing as government mandates. The Japanese military and the government frequently encountered obstacles because of Japan's multifaceted approach to propaganda. Since no single agency had control, different agencies often competed with divergent messages for the same target audience. Within the military, the army competed with the navy; within bureaucratic circles, the Ministry of Foreign Affairs competed with the Office of the Prime Minster, the Diet, and various cabinet agencies that arose to conduct propaganda campaigns. During World War Two, the United States faced similar difficulties. Numerous offices like the Office of Strategic Services (OSS), the Office of War Information (OWI), other independent military and civilian agencies such as the Allied Translator and Interpreter Section (ATIS, the US military translating bureau in the Pacific) and even Hollywood censorship boards competed for a piece of the propaganda action.

Wartime Japanese propaganda has frequently been labeled a failure, but I maintain that Japan was a "successful failure" because wartime Japanese propaganda did not cease at the end of the war with the fall of the Japanese empire. Not only did wartime Japanese propaganda stoke the fires of a battle that raged for fifteen years, but more importantly, the same propaganda also helped Japan accept the defeat, urged Japan to rebuild in the immediate postwar, and assuaged a Japanese psyche that later erected the world's second largest economy. How wartime Japanese propaganda achieved this is far from a dormant issue, and it behooves us to examine the topic more carefully.

Imperial Propaganda as War Propaganda

Japanese wartime propaganda developed out of a dynamic interaction between official propaganda policy and the people. This symbiotic relationship between plan and reality often grew rancorous. Japan readied itself for war in a myriad of ways, with a variety of appealing messages for all groups. With few exceptions, wartime Japan rarely experienced charismatic political personalities who galvanized the nation. Japan did not experience a cult of Stalin, Hitler, or Mussolini. At the same time, although a bucktoothed emperor and a caricature of General Tōjō Hideki became central to US propaganda against Japan, comparable figures never played a principal role in domestic Japanese propaganda. Instead, Japan became obsessed with its vision of the future. For a few—the staunch militarists and imperialists—the emperor may have remained the central icon behind mobilization for the war. Indeed, after the war former Prime Minister Konoe Fumimaro committed suicide, and General Tōjō attempted it, but most military as well as most civilians accepted defeat and went on with their lives. For the vast majority, Japan's war propaganda had stimulated feelings not about the emperor, but about Japan's modernity that they believed culminated in a beneficent empire. Wartime Japanese society envisioned the empire, with Japan at its pinnacle, as hygienic, progressive, scientific, the harbinger of civilization that Asia should strive to emulate. Japanese wartime propaganda unified the public to support this idea of a modern empire while aiding the war effort, and the idea of empire became crucial to the success of wartime propaganda.

Japan launched its first imperial experiment when it acquired Taiwan from the Qing court following the Treaty of Shimonoseki in 1895. Within a decade Japan had defeated the Russians and later obtained large land leases in northern China. By the time full-scale war with China exploded in the summer of 1937, the Japanese empire was already several decades old. During these wartime years, Japanese propaganda should not be seen as mere war propaganda —it was imperial propaganda.

Japan administered an empire for a half a century, but contemporary scholars and the Japanese public have not dealt adequately with the issue of how empire intersects with propaganda. In fact, the notion that wartime propaganda is a special extension of imperial propaganda explains how Japan's wartime propaganda structure did not just suddenly appear in the 1930s when Japan began to face what it called its crises, or *hijōji*. The Japanese propaganda of World War Two is actually a subset of the imperial propaganda project that dates back to the 1890s. Although this book examines only the propaganda from 1931–1945, long before the start of the war with China the idea of empire attracted well-known writers, politicians, educators, and businessmen to imperial propaganda, and these people maintained their interest even after Japan's defeat. In the first decades of the twentieth century, not only did many of the nonmilitary educated Japanese elite support Japan's imperial aims, but Japan's message of "Asia for the Asiatics" also held broad popular appeal.

Domestic Japanese propaganda slogans alone did not motivate the population to wage war for a decade and a half.[20] In line with the Japanese prescription that empty rhetoric mobilized few, wartime propaganda often specifically depicted an advanced and modern Japan. This image suffused the daily routine, crossed oceans, traversed cultures, and influenced ideologies. The propaganda was so potent that its legacy persists today. In contemporary Japanese society the advertising slogan that frugality helped the war effort—"luxury is the enemy"—is still remembered by those who lived through the war. In contrast, it is interesting to note that "the Emperor whom the wartime generation had been taught to worship as a living god, and in whose name so many had died," was rarely mentioned by individuals at the time as a motivating factor behind Japanese support for the war.[21]

A cross section of urban and rural Japanese created Japanese wartime propaganda. Propaganda provided an outlet for motivated advertisers to work for the government and sponsor new magazines. Intellectuals debated the merits of wartime propaganda, discussing ways to better mobilize the country. The elite published articles on such themes not only in government journals but also in popular magazines and newspapers for the nation's readers to digest. Obviously Japan failed ultimately in its military conquest, but military failure denotes only that. Militaries quickly demobilize, whereas societies do not. Wartime propaganda ideals had become so much a part of Japanese daily life that many of its effects lasted well beyond the surrender and even the occupation.

As in Vichy France, many Japanese embraced the war in the early years because Japan seemed to be the winning side. In the beginning of the Nazi seizure of Europe, it was highly likely that many French were collaborationist, just as by mid-1944, when the tide turned, many switched allegiance to the Free French.[22] It is true that many French may have engaged in realpolitik and felt they had no choice, even though many historians take issue with that conclusion. However, in contrast to Vichy, Japanese continued to mobilize and support the war even when the situation appeared increasingly hopeless from 1943 until the surrender in August 1945. The Japanese fervor for war cannot only be explained by realpolitik, given the fact that enthusiasm lasted well beyond the time when winning appeared as a salvageable option.

Wartime Japanese propaganda developed through trial and error and also through competition. Moreover, it took place within the various domains of the Japanese empire. Propaganda campaigns that worked in China or met with resistance there often influenced domestic decisions, while domestic mobilization programs that achieved good results often carried over across to the Asian continent and elsewhere.

Reports sent back from Japanese propaganda platoons in China and Southeast Asia continually influenced the way in which Japan mobilized the domestic population. These exchanges spurred the continual development of new propaganda plans and methodologies. This production of propaganda and feedback about its effectiveness did not always translate into a centralized administration throughout the empire on the Japanese side, but Japanese propaganda remained a potent force.[23] During the war and for some after they achieved independence, leaders in Burma, India, the Philippines, and Indonesia employed Japanese rhetoric and often accepted Japanese assistance to further their own causes. Even Vietnamese patriots recognized some of the validity in Japanese propaganda claims while opposing the war's aims.[24]

False Accusations

As much as some pan-Asianists like Indian Independence leader Chandra Bose and Burmese Prime Minister Ba Maw supported elements of Japanese propaganda, wartime Japanese propaganda is still poorly understood. Americans caricatured Japanese wartime propaganda, hampering later analyses. They considered the English-language propaganda the Japanese produced to be inept.[25] And indeed, Japanese propaganda in English frequently appeared incompetent. American GIs who saw Japanese efforts firsthand fueled much of this sentiment. One Japanese leaflet, for example, had a beautiful nude woman on one side (presumably to command the soldiers' attention initially) and on the other listed thirteen "dangerous actions." The leaflet apparently sought to scare the soldiers, but the sheet had such outlandish content and so many grievous spelling errors that it probably became the butt of many platoon jokes. "Don't fall into the habit of glancing sideways at your comrades in arms," the leaflet warned. "Your surgeon dislikes such a habit, as it predicts the approaching menace of neurosis." Nothing, however, produced more guffaws than "Don't eat your own excrement or drink your own urine in the presence of others. If you do, you are sure to be branded a lunatic, however warmly you may protest."[26]

Allied soldiers were not the only parties who believed the Japanese incapable of effective wartime propaganda. In a postwar book, Phyllis Argall, a resident of Japan in the 1930s, felt the need to criticize several Japanese government agencies that produced English-language propaganda for dissemination abroad. One Japanese agency, for example, failed to grasp the double meaning of the statement: "The Welfare Minister promised to do all in his power to increase the birthrate on the train to Atami, and stated that public funds would be available for that purpose."[27]

After the war, the popular American fixation on Japanese propaganda as the work of the *yakuza*, the Japanese mafia, and the secretive Black Dragon Society obfuscated the real story.[28] Marius Jansen's treatise on Sun Yat Sen and the Japanese demonstrates that strong connections did exist between underworld figures from China and Japan; a conspiracy, however, did not.[29] The American obsession with the Black Dragon Society and organizations of that ilk, as the instigators of the war, ran deep throughout the Allied occupying forces. The postwar interrogation of General Doihara Kenji, the supposed Lawrence of Arabia of the East, demonstrates the extent to which the occupation forces believed this myth. The reports make it seem as if the occupation forces almost needed him to admit that the Manchurian Incident and the

Black Dragons were connected.[30] The skewed American perception of Japanese propaganda prevented the United States from recognizing that Japanese propaganda was not relegated to a small junta of military men, bent on evil machinations. The agencies that actually drafted, produced, and distributed Japanese wartime propaganda consisted of well-intentioned intellectuals, rural women, stage performers, police officers, and other average Japanese eagerly participating in a society that wanted to support the war. The entire propaganda structure was grounded outside of the government.

Japanese wartime propaganda evolved over decades, as the product of empire-building. Published Japanese comedy routines about the war sold well during the first Sino-Japanese war (1894–1895); pamphlets mocked the Chinese and colorful pictures depicted battlefield victories.[31] During the Russo-Japanese war Japanese authorities prevented foreign journalists like Jack London from observing the war firsthand. However, pictures championing Japan's victories drawn by Japanese journalists and military artists were readily available to rural and urban consumers.[32] In what became a standard operating procedure later on, the Japanese government during the Sino-Japanese war paid Reuters bribes to print articles that portrayed the Japanese in a positive light. Japanese officials solicited American news reporters with offers of high salaries to speak favorably of Japan in both domestic and international papers. The Japanese government took these measures in response to negative international press after the massacre of Chinese troops and civilians at Port Arthur in late November 1894.[33]

In the early 1930s Japan's reliance on social mobilization to solve political problems played into Japan's escalating militarism and added to the Japanese desire to look beyond politics for the answer to Japan's problems. The preconditions for the rise of Japanese militarism—an emasculated political realm and a beleaguered economy—were already well in place by the time of the Manchurian Incident on September 18, 1931. Throughout the 1920s labor- and rural-based political parties continually failed to create a stable political coalition. By the early 1930s a stumbling economy and strengthened military had forced the political parties into a defensive posture. When Japan's Kwantung Army in China realized that the civilian government back home had no ability to hinder its expansionist goals, military aggression on the Chinese mainland continued to escalate.

For the domestic population, the gnawing sense that social unrest was imminent fed social anxiety to seek answers beyond the apparently inept civilian government. Disgruntled military personnel, imperialist politicians, and dissatisfied portions of the public therefore took it upon themselves to change a political system they deemed inadequate. Between 1921 and 1936 mutinous Japanese assassinated a half dozen government ministers in office. These actions destabilized an already precarious situation. Japanese socialist and communist efforts to oppose the government provided the upper classes with even more reason to fear domestic unrest.[34]

The Thought War

During the restless 1930s Japanese propaganda efforts on the part of all parties multiplied exponentially. Japanese authorities had become aware of the need to maintain popular support when they sent masses of forces to China in 1932 and 1937 and later when war began against the Allies in 1941. This large-scale dispatch of forces helped to increase bureaucratic, civilian, and military attention to propaganda.

For Japan, the entire process of convincing China that Japan's mission was to liberate Asia hinged on the idea of the "thought war," or *shisōsen*.[35] The Japanese consistently used the term "thought war" to describe the fight for ideological supremacy in Asia and later against the West. As one wartime author described it, Japan waged war over various differences in "world view," most importantly against democracy and individualism.

> What kind of ideology is democracy? It is an ideology that bases itself on the individual. It is an ideology that began for the existence of the individual, for the individual's profit, and to protect the individual. If one promotes this idea, we will end up with a society wherein women and men are equals, the old and young, adults and children, are all treated as separate individuals. This will lead to conflict.[36]

Civilian and military leaders in Japan constantly spoke of the need for action in the thought war, and the duty to refine and hone their propaganda skills. Realizing that the public could not be ignored, government officials wanted the population to be enthusiastic about the war. Leaders saw propaganda as a force behind stimulating and supporting such enthusiasm.

Wartime Japanese propaganda created an image of Japan as the modern leader of Asia. The Japanese people believed the propaganda because that image reflected a Japan that could guide Asia through the twentieth century. While the goal of Japanese propaganda was to unite the military front and the home front, wartime Japanese propaganda remained effective for three main reasons. First, the production of wartime propaganda was not limited to military and fascist circles. The men and women who wrote and produced the propaganda came from a range of backgrounds. These bureaucrats, writers, photographers, and advertisers also had a variety of rationales for accepting or helping to develop the propaganda. Fear of opposing the government played a role, but many Japanese also believed in Japan's mission of modernity in Asia. Second, wartime propaganda seeped into the fabric of daily wartime life, and civilians cooperated in its growth. Japanese propaganda worked at many different levels of society and across many different venues. The propaganda appealed to a mass audience, but that audience also helped produce the propaganda. Comedians voluntarily employed propaganda terminology in their routines. Rural inhabitants wrote letters to magazines and to their government representatives, enthusiastically offering suggestions for improved propaganda. Third, no organization took domestic support for the war's aims for granted. The Japanese worked tirelessly throughout the war and afterward to mobilize the population. Bureaucratic agencies continually monitored the populace for dissatisfaction. The police constantly took the pulse of the people, trying to assess their understanding of the war's aims and requesting feedback through interviews, interrogations, questionnaires, and eavesdropping. Even the Japanese military believed that it had to stay constantly in tune with the public psyche. The Japanese military commissioned innumerable military and civilian studies that monitored and gauged public opinion.

Japanese wartime propaganda developed like a spoked wheel. The authorities provided the center hub with their plans and programs. The population provided the structure that supported and reinforced. Without both parts the resulting propaganda would have collapsed.

This book consists of six chapters, each describing an element within wartime Japanese propaganda. Chapter One discusses the evolution of propaganda as a profession in Japan. Detailing the underlying rationale behind the propaganda initiatives assists in understanding the goals Japanese propaganda espoused. Chapter Two analyzes how the police and the military defined the socially acceptable, and how, through their supervisory role, they watched society for signs of dissatisfaction and malcontents. Chapter Three looks at the advertising industry's propaganda products. Censorship helped to stifle recalcitrant social elements, but without a forceful visual representation of their goals, the propagandist's efforts would have been hampered. The relationship between the advertising industry and Japanese authorities explains how Japan propagated its image as the leader and modernizer in Asia. The fourth chapter explores how popular culture and the entertainment industry supported the war. Japanese wartime propaganda did not confine itself to slogans and government-sponsored exhibitions. Successful professional entertainers often incorporated wartime propaganda as part of their own routines to help popularize their careers. These propaganda messages filtered down to the society and took hold. Chapter Five explains how Japanese propaganda dealt with the competition it faced abroad. How exactly did China and the United States react to Japanese propaganda efforts and what did these responses reveal? The Japanese government and military became keenly aware that Japanese abroad faced a threat from foreign propaganda, so they sought to combat such efforts with propaganda that was both defensive and proactive. Even though the Japanese empire controlled more ground than just China and threatened more countries than just the United States, I focus on the responses of these two nations for two reasons: the Chinese posed the largest and greatest propaganda threat to the Japanese, and proved more difficult to convince than the Japanese had originally anticipated. Analyzing the Chinese response to Japanese propaganda helps us fathom the obstacles that Japanese wartime propaganda faced within its empire. America, on the other hand, presented the greatest military threat to the Japanese. In addition, American culture and history were so far removed from the Japanese and average Asian experience that the United States, too, stood as a major obstacle, impeding the claims of Japanese propaganda. It grew difficult in some regions to claim the Japanese were bringing liberty for Asians, taking them out from under the tyranny of white rule, while the Japanese themselves instituted much of the same racial hierarchy they supposedly disparaged. While Japan could essentially ignore Burmese, British, and Philippine propaganda threats because these countries were not as militarily powerful or culturally dominant in Asia, it could not as easily dismiss the Americans and Chinese. Chapter Six seeks to explain connections between wartime and postwar Japanese propaganda. The Japanese prepared for defeat using many of the same propaganda agencies and techniques that had been employed during the war. The individuals who worked for these agencies later worked in positions of power and shaped the postwar Japanese media and advertising industries.

Postwar Japanese commentary on wartime Japanese propaganda has generated a failure myth that asserts Japan lacked efficient propaganda programs. Until recently this myth masked the actual scope and effectiveness of the propaganda projects. The very structure of the Tokyo War Crimes Trials forced many to examine only what the Japanese military had done, but not at relations among the government bureaus or reactions from the private sector. The key to understanding the full range and depth of wartime Japanese propaganda and its impact on postwar Japan requires that we look beyond the military.

Advertising agencies became subcontractors for military poster campaigns. Comedians and entertainers unilaterally mobilized themselves to travel to China and amuse the Japanese imperial troops. Youth groups and children conducted recycling campaigns, and married women's associations collected records and books to send to wounded soldiers. Japanese propaganda poured from a multiplicity of official and nonofficial venues.

The Japanese supported a war that lasted fifteen years and stretched to include virtually half the globe. A war of this magnitude, ferocity, and breadth demanded active participation from a population that believed in the cause. Although the war years were often bleak, that was not the only image, nor does it adequately describe wartime Japanese society.

CHAPTER ONE

Master Propagandists and Their Craft

In January 1940 the conservative Japanese magazine *Bungei shunjū* published the results of an extensive poll concerning how Japan's population viewed the political situation. Pollsters queried the public with questions ranging from "Do you think that the current Konoe cabinet is doing a good job?" to "Would you consider working on the Chinese continent?" One revealing part of the survey charted how Japanese regarded government regulations in light of the continuing war on the Chinese mainland. An overwhelming two-thirds of the urban respondents suggested that social controls should be *further strengthened* to help support Japan's aims in China. At the start of 1940, almost two years before the war with America began and several years after the invasion of China, the Japanese public supported measures that limited its own ability to oppose the war. Japan's residents seemed to agree that sustained efforts to galvanize the society to support the war mandated the shaping of public opinion.[1]

Japanese Propaganda Shapes Public Opinion

Japanese wartime propaganda consisted of two subsets—official and unofficial. Official propaganda emanated from government channels and related agencies. Unofficial propaganda developed within nongovernmental institutions, such as private companies that cut records, produced advertising, etc. Both types of propaganda thrived and attracted audiences. A host of bureaucrats and professionals, most belonging to the educated, cosmopolitan, urbane and skilled classes, worked on this propaganda, This chapter analyzes the growth and structure of the government's plans to promote official propaganda and examines the professionals who worked behind the scenes on the unofficial side.

Japan's propaganda comprised a mix of messages, from nativist to promotion of the modern, which were developed by an increasingly professional staff. The messages conveyed a sense not only of Japan's modernity, but also of its mission to bring culture and progress to the rest of Asia. Japan was touted as a civilizing force, but also as a prime tourist destination. In fact, Japanese wartime propaganda often sought to elicit support for commercial gain as much as it did to enlighten audiences about Japan's "modernization mission in Asia."[2]

Wartime propaganda depended on the mass culture and the drive for mass consumption that developed during Japan's era of Taisho democracy in the 1920s. Reliance on new media technology to reach the masses also set propaganda apart from its antecedents. Japanese propagandists did not have to instruct the Japanese about nationalism and patriotism; the public had already learned them in Meiji- and Taisho-era schools and educational programs. A literate population that read magazines, newspapers, watched movies, listened to music and regularly devoured vast quantities of consumer products made targeting of propaganda easy.

Misconceptions concerning Japanese propaganda conjure up an image of "Big Brother" and an Orwellian model of an oppressive regime that censored the media and forced the people to adopt certain lines of thinking. Actual Japanese wartime propaganda proved more subtle. Japan desired to broadcast to its neighbors the simple message that Japan was the most modern country and race in Asia and that it alone could lead Asians through the twentieth century. The shape and tone of the message took many forms. It could be entertaining, frightening, threatening, or pleading. Domestically, the Japanese often needed to convince themselves of their own superiority, but when reaching to the far corners of the Japanese empire, the Japanese had to feed the conquered areas a propaganda diet of Japanese vitality and dominance.

Western understanding of Japanese propaganda developed primarily at the start of World War Two within the American armed forces. While the Americans noted that the Japanese seemed capable of mobilizing their society to an unprecedented degree, the actual mechanics of the process, other than force and terror, seemed to evade US comprehension. Studies of Japanese mobilization failed to understand Japanese propaganda methods because Americans had exaggerated ideas of Japanese culture's supposedly slavish devotion to the emperor.[3] The influence that the Shōwa emperor exerted in wartime Japan cannot be completely discounted, but it must be placed in context. An effective mobilization campaign, Japanese propaganda researchers stated, contained messages that spoke to the common people—indeed, it frequently originated from them. For the professional propagandists who worked on wartime propaganda, discussion of the emperor seldom figured in their work. Talk centered more on mundane issues like paper quality, font choice, and editing decisions. Propagandists concentrated on the content of their propaganda, but the emperor rarely made an appearance in it.

Proposals and suggestions for improved propaganda products came from around the Japanese nation and from a variety of organizations. Advertising agencies and executives bombarded the authorities with proposals to help the government achieve better levels of social mobilization and produce more effective propaganda. In 1937 a collection of advertising groups banded together to publish a magazine entitled *Puresuaruto,* or *Press Art.* From 1937 to 1945 this privately managed magazine produced dozens of issues concerning how Japanese advertising could be altered to attract foreign audiences, namely, the Chinese. The journal also ran advertisements that it claimed would promote tourism and protection of the roads, trains, and waterways considered essential to the war effort. Writers who toured the country for the magazine assiduously carried out research and penned editorials about successful campaigns to promote "wholesome entertainment" in the more rural areas of southern Japan. Writers who had been mobilized for military propaganda work in China and Southeast Asia periodically reported from the battlefront. These items frequently received prominent display in the magazine.[4]

A privately owned magazine promoting government propaganda is an example of what historian Yoshimi Yoshiaki identifies as "grass-roots fascism."[5] The grass roots of this brand of propaganda demonstrate that there was popular support of the war to dominate Asia. In many cases Japanese saw the Fifteen-Year War as a positive development where Japan would display its civilian and military might to an international audience.

Propaganda as State Management

Unlike World War Two in America, which lasted from December 1941 to August 1945, for Japan the war lasted more than three times as long. Only during the last three years did military setbacks become a daily occurrence. Until the late summer of 1942 and the Battle of Midway, the Japanese had been exceedingly successful in all their military endeavors. Their feeling of achievement and entitlement ran deeper than commonly assumed, if we observe how the victories over China in 1895 and Russia in 1905 reinforced a psychology of superiority. The feeling of euphoria among the Japanese that produced the songs comedian Kawayanagi Senryū sings today carried with it Japanese emotional attachment to victory into the early 1940s.

A definition of propaganda as a product of the interaction between state and society has taken root in recent years as studies on fascism and theories regarding social mobilization have developed. Theories using such a definition assert that social policy is actually not state-mandated but the result of a relationship between the government and the people. The Japanese state's primary goal, both before and during the war, was to "transform the Japanese people into active participants in the state's various projects."[6] Japanese campaigns to bring the people in line with official state policy have been described as a form of "moral suasion," a translation of the Sino-Japanese term *kyōka*.[7] *Kyōka* movements from the 1880s to the 1930s were key to the Japanese bureaucracy's effort to get Japanese to identify as citizens of a national entity. By 1929, as the world economy slid downward in a rapid spiral, the Hamaguchi cabinet initiated its National Moral Suasion Mobilization Campaign, based on the twin goals of "improving the economic lifestyle," and "cultivating national strength."[8] The rise of the politically and socially influential youth training camps and the military reserve associations suggests that the government and military wanted to affect social change and create a base for war support.

Bureaucratic campaigns to motivate the civilian public into action, however, took precedence over the military associations. The growth of mass social management stemmed originally from the chaos that ensued after the great Kantō earthquake of 1923 that leveled Tokyo and refashioned local politics. After the Kantō earthquake widespread looting occurred, as did the mass murder of Koreans falsely suspected of poisoning wells. In an effort to bolster the weakened social order and prevent looting, the Japanese government implemented several important programs. It sponsored a decree, called the Imperial Ordinance for the Promotion of National Spirit, which aimed to "assuage the hearts of the people" in their time of grief and panic. Public ordinances of this kind obviously predated the government's propaganda campaigns in the 1930s.[9]

The *kyōka* movements, and their antecedents in Confucian moral doctrine, later developed into a more scientifically savvy system of social management to bring the people into conformance with what officials felt was their own more educated reasoning. These movements, too, preceded Japan's stupendous growth in propaganda agencies and inspired the enormous number of subsequent campaigns that focused on *senden*. The Japanese believed that the British, the first masters of propaganda in the twentieth century, reigned supreme in that realm due to one key factor: the British realized the need for propaganda in ways that other participants in World War One had not envisioned.[10] It was a miscalculation few would later make. In the 1920s the Germans, the Japanese, and the Americans all began to emulate the British form of wartime propaganda. Japanese crews in the Ministry of Foreign Affairs busily translated British works and learned from British mobilization efforts during World War One. In the early 1930s Japanese government agencies began large-scale translation projects of English and German propaganda studies. These studies employed the word *senden* for the term propaganda. The idea of a technological and scientifically based *senden,* replacing the traditional morally based *kyōka,* reflected an empire focused on linking the will of imperial subjects to the will of the nation and the splendor of its expansion. Although the term *kyōka* survived into the early 1940s, by the mid 1930s the term used for propaganda had become the one that originally denoted advertising, *senden.* The names of government campaigns reflected this shift, changing from the traditional Sino-centric notion of a government morally leading its people, as the *kyōka* term denotes, to a technologically advanced, more modern system of propaganda that *senden* implies.

Given this evidence of early Japanese efforts to mobilize society, it seems bizarre to note that many Japanese remained convinced that, culturally speaking, they were incapable of producing propaganda.[11] This strange notion appears in prewar journals as well as postwar interviews. In the May 1942 issue of *Propaganda,* famed Japanese intellectual Hasegawa Nyozekan mourned Japan's inability to muster effective propaganda in radio, film, leaflets, and other media. According to Hasegawa and others, Japan's failure stemmed from the fact that propaganda campaigns were a "foreign element." Japanese could not implement propaganda because telling lies was not in their nature, Hasegawa wrote.[12] His article exposed a fascinating paradox in Japanese attitudes toward propaganda. On one hand Hasegawa described the Japanese as inadequate to the task of creating effective propaganda, which explained their supposed failure to create a feeling of allegiance among other Asians. At the same time he explained that the Japanese themselves were easily led by propaganda, which was why the country was so unified in its support for the war. Wartime Japanese advertising executives espoused similar opinions. These men also asserted that the Japanese warrior ethic equated lies with blasphemy, an attitude that supposedly impeded Japanese efforts to develop excellent wartime propaganda like the west.[13]

Hasegawa's opinion notwithstanding, it is obvious that the Japanese were excellent propagandists. Examinations of wartime Japanese magazines demonstrate that the entire Japanese public discussed propaganda. While many may have been discussing whether it was virtuous or not to mobilize, there were just as many other voices chanting for stronger, more effective propaganda as a national necessity. Joseph Newman, a longtime reporter in Tokyo for the *New York Herald Tribune,* had a unique take on Japan's preference to downplay its propaganda. In the months just after Pearl Harbor Newman wrote that the "Japanese always complained that they were poor propagandists. In best propaganda style, they complained so persistently that they convinced many foreigners it was true. Japanese like nothing better than to be told they were poor propagandists. It assured them that their propaganda was working."[14]

A postwar sociological study of Japanese wartime psychology asserted that the Japanese of the 1930s were overly obedient to authority.[15] Claims that "the majority of Japanese responded to the Cabinet Board of Information Bureau's propaganda with quiet acquiescence, at least on the surface," and that the Japanese "had no choice but to follow the policy in silence" leads readers to the misguided conclusion that the Japanese military duped the Japanese masses.[16] Such notions about Japanese passivity mirror an immediate postwar book on Japanese propaganda and mobilization in which the author stressed that the Japanese failed in World War Two because the Japanese based propaganda on lies while the Allies' propaganda was truthful.[17] More cynically one might say that Japan's stance that it implemented inefficient propaganda lifted the burden from postwar Japanese society that perhaps civilians were complicit in supporting the war. Postwar scholarship incorrectly labeled the wartime Japanese propaganda campaigns as artifacts of the military and government and not as products of collusion between the civilian society and its leaders.

Recent cultural studies observers have noted that the American occupation and postwar Tokyo War Crimes Trials, officially known as the International Military Tribunals for the Far East, hindered historical inquiry into Japanese wartime propaganda. The trials determined Japan's wartime goals and actions to be the result of an oppressive military junta that misled the otherwise peaceful Japanese masses. The Tokyo Trials clearly helped establish a Japanese historical amnesia that make it possible to deny the existence of a collusive populace.[18] Postwar Japanese education also taught that the military led the population astray; few texts mentioned mass participation in voluntary propaganda activities. However, censorship and terror alone did not characterize the war years. In actuality the people were not duped, nor were they passive. The masses understood the situation not only because the government explained it, but also because the population itself helped create the propaganda environment.

Japanese Notions of Propaganda: *Senden* vs. *Kyōka*

The Japanese translated numerous English and German propaganda studies and conducted their own research to arrive at a workable understanding of propaganda to promote their expanding empire. In several ways wartime Japanese theories concerning propaganda parallel the theory of postwar French propaganda researcher, Jacques Ellul, who pronounced that propaganda existed "to provoke action." Wartime Japanese theorists would have agreed with Ellul that propaganda ". . . aimed to make the individual cling irrationally to a process of action. It is no longer to lead to a choice, but to loosen the reflexes. It is no longer to transform an opinion, but to arouse an active and mythical belief."[19] In short, propaganda served to generate an artificial environment that helped to sustain a socially dominant ideology.

Japanese theories of propaganda predated Ellul's concepts, but the two appear remarkably similar. By the 1930s the Japanese had already recognized that propaganda grew from a relationship between the state and the people and could not simply be imposed on them. Yokomizo Mitsuteru, the director of the Japanese government's influential Cabinet Board of Information, said this explicitly. While attending a September 1937 conference held to educate the public concerning the importance of the *shisōsen*, or "thought war," Yokomizo expounded on the need to recognize propaganda as a way to wage battle without weapons. *Senden*, or propaganda, Yokomizo explained to the Japanese public, was not the act of spreading lies or falsities. Instead, by "disseminating credible facts propaganda creates a situation in which one can seek understanding and resonance, in order to reach a certain goal."[20] Arai Zentarō, Home Ministry bureaucrat, former governor of Kagoshima, mayor of Kyoto, and later an official purged by the postwar occupation, elucidated further the government's position on propaganda. Arai claimed that to make the people independent in spirit the government intended to push through propaganda programs "putting more and more strength into arousing national spirit which was key to urging the people to solve national problems on their own initiative."[21] The Japanese did not view the goal of propaganda as the creation of a dependent population. To Japanese officialdom in the 1930s, propaganda meant the cultivation of cultural values and attitudes that would be held so deeply they would appear innate and not imposed.

The 1937 exhibit on wartime propaganda demonstrated that the government did not keep the Japanese masses in the dark but continually educated them about the war with China. The government and military openly explained the propaganda campaigns to the masses; they invited the people to ingest, enjoy, and respond to the propaganda. Propaganda was not a dirty word, nor was it a concept to be challenged, quite the reverse. Even though agencies in charge of Japan's propaganda overtly managed the campaigns, the government wished to draw as much individual participation as possible from the Japanese population.

According to the government's own statistics, each day approximately 70,000 people attended the three-week-long propaganda exhibit. The Home

Ministry sponsored the event because it felt the population did not fully grasp the rationale behind the need to mobilize for war on the Chinese continent. The authorities also wanted to define fully the threat that Chinese propaganda posed to Japanese goals. After its Tokyo debut the exhibit toured the country, usually hosted in department stores, with stops in Osaka, Kyoto, Fukuoka, Sagashi, Kumamoto, Sapporo, Omiya, Sasebo city, and Seoul, Korea.

The government never banked on the people's blind allegiance. Moreover, early on, the Japanese authorities realized that government-sponsored propaganda had to compete with a range of other consumer activities. In Osaka, for example, the Mitsubishi department store's exhibit on "National Policy Textiles and Goods" and the well-attended movie *Nanjing* rivaled the propaganda exhibit.[22]

The 1937 national propaganda exhibit, and the extent to which the coordinating agency tried to enlist the cooperation of other ministries, demonstrates that the exhibit attempted "to educate" rather than pander to the people.[23] This relationship between government and people produced propaganda that may best be understood as "democratic fascism." The media created an environment in which Japanese individuals felt they participated in something larger than themselves. The value of such participation was that the masses were "not solely a depository for information, but acted as soldiers within the 'thought war'; they should be able to be actively engaged" with the propaganda war.[24] Japanese propaganda programs demanded active participants, not drone-like followers.

Bureaucratic Groundwork for the Creation of Propaganda

In the early 1930s government policy concerning propaganda stood in disarray, and the government grew anxious that it had failed to promote a unified face to its own public and to international opinion makers. The entire system lacked unified coordination. Officials complained that mixed messages existed even on the local level. Efficacious propaganda seemed as far away as a dream.

By January 10, 1935, a research group under Cabinet auspices proposed a plan to establish a government agency that would coordinate propaganda efforts. The plan charged the agency, which would be under the authority of the prime minister, with six main duties. These included "unified planning of all propaganda efforts," "analysis of international and domestic propaganda," and "research on the 'thought war.'"[25] In September 1937 the agency rose in profile to a Cabinet Information Office, finally later to become a Cabinet Board of Information. Essentially the agency coordinated propaganda policies among the Foreign Ministry, the Army Ministry, Army General Staff Headquarters, the Navy Ministry, the Navy Command Center, the Home Ministry, the Ministry of Education, and the Ministry of Telecommunications. However, it possessed no regulatory status and little authority. It was an unofficial, voluntary bureau set up to manage information and maintain contact among the reluctantly cooperative government bodies. By the late 1930s the Cabinet Board of Information had assumed the additional task of managing propaganda aimed abroad. Previously, propaganda aimed abroad had been under the aegis of the Information Office within the Foreign Ministry, a territory the ministry fiercely protected and never fully relinquished.

As previously noted, Japan never successfully organized all of its official propaganda organs under one roof, and competing offices continued to struggle for supremacy throughout the war. On November 7, 1935, the Ministry of Telecommunications and the Foreign Ministry jointly created the Dōmei News Agency (Dōmei Tsūshin) to provide a single voice through which Japan would be heard abroad. Leaders attempted to corral the assortment of messages and messengers emanating from the country. In part, Japan feared that on the international front China was winning greater western support with superior propaganda. And in fact, China was gaining the very western support that Japan so dearly desired. In the United States, General Chiang Kai Shek and his American-educated wife Soong Mei-ling appeared on the cover of *Time* magazine in January 1938 as husband and wife of the year. China benefited from an outpouring of public sympathy over its plight and this frustrated the Japanese.

Like its predecessors, the Cabinet Board of Information promulgated numerous campaigns to mobilize the people in support of Japan's imperial aims across Asia. One early plan, proposed at a November 9, 1936, meeting, decided to "consider policies for national *kyōka*-propaganda." The committee outlined nebulous goals to "raise awareness, strengthen the national spirit, promote the idea of the national polity, etc." The necessity to draft a more concrete propaganda policy did not surface until after the Japanese military forces launched their all-out offensive on the Chinese mainland in the summer of 1937.

On July 1, 1937, the civilian arm of the propaganda war was born. Yokomizo Mitsuteru, the man designated as director of the Cabinet Information Office, spoke at the second General Information Committee Conference and outlined the three major duties of the Cabinet Information Office. Officials felt the threat of war with China required an agency to "coordinate communication concerning basic information relating to the implementation of national policies, organize communications regarding foreign and domestic information, and manage communications pertaining to enlightenment propaganda."[26] The escalating war with China introduced the need for immediate and effective propaganda. The military crisis Japan faced in the summer of 1937 saddled the agency with the unenviable task of bringing sense and consistency to the often contradictory messages issuing from a multitude of civilian sources, government bureaus, and the military. The Cabinet Information Office's mission also included informing other government bureaus—which were very protective and secretive about their own propaganda projects—about activities in related government branches. To disseminate its message the Cabinet Information Committee began publishing a magazine called *Weekly Report (Shūhō)* on September 21, 1936. In July 1937 readership hovered at 160,000, but neared 1.5 million by March 1943.[27] The magazine primarily published news and other information from government agencies. The Information Committee also published a photo magazine with similar content entitled *Weekly Report in Photos.*[28]

Propaganda in Japan never came under the sole jurisdiction of a single agency; no single Ministry of Propaganda ever existed. And although the Cabinet Board of Information may not have been as successful as the Nazi Ministry of Propaganda, on which it was modeled, it nonetheless had considerable impact on the dissemination of propaganda. It is through the hazy relationship between government and nongovernmental agencies, however, where wartime Japanese propaganda reached into the heart of Japanese society.

Japan recognized that the war in China was going to take longer than originally planned and that a fierce propaganda war had to be waged to combat the Chinese. On August 24, 1937, the Japanese government embarked on its National Spiritual Mobilization Campaign to preempt domestic dissent against the war in China. The campaign did not produce the desired results for the Japanese so officials drew up a second program, the Imperial Rule Assistance Association (IRAA) (Taiseiyokusankai). The IRAA later expanded into a superstructure that encompassed much more than several propaganda agencies. Under its umbrella the government brought together all political parties into a mass organization and herded them toward a unified mandate. The IRAA did not create any new agencies; instead it ruled over preexisting local associations. One Japanese scholar compared the situation to a puppet master manipulating the associations as puppets to act out programs the master selected, where one kind of rule is quietly placed on top of an already existing structure.[29]

The Imperial Rule Assistance Association employed the new discipline of social science and the techniques of statistics to craft its propaganda. It persistently polled domestic public opinion to determine the effect of the government's messages. Periodically, at urban and rural lectures the organization sponsored around the country, speakers distributed postcards to those who attended and asked for their frank comments. A tabulation office within the Imperial Rule Assistance Association collected and tallied the responses, trying to read the pulse of the nation. Frequently, the statisticians graded a listener's responses into categories such as "positive concern," a euphemism for criticism. Often listeners wrote explicitly that while they had enjoyed the lectures, the theories discussed had been too vague and not concrete enough. One respondent castigated the government's entire 1930s program for renovating Japan, with its "new political system" that the respondent identified as "Japanese-style Communism." The most common complaints surrounded the incomprehensibility of the lectures. The ordinary people in rural areas often had minimal understanding of the terms used to explain why Japan was the leader of Asia, why it needed to wage war in China, and why the international community had isolated Japan.[30] Slogans the government developed like "Eight Corners of the World Under One Roof" *(hakkō ichiu)* or "One Hundred Million Souls with One Mind" *(ichioku isshin)* failed to strike a resonant chord with the people. The failure of these slogans enhanced the propaganda value of other activities that might stimulate support for the war, such as entertainment, music, sports, and health programs.

The Imperial Rule Assistance Association frequently sponsored town meetings that drew large crowds. One such talk, "A Lecture about the Repercussions Stemming from Foreign Problems," offered near the winter of 1940, produced responses from a diverse group of fifty-seven attendees including a seventeen-year-old high school student and a forty-two year-old chauffeur. Participants had expected the lecture to be propaganda, and they looked forward to the event. Afterwards the audience politely suggested how to improve the propaganda. One thirty-nine-year-old designer recommended:

> . . . while a lecture is one form of propaganda, at the same time it also has to have entertainment value. It is absolutely mandatory, especially with this type of lecture, that it manifest a great emotive outpouring and convey a sense of leadership. In this sense, we expect prudence in the choice of lecturer. In conclusion, more important than the number of attendees, it is rather the speaker's passion, spirit, leadership, and polish that should be able to arouse the nation.[31]

Throughout the war years letters concerning the Imperial Rule Assistance Association's propaganda continued to flood into the agency's offices. IRAA files suggest that clerks recorded and analyzed each one. A Tokyo respondent felt that the whole scheme of the IRAA was superfluous. Everyone in Japan loves the country and is loyal to the emperor, and hence the association is a waste of money, the writer grumbled. Instead, he suggested, the money should be given to the poor and Japan would become a much happier place to live.[32]

The hierarchy of government agencies mobilizing the population consisted of associations cascading down to the smallest unit, the neighborhood association. Internal IRAA documents reveal that the organization felt its main responsibility was to lead the village associations *(chōnaikai)* and neighborhood associations *(tonarigumi)*. At the lowest level, neighborhood associations were used for mutual surveillance and to promote peer pressure. One step up, the village association managed the distribution of rationed goods and promoted collective action among the residents.[33] Village and neighborhood groups instructed the families and individuals on its roster that because Japan was facing a time of crisis in its war with China every aspect of life had to help the war effort. Lectures, magazines, and other media educated Japanese to think about when and what they purchased, and when and what they used and ate. Japanese told one another to believe in the greater common good and the glory of a victorious Japan in Asia.[34]

Reaching the People

The government used a variety of vehicles to inform the public of the new official information agencies and their roles. One favored strategy was contests. During the war, contests took place in every conceivable category of entertainment—dances, posters, movies, etc. Musical contests attracted some of the largest numbers of contestants, and many of the songs comedian Kawayanagi Senryū sings today won prizes in these contests. In October 1937, the Cabinet Information Office advertised a song contest for the creation of a national patriotic march. Advertisements urged contestants to draft a song that "the people could sing with heartfelt feeling for all eternity." The song needed to contain lyrics that "beautifully, brightly, and bravely had the air of a marching song." The contest directions suggested that what was clearly a propaganda song "should be a representation of the truth about Japan, symbolize the eternal life force and ideal of the empire, and be equal to the task of arousing the national spirit." Quite a task! The bureaucracy strongly supported many of these wartime contests with significant cash and prizes. More interestingly, this contest did not confine itself to the Japanese. Rules specifically detailed that participants could be from anywhere in the Japanese empire—Manchukuo,

Korea, Taiwan, etc. The results, announced in November of the same year, suggest that entries arrived from throughout the empire.[35]

In the 1937 contest a man from Tottori prefecture on the southwest coast of Japan placed first while someone living in Dalian, one of Japan's outpost cities on the Chinese Liaodong peninsula, won second prize. An individual from Yamaguchi prefecture in the south of Japan's main island won third prize. After the contest for the lyrics, the Cabinet Information Office held a second contest for accompanying music, with the same rules and prize money. The Cabinet Board of Information announced the final results on December 24, 1937, and staged a concert at a hall in the prime minister's residence. Aside from masquerading as fun, and offering monetary rewards, the fact that contestants emerged from around the Japanese empire demonstrates that Japanese propaganda did assist in connecting the home front with the battlefront and aid in the flow of information between colonial outposts and the home islands.

By the summer of 1941 Japan had already been embroiled for four years in an openly declared war on the Chinese mainland and had moved to occupy Indochina after the French lost possession of it when they surrendered to the Nazis. War with the Allies, however, was still six months away. The June 1941 issue of the magazine *National Drama (Kokumin engeki)* contained a full-page, red-ink announcement calling for scripts. "In these times of crisis," it announced, "the role film and drama play is unusually great. In this situation we face a grave shortage of what we need most—good scripts. Thus, the Cabinet Board of Information is issuing a wide appeal for excellent scripts in this quest to help assist with creating national films and theater. This will be no easy task."[36] As with the song contest, the agency offered monetary prizes to the winners.

A primary reason for the prevalence of contests seems to have been the dearth of entertainment in local villages. In order to satisfy this hunger the Japanese government and the IRAA created traveling theater groups that journeyed deep into the hinterland to entertain and educate audiences. These bands sometimes performed their own material, but frequently used prize songs produced by contests promoted in another government-sponsored magazine *Ie no hikari* (Homelight), the magazine of the enormous agricultural cooperative movement. Titles like "Fields are Battlegrounds Too" and "Song of the Farmer's Wife" proved popular.[37] Larger film and entertainment companies like Tōhō and Shōchiku financially supported their own traveling groups. The IRAA regularly dispersed funds, and each village also assisted with remuneration. Many companies felt it their patriotic duty to support these propaganda/entertainment recitals.[38] As the number of troupes and performances increased, the situation became less financially tenable for most entertainment organizations, and companies directly petitioned the government for reimbursement. The Cabinet Board of Information and the IRAA agencies, in cooperation with businesses and the community, permitted organizations a certain latitude to develop appropriate programs they wanted.

Japanese government organs responsible for propaganda constantly competed with other government agencies, lessening their overall efficacy. Competing bureaucratic administrations did the job one bureau could easily have done and the increased number of rules meant a diffusion of authority. This situation gave rise to the whimsical, antipropaganda slogan, "verbally agreeing but secretly desiring something else," a play on words with the abbreviation for the IRAA.[39] Struggles for supremacy among agencies producing propaganda also reflected the larger struggle within the Japanese military between the army and navy for control over foreign policy and war plans. Even with the arrival of the Cabinet Board of Information, designed to coordinate communication between government departments, the military refused to relinquish even a modicum of control over information relating to its activities. As a consequence a dual system of propaganda developed in Japan and continued throughout the war. The military continued to staff and disseminate propaganda through its own press department at the Imperial General Headquarters (Daihonei Hōdōbu) as well as through its intelligence platoons that worked abroad collecting information and writing and photographing what Japan's armed forces were doing. Civilian reporters worked for both the government and the military, but each staff was managed separately and operated under different internal regulations.

Professional Japanese Propagandists

To westerners the wartime Japanese behaved like docile sheep, blindly worshipping the emperor, soldiers shouting his name on the battlefield with their dying gasp. In contrast to this image held by the west, the Japanese who worked on wartime propaganda realized just the opposite. Japanese discriminated. They listened to some propaganda messages, ignored others. Effective propaganda that actually motivated people did not just appear, it required careful study, analysis, and production. Achieving this goal necessitated a staff of professionals who understood social psychology, public opinion, polling, industrial publishing, and a variety of other media skills. These men and women came from diverse backgrounds, liberal and conservative, and the range of their experiences and attitudes supports the label of "democratic fascism." Participants in propaganda activities joined for a range of reasons: some felt it would help advance their careers; some ardently believed in the messages; some may have been merely caught up in the moment; others saw opportunities ripe for the taking.

The most significant figure who helped construct Japanese conceptions of propaganda and formulate its practice was Koyama Eizō. Koyama was a prolific scholar, translator, professor, researcher, and government consultant on projects ranging from education, race and population studies, entertainment mobilization, health and urban issues, to media studies.[40]

Koyama began life as an elite in Japanese society. Born March 12, 1899, on the northern Japanese island of Hokkaido, his family did well enough in commerce during World War One to support Koyama through top schools, an education that culminated in his graduation from Tokyo Imperial University, Japan's flagship institution for higher education. Always interested in foreign cultures, Koyama took part in a trip in the 1930s sponsored by the Navy Ministry to Micronesia, Borneo, and western Asia. By 1938 he had joined Rikkyō University as a professor in the economics department, and in 1939 he began a consulting career with the Health and Welfare Ministry's Population Problems Research Institute. In 1942 Koyama joined the investigation section of the Kikakuin, or Cabinet Planning Agency, while at the same time continuing to examine questions of ethnicity and culture for the Ministry of Education's division of ethnic research. In his investigations at this research facility Koyama had an opportunity to analyze anti-Japanese mainland Chinese propaganda that had been collected and sent back to Japan for analysis.[41]

In the midst of this busy schedule Koyama found the time and means to pen several important books concerning propaganda: *Theories on the Craft of Propaganda* (1937), *Theory of Wartime Propaganda* (1942), and *Propaganda War* (1943). He did not limit his work to purely academic speculation regarding social mobilization. Race also intrigued Koyama. In 1943, as part of his consulting work for the Ministry of Health and Welfare's Population Problems Research Center, Koyama helped complete the lengthy six-volume report entitled *An Investigation of Global Policy with the Yamato Race as Nucleus.*[42]

In his 1937 work on propaganda, Koyama broke propaganda down into minute detail, explaining exactly how music could operate as propaganda, how to gauge whether campaigns were successful or not, as well as how tourism and advertising related to propaganda. Koyama's earliest work on propaganda clearly parallels the views expressed by the French theorist Ellul some thirty years later. Propaganda should be understood as a way to mold the minds of men, Koyama wrote. In the introduction to his treatise on propaganda Koyama asserted that propaganda existed as a fight for the "hegemony of an ideology." It must bring the people together under a unified concept of society and goals.[43] Agitation, on the other hand, is merely destructive and does not serve to motivate. Advertising, Koyama admitted, is related to propaganda, but it exists with the sole goal of furthering personal profit and is not necessarily aligned with national interests.[44]

By his 1942 work Koyama clearly felt the effects of Japan's stagnation in the propaganda war with China. His book began with accolades for Japan's war of liberation, which broke the chains of imperialism that had tied Asia to the west since the previous century. Koyama described how propaganda was intricately tied to the "thought war," or *shisōsen*, between Japan and the west. The thought war is important, Koyama cogently observed, because it plants the belief in the masses that victory is assured and that makes it possible to endure hardships in the meantime. Not only does effective propaganda in the thought war incite hatred of the enemy, Koyama proclaimed, it painstakingly points out the enemy's own hypocrisy, thus validating disgust with the enemy.[45] Koyama's book basically doubles as a piece of propaganda. Included in the back was a short and choppy article in English entitled, "China's Anti-Japanese Propaganda." Even though Koyama wrote numerous articles outlining and guiding Japanese propaganda programs during the war, as did so many other academics, he bemoaned Japan's inability to wage an effective propaganda campaign. "Now the Japanese is [sic] a people who honor truthful action rather than talking. They look at mere lip service as a sign of insincerity. Of all peoples in the world, theirs is a race gifted least with the art of talking well for and about themselves."[46] Koyama wished to convince others that Japan should be pitied because he felt that the Chinese were so much more capable on the propaganda front.[47] From 1937 on, Japan found itself roundly criticized in the international arena for its actions in China. Japanese officials and propagandists recognized that it would take high-quality English-language propaganda to convince the outside world of its supposedly peaceful aims.

Koyama also strenuously advocated the role of tourism in shaping international opinion. Japanese tourism came under the supervision of the Ministry of Railroads, which sponsored the Japan Tourism Bureau. But the Ministry of Foreign Affairs also had a hand in activities relating to foreigners visiting Japan. The opening leaf of the Japanese magazine *International Tourism (Kokusai kankō)* underscored the strategic importance of tourism. Tourism helped sway international public opinion and brought financial rewards in the form of convertible international currency.

> Those of us who are involved in international tourism do not only wish to correct and improve foreign understanding of Japan, but desire to raise the overall level of awareness abroad concerning Japan's proper actions during this holy war. At the same time, it is also difficult to conceal the pleasure of inviting to Japan

friendly foreign guests whose expenditures would offer some measure of relief in this time of economic emergency.[48]

In the same tourist magazine Koyama specifically noted how tourism could help bring about better relations between China and Japan. In order to understand the Chinese, the Japanese would have to analyze how the Chinese live and comprehend their ethnicity, Koyama wrote. Japan's military strength had expanded its zone of tourism and created a bloc, he said, and it is important to take advantage of the "new order," a Japanese-dominated East Asia.[49]

As with the song and script contests, supporters of propaganda and tourism ran numerous contests in tourism magazines for picture postcards and tourism posters. One 1939 contest announced:

> We are currently entering a new phase in our long bid to establish a new order, and we hope to raise the banner of Japanese national culture through international tourism and assertive propaganda. We have reached the increasingly significant juncture where, in line with national policy, we need to draw in foreign cash from the foreign guests whom we entice to Japan. Moreover, next year we celebrate the 2,600th-year anniversary of our country's founding . . . the great task of international tourism, as one wing of this holy war, is to propagate both abroad and domestically the true image of our youthful Japan with an old history.[50]

Koyama realized that producing effective Japanese wartime propaganda meant keeping track of what the enemy produced. In 1944 he published a book entitled *Trends among the Chinese Masses during the Greater East Asian War.* Years earlier Koyama had already begun analysis of the propaganda Chiang Kai Shek's Nationalist Party (KMT; Guomindang) produced in the war against Japan.[51] In the 1944 book Koyama specifically mentioned the high degree of influence Chinese wielded on the international front. He believed that the Chinese succeeded because they understood that the key to propaganda was organization.[52] Koyama felt that too often Japanese agencies, both government and private, competed unnecessarily. For example, the Ministry of Foreign Affairs and the Cabinet Board of Information both distributed propaganda abroad and their overlapping messages confused audiences.

Tsurumi Yūsuke, Intellectual Propagandist

Numerous Japanese intellectuals also assisted in wartime propaganda enterprises. Unlike Germany and elsewhere, where many intellectuals fled or disassociated themselves from the war project, many Japanese intellectuals lent their time, expertise, and money to the war. These men and women were educated, often internationally, well-traveled, multilingual, cosmopolitan individuals. They were not shrill fascists, but they did believe that Japan should be the leader in Asia. Many honestly asserted that Japan's "three-thousand-year history" and "unparalleled racial superiority" bestowed a civilizing mission on the country.[53]

Many wartime Japanese propagandists do not fit the negative postwar stereotype often attributed to propagandists such as Joseph Goebbels, head of the Nazi propaganda programs. Tsurumi Yūsuke was such an individual. He was a bureaucrat, a public intellectual, involved in promoting tourism, and at times he worked in high offices within the Ministry of Railroads. Tsurumi was not a hawk; he had traveled to China and counted among his acquaintances the famed Chinese writer Ba Jin. At one time Tsurumi had a personal audience with US President Woodrow Wilson. That meeting convinced Tsurumi to go into politics, and he later toured the United States with famed Christian intellectual internationalist Nitobe Inazō. He wrote poetry and novels, one of which, entitled *Mother,* later became a movie with the same title financed by Shōchiku pictures.[54] He also sent his two children to America for higher education.

Tsurumi Yūsuke remained a Japanese imperialist while supporting the virtues of a first-class elite American education for his children. According to the testimony of others, Tsurumi spoke fluent English. He told friends that before he delivered a talk in English, he performed facial exercises and actually massaged his face so that he could pronounce the words well. While on a seventy-day tour of China in 1923, Tsurumi had met with China's elite, including Hu Shi, Wu Yu, Zhou Zuoren, Xu Shichang, Cai Yuanpei, Wang Chongjiu, and the warlord Yan Xishan.

Tsurumi declared that Japan should strive for friendliness and openness toward China, but he attacked what he considered the outdated notion that the two countries shared a common race and historical cultural past.[55] Japan had grown powerful in Asia, he said, and this new friendship with a dominant Japan necessitated changing attitudes toward East Asian security.

In short, the cosmopolitan, well-educated, sophisticated Tsurumi contradicts the stereotype of a wartime propagandist touting Japanese supremacy. Tsurumi's behavior is an indicator that Japanese propaganda entailed more than Japanese military dominance of the world. Frequently wartime propaganda appealed to rational intellectuals because it reflected Japan as a civilizing force in a backward Asia. The fact that Tsurumi and others eagerly participated in seminars, tourist organizations, and lecture series to promote Japan's war aims demonstrates that many Japanese intellectuals in the 1930s believed in Japan as the leader in Asia.

The participation of intellectuals in the propaganda activities widened the sphere of propaganda's appeal. Tsurumi was certainly no Koyama Eizō. At times he worked for various government agencies, but Tsurumi represents a portion of elite society and the intellectual world who supported wartime propaganda aims behind the scenes. In the October 1939 issue of *International Tourism,* in an article entitled "Diagnosis of Tourism Propaganda Aimed at America," the well-traveled and influential Tsurumi penned arguments very similar to those Koyama espoused in his writings on tourism and propaganda. As Tsurumi observed, Japan was moving closer to Germany and away from friendship with the United States. This shift affected the types of tourist propaganda that he felt Japan should aim toward the United States. If the United States joined the war in Europe, Tsurumi noted that times would be tough because there would be fewer tourists. But, he speculated, what if the United States did not enter the fray and Japan maintained its own neutrality? Tsurumi cheerily suggested that because war had closed Europe to travelers, more tourists would therefore come to Asia. Tsurumi felt that Japan used to produce tourist literature targeted to foreign intellectuals or the upper class, emphasizing items like *nō* theater, kabuki performances, and the tea ceremony. Having scrutinized the situation, Tsurumi concluded that most people were satisfied with just reading about such pastimes.

Instead, Tsurumi recommended that Japan focus on America's middle class. He suggested that companies publish articles in popular magazines like the *Saturday Evening Post.* Tsurumi urged that Japan educate the US public to think of Japan in contrast to China with its starving filthy peasants. Tsurumi wanted the world to know that "Japan is at peace, we have bathtubs. We have paved roads. We also have stamps. You can find and eat Western food. There are no poisonous insects here. Cholera does not run rampant."[56] Tsurumi wished to show the world that Japan was modern. He admitted that such propaganda still necessitated using images of cherry blossoms and Mt. Fuji because he did not want the image of Japan to be just like America. As a champion of Japan's modernity, Tsurumi also realized that something had to be done about Japanese toilets, or all propaganda efforts would be in vain. He complained that the first thing that bothered him when he returned from his numerous trips abroad was the stench. Japan could not put all that effort into propaganda, Tsurumi wrote publicly, and then lead foreign tourists to a stinky toilet in a private house.

Japanese intellectuals simultaneously cherished Japan's modernity and praised its expansionist goals in Asia. Tsurumi may have been liberal, but he was still a 1930s imperialist, and he created an organization called the Pacific Association to fund imperial aims. One subordinate who worked for the group remembered Tsurumi's remarks concerning the 1937 "China Incident," the occasion in July where Japanese soldiers clashed with Chinese at the Marco Polo Bridge some miles outside Beijing, which signaled the beginning of the major Japanese military offensive on the Chinese mainland:

> Now, due to the China Incident, Japan is stuck in a quagmire on the mainland— we cannot advance, we cannot retreat. If we continue in this manner Japan will fall into dire straits. But, even if we withdraw from China, we Japanese cannot live only on this small island nation. Shifting our national sights from the Chinese continent toward the south, Japanese should make a peaceful advance toward the South Seas. Particularly in New Guinea, where natives are not numerous and the society is underdeveloped, if the diligent Japanese make it a colony, it would be much cheaper in the long run than the finances needed for war in China. However, in order to succeed in this endeavor we need, more than anything, to open a dialogue with the United States. I myself have many close friends in American political circles, and I would like to dedicate the remaining years of my life to promoting Japanese advancement in the South Seas amidst a peaceful US-Japan rapprochement.[57]

Tsurumi's attitudes closely parallel descriptions of Japan's charismatic postwar Prime Minister Yoshida Shigeru as an "imperialist," and Tsurumi perhaps most vividly embodies the concerns wartime Japanese intellectuals voiced.[58] While he was a liberal and international personality Tsurumi still revered the emperor and supported Japan's imperial claims. Members of Japan's cosmopolitan elite did not distance themselves from wartime propaganda; they embraced it and involved themselves in its creation. Intellectuals were not misled; they actively helped convince others because they believed in Japan's war in Asia. When the declaration of war against America was announced over the radio, one of Tsurumi's subordinates was sitting in his chair at work. Tsurumi came out of his office and yelled at this individual in a loud voice, ordering him to stand up and lower his head because one needed to stand at strict attention when an imperial declaration was being broadcast over the radio.[59] Despite advocating close relations with America, for Tsurumi the empire took precedence.

Tourism as Propaganda

Nothing illustrates the interconnectedness among government agencies, civilian bureaucracies, and the military more than the wartime tourist trade. A wide spectrum of the Japanese population—from government officials to military officers to the man on the street—wholeheartedly believed that Japan had to publicize its modernity. Tourism became central to this publicity campaign. In 1938 a campaign was undertaken to alter the opinions of those who had denounced the December 1937 Nanjing massacre. As part of this, the International Tourist Bureau, an agency under the aegis of the Ministry of Railroads, sent propaganda film troops into China. Among their numerous projects they produced a series of films entitled "The Japan You Don't Know," which they distributed along with Chinese language pamphlets and postcards. The unit distributed 20,000 pamphlets emblazoned with pictures of Japan and charged a Japanese army pacification platoon, or *senbuhan* (a unit specifically responsible for keeping order in occupied areas), to distribute the pamphlets to the Chinese public.[60] The pamphlets spoke of the friendly history between China and Japan. The same tourism bureau also printed and delivered 360,000 picture postcards.[61]

A close relationship between the government and the tourist industry enabled the industry to seek government aid to promote its products. Years before the invasion of China in 1937, but only a few years after Japan's initial military foray into Manchuria in 1931, the Japan Tourism Bureau (JTB) asked Amō Eiji, head of the Foreign Ministry's Information Bureau, to contribute a letter to the magazine *Tourist*. Amō Eiji was a well-known Japanese, an internationally educated bureaucrat who had caused an international stir with his declaration of Japan's "Asiatic Monroe Doctrine."[62] As a spokesman for the government, Amō announced that since order in East Asia was Japan's responsibility, the west should refrain from providing assistance to China.[63] On November 20, 1934, Amō wrote the requested letter for the magazine *Tourist*. Amō sent copies in both English and Japanese to the JTB, with the English title of "Impressions of the Tourist Industry." Amō took pride in his Japanese heritage, saying that the Japanese were an "Asiatic people living in an insignificant archipelago, yet maintaining a superb national unity, and accomplishing unparalleled development in three quarters of a century." Amō felt that international tourists did indeed come to Japan to witness this growth firsthand, but that obstructive police and linguistic barriers sometimes made this travel difficult. To surmount these hurdles, Japan needed to polish its image.[64]

Compared with his counterparts Tsurumi and Koyama, Amō was even more outspoken about the role tourism played in generating a benevolent international attitude toward Japan. In an internal Ministry of Foreign Affairs memo, Amō emphasized that tourism was not only a profit-making venture, but that it had significant cultural and political implications. More and more foreigners are visiting Japan, he wrote, and since "seeing is believing," he reasoned, once they arrive in Japan they will see what the foreign press spouts is untrue because Japan is a peaceful and great nation.[65]

Since Japan lacked international resorts, such as those found in Paris or

Shanghai, in 1935 the Ministry of Foreign Affairs and the Railroad Ministry had floated a plan to construct an enormous resort just off the coast of Atami, about an hour and a half away from Yokohama. The blueprint called for a "city that never sleeps," with movie theaters, tea rooms, dance halls, bars, indoor exercise rooms—so many different attractions that visitors would think they had arrived at "paradise."[66] Unfortunately, the project never made it past the planning stages, and the blueprints still await funding in the Ministry of Foreign Affairs archives. Instead, in an effort to secure positive American opinion for its growing Asian empire, Japanese government agencies invited prominent American editors from well-known magazines such as *Harper's Bazaar, Traveler, Atlantic Monthly, Time, Fortune,* and others to visit Japan, Korea, and Manchuria for two months, all expenses paid.[67]

In contrast to the Cabinet Board of Information, the two agencies most concerned with public opinion—the Ministry of Foreign Affairs and the Railroad Ministry—went to great lengths to conceal their hand in propaganda campaigns. A 1938 top-secret internal report from the Ministry of Foreign Affairs came with specific instructions not to release any of the contents to the public. The memo discussed the methods by which Japan could increase positive public exposure. By this time, in September 1938, Japan was already facing caustic international criticism for all-out war against China, following the July 1937 China Incident. This secret report, entitled "An Outline of Propaganda and Intelligence Operations Relating to the China Incident," underscored the prominent position American public opinion occupied in the Japanese quest for international acceptance.

Having acknowledged that propaganda operations directed at North America were central to Japan's success, Japanese officials felt empowered to use every available means, including employing Japanese-Americans and mobilizing Japanese consulates in San Francisco, Los Angeles, and elsewhere to gain support.[68] The Japanese government maneuvered to have favorable articles concerning its movements in Asia and explaining why boycotts against Japan hurt everyone printed in prominent American newspapers. The Ministry of Foreign Affairs targeted Black American newspapers for specific attention in the hope that disenfranchised minorities would seek solace in Japan's championship of the "colored races."[69] The goal to manipulate foreign media focused on "guiding world opinion concerning Japan," "splitting world opinion regarding Japan and the China Incident," and "breaking the front of unified anti-Japanese opinion."[70]

Following Japan's military invasion of China in the summer of 1937, Japan had faced harsh international criticism. News of Japanese atrocities, primarily in Nanjing in December 1937, was broadcast worldwide. The Japanese government sought to discredit what it considered exaggerated accounts foreign missionaries provided to the outside world.[71] One American in particular, journalist Frederick Vincent Williams, worked for Japan by producing in 1938 a book called *Behind the News in China.* Williams suggested to the American public that overzealous missionaries had fabricated the reports of atrocities in China. In his forward, he wrote that he "saw both sides" and "was able to judge for himself," and hence presented his book as free of bias. "I have spoken freely and directly and with the idea in mind that it is better to know the truth than to continue to kid ourselves along."[72] To profit from such "neutral," third-person reporting, a Japanese newspaper, the *Osaka mainichi,* then republished what Williams wrote as pamphlets, bearing titles such as "Common Sense and the China Emergency." These pamphlets featured articles suggesting that the behavior of the Japanese military was beyond reproach and that Japan had no role in the instigation of any problems in China.[73]

Williams was as prolific in his denial of Japanese atrocities as the Japanese. Unfortunately, however, neighbors frequently saw him at the bank depositing money, which aroused suspicion as to his allegiance and journalistic objectivity. After a three-week trial, on June 1, 1942, the Washington DC Federal District Court convicted Frederick Vincent Williams of conspiracy and nine violations of the Foreign Agents Act. The court concluded that a secret Japanese propaganda organization, the Jikyoku Iinkai, Committee for the Current State of Affairs, also known as the Japanese Committee on Trade and Information, had employed Williams. The US media believed that the Japanese government financed and controlled the organization, "which spent some $195,000 for the purpose of spreading propaganda in the United States through radio speeches, a monthly magazine and pro-Japanese booklets."[74]

Evidence on the Japanese side corroborates Williams's culpability. Williams did not begin penning laudatory articles for the Japanese government in 1938; he had been working for Japan years prior to the outbreak of war with China. Moreover, Japanese government officials had similar relations with other journalists well before the onset of war into China in 1937. Records from Japan's Ministry of Foreign Affairs verify that Japanese officials contacted Williams and other non-Japanese journalists as early as December 1932. In that year the Japanese consul in Portland, Oregon, Nakamura Toyoichi, wrote a memo to Ministry of Foreign Affairs Information Bureau Chief Shiratori Toshio, saying that a newsman, Frederick Williams Vincent, Jr. (they slightly jumbled his name), was traveling to Manchuria and desired introductions. The memo noted that Williams "is well disposed toward us," is a good friend of an influential American Chamber of Commerce member in Portland, and writes for numerous papers across the country.[75]

In January 1933 the second-in-command at the consulate wrote directly to Vice-Minister of the Railroad Ministry Kubota Keiichi to request unlimited rail passes for Williams. The Japanese government should treat Williams well, Vice Consul Arita wrote, since Japanese officials anticipated that Williams would provide Japan with good press abroad, to "enlighten" the world concerning Japan's projects throughout Asia.[76] The Railroad Ministry later sent Williams a one-month first-class rail pass. In 1938 Williams showed up again in Manchuria, this time in the capital of Japan's puppet kingdom Manchukuo, requesting an interview with the emperor Puyi. Puyi, the last emperor of the deposed Qing dynasty, was Japan's choice to be emperor of the newly created "country" of Manchukuo. Japan's Kwantung Army, which essentially ran the country, did not take kindly to nosy foreign journalists and refused. The situation seemed sufficiently disturbing to the civilian government in Tokyo, which had long courted Williams, that Japan's ambassador in Xinjing, the capital of Manchukuo, General Ueda Kenkichi, sent a missive to the Minister of Foreign Affairs Hirota Kōki explaining the state of affairs and asking for guidance.[77]

A top-secret cable from Japanese Consul Satō in San Francisco, in September 1940, to then Minister of Foreign Affairs Matsuoka Yōsuke emphasizes the importance the Japanese Ministry of Foreign Affairs and related agencies placed on favorable reporting by non-Japanese Americans in the world of public opinion. As an alumnus of the University of Oregon, Matsuoka understood the implications of the cable clearly. He understood America and the need to shape international public opinion. After graduating from university in the United States and returning to Japan, Matsuoka had served as head of the South Manchurian Railway, whose offices frequently served as propaganda conduits on the Chinese mainland. Satō explained to Minister Matsuoka that since the start of the China Incident enlightenment propaganda directed toward America had generally been under the guidance of the Jikyoku Iinkai. However, Satō had recognized that the FBI had redoubled efforts to root out "fifth columns and enemy agents" in the United States. He therefore suggested that the Japanese government disassociate from the Jikyoku Committee—actually disband it—and inform the US State Department that it would soon cease to exist. In addition, Satō suggested that since these changes placed Frederick Williams in a difficult predicament, the Japanese government should consider changing his title, or employ him directly as a special correspondent for *The Japan Times* to avoid the appearance of impropriety.[78]

Williams was not the only instance in which Japan courted non-Japanese journalists. The Ministry of Foreign Affairs and tourist agencies had financed at least two other Americans, David Warren Ryder and Ralph Townsend.[79] A top-secret June 1936 telegram, from Ambassador Saitō Hiroshi in the United States to Minister of Foreign Affairs Arita Hachirō, detailed how many influential US journalists Japanese consulates employed. The New York consulate supported Fisher, a writer for *The New York Times;* the San Francisco consulate received services from Thompson, as well as Henry Cotkins, foreign editor of the *San Francisco News;* the Japanese government had paid for Newton Bull, an orator, to journey several times to Japan and Manchuria; the New Orleans' consulate employed a man under the name of Dr. Townsend; the Washington Embassy enlisted Dr. Brooks Emeney; and the Portland consulate retained David Wilson. The telegram also listed other non-Japanese journalists who had no specific affiliation.[80]

The Japanese government also used tourism as a way to mold international and domestic public opinion. On September 19, 1938, influential members of the tourism industry, the media, and the government met at the Railway Hotel in Tokyo to "discuss the international tourism industry under the present circumstances." Participants included the head of the foreign division of the nascent Dōmei News Agency, Iwamoto Kiyoshi; the section chief of the Entertainment and Literature section of the Japan Broadcasting Association, Ono Kenichirō; Viscount Konoe Hidemaro, secretary to Prime Minister Konoe Fumimaro; noted department store magnate and creator of the hugely popular female review Takarazuka, Kobayashi Ichizō; and *Asahi shimbun* editor, Suzuki Bunshirō.[81]

The meeting examined two perplexing issues facing tourism and propaganda. First, what methods should be employed to create effective propaganda? And second, how should this propaganda be presented to foreign customers? Den Makoto, head of the International Tourist Bureau, opened the meeting bemoaning the world's ignorance of Japan and the gross misinformation concerning Japan in the foreign media. Den argued that pictures and pamphlets made good propaganda, but the best method was to bring foreigners to Japan itself to show them the real Japan. Den remarked that Japan had to spread the notion domestically that tourists should be treated well because they were important sources for positive international public opinion. Near the end of the meeting Kobayashi Ichizō interrupted to propose that his Takarazuka performance troupes could serve as an effective method for promoting excellent propaganda abroad, not to mention the generous profits that would follow. With several months of touring, good performance venues, and support from the government, these performances could have a great impact, Kobayashi suggested.[82]

A meeting held about nine months later discussed a similar agenda. A Who's Who of the intellectual elite and the politically influential presided at the June 19 meeting. Ashida Hitoshi from the Ministry of Foreign Affairs, Baron Kuroda Kiyoshi, Tatsuno Yutaka, a professor of literature from Tokyo Imperial University, and Tsurumi Yūsuke, an internationally known intellectual, were among the participants. A representative from the tourist bureau opened the meeting with the observation that since the China Incident world public opinion had been growing against Japan, especially in the United States. Echoing comments he had written in the tourism magazine, Tsurumi reminded the others that the content and style of propaganda depended on the country where one was trying to peddle influence. Tsurumi mentioned the fact that the tourist bureau often met with the Cultural Affairs section of the Ministry of Foreign Affairs for informative meetings and that this was one way to prepare the groundwork for effective tourism propaganda.[83]

Tourism, Trains, and Dreams of Empire

Tourism plans in 1930s Japan surpassed the wildest dreams of even its staunchest supporters. As part of its propaganda plans for the 1930s, Japan was seeking to prove that it was the most modern, most advanced, and strongest nation in Asia. The country hoped to demonstrate this with the ultimate expression of imperialism and technology—construction of a rail line under the Sea of Japan between Japan's southern tip and its colony Korea. Why not? After all, Japan's vast multinational conglomerate, the South Manchuria Railroad Company, already owned and operated one of the sleekest and most aerodynamic trains in Asia, the first all-air-conditioned Ajia.

Japanese travel brochures touted Xinjing, the new capital of Manchukuo, as a planned utopian city of the future.[84] Trumpeted as the apex of urban modernism, Xinjing was to have tree-lined streets and a citywide sewer system, among other recent innovations, that would demonstrate to the world the modernity Japan was bringing to Asia.[85] City planning for Tokyo and Manchukuo also tied into Japan's colossal projects for its hosting of the 1940 Olympics, which was to occur simultaneously with the 2,600th year anniversary of the nation's founding. The internally published blueprint of the government's plans for the combined celebration of the 2,600th anniversary and the Olympics clearly stated that Japan should seize the occasion to "strengthen the nation's awareness of the true Japan, and unveil the correct image of Japan to other countries as well as demonstrate our increasing national power, might, and national prosperity."[86] In many ways Japan's emphasis on trains as propaganda indicative of its imperial prestige had begun at the turn of the century with Japan's initial forays into Manchuria.[87]

The years leading up to Japan's victory in securing sponsorship of the

1940 Olympics recorded tremendous growth in Japanese travel to Manchuria. By 1930 several major hotels, coping with the growing influx of Japanese tourists, opened luxurious buildings in the city of Dalian. By 1941, before the outbreak of the Pacific War, the rising number of Japanese tourists forced the Japan Tourism Bureau to resort to hiring local Chinese staff to keep up with demand. While a majority of the travelers came from the wealthy classes, many were also students on school trips or organized group tours from rural areas. From 1930 to 1939 Japanese travelers to Manchuria alone rose from 530,000 to just under one million. Dalian hotel occupancy rates leapt from a mere 20,000 in 1934 to around one million by 1939.[88] Nor, apparently, did Japan's full-scale invasion of China in 1937 deter foreign visitors, who continued to choose the Japanese empire as a destination. In 1940 a record number of travelers visited in the summer months of July, August, and September.[89]

With increased Japanese travel, rail lines grew in importance. They provided the Japanese with greater flexibility to promote "healthy activities," like sports and leisure pursuits. This "expansion of Japan's railway networks combined to open more and more mountain areas to summer and winter sporting activity."[90]

At the same time the widening military crisis in China after the summer of 1937 placed heavier demands on trains to transport troops and material. This, combined with increased passenger transport on the rail lines, forced Japanese bureaucrats to discuss how to organize the system and make it more efficient. Why, for example, were connections not better coordinated? Why should it take an express train so long to get from Tokyo to Shimonoseki, the southernmost tip of Japan's main island? Numerous officials argued that if transport could be efficiently linked to Manchuria, then many of Japan's economic modernization programs could be more seamlessly integrated. Manchuria had gradually come to occupy Japan's popular consciousness as a necessary source for economic prosperity and a pressure valve to relieve tensions from the expanding Japanese population. The answer to railway problems, many felt, lay in not just reorganizing train schedules and track switches, but in building an entirely new system of train transport that would combine speed, efficiency, and mobility.

One plan called for a high-speed train line that would originate in Tokyo, cut through the mountains south to Shimonoseki, and then, *going under the ocean floor,* would shift west to Korea to arrive above ground near Pusan. From there the train would continue on to Hōten (Mukden, now Shenyang) and Xinjing (now Changchun).[91] The plan would simultaneously accomplish two goals: it would help Japan alleviate congested transportation conditions, and it would highlight Japan's technological superiority, a concept to be showcased at the 1940 Olympics.[92] Rail Minister Murata Shōzō declared at a press conference that this plan had to be implemented or the Chinese continent's economic future would fail.[93]

The train was called the *dangan ressha*, or "bullet train," because it would travel quickly, making the trip from Tokyo to the capital of Manchukuo in under three days.[94] Its conception did not stem altogether from wartime urgency, though fear of losing goods due to sea battles and bombing raids did force the issue. Actual feasibility studies had already begun in 1935, two years prior to the full-scale Japanese military incursions into China. The bullet-train project soon became part of the popular consciousness. Newspapers described it in detail, and at least one author devoted a book to the subject. The Tōei film company went so far as to produce and market a film, titled *Otoko*, about the building of the train line, in which the director included actual footage of the first tunnel dug.[95] Visions of a modern, healthy Japan captured the imagination of the country.

The project mesmerized more than just the railway officials, it captured the imagination of the nation. The glory Japan could achieve with the success of such a venture fascinated bureaucrats, who spoke of the plans in hushed tones of awe at Japan's technological audacity. One such bureaucrat spoke at a September 8, 1939, Imperial Railway Association meeting. Mirroring comments that Tsurumi Yūsuke had made earlier, concerning how the war in Europe might prove to be a bonus for Japan, this tourism bureau official tried to convince the participants that war in Europe would render many transcontinental train lines obsolete. Since long flights were neither financially or physically possible at that time, the new order of East Asia mandated laying down new rail lines, he said. This underscored the immense importance of Japan's sea-tunnel project.[96]

Though committed to high-speed travel as a showcase for Japanese modernity, Japanese officials were also intensely concerned with public hygiene and health. This anxiety stemmed from continued apprehension over how the west, and other Asian countries and colonies, perceived Japan. The Japanese government wished to present itself as a country unlike the rest of Asia, specifically China; Japan was a sanitary country as strong and healthy as the west. Success at sports, a concrete indicator of strength and national health the Japanese felt, would serve as a barometer for international acclaim and prestige. Japanese society hoped the 1940 Olympics would prove irrefutably that Japan had entered the circle of modern nations.

The Japanese government's increased concentration on the health and strength of the individual Japanese—seen as a strategy to produce a more resilient and powerful nation—was reflected in the variety of new health plans initiated by the Diet and social organizations. Physical education programs conducted in schools and broadcast on radio buoyed this national interest in health. Through this national attention to health and hygiene the Japanese nation saw itself as modern, and thus not Chinese or Korean. The Japanese government urgently desired to separate itself from the stereotypical image of a dirty, stagnant, squalid, backwater Asian country, and replace that vision with one of a clean, hygienic, technologically advanced Japan. The government understood that the fundamental base of a healthy nation was a healthy individual. As the Japanese government conceived of it, national strength demanded a strong, healthy populace. With such careful attention paid to them, it is no wonder that a majority of Japanese citizens reacted favorably to the programs that placed them at the center of the success of the nation. As the 1940 *Bungei shunjū* magazine survey noted, the Japanese did not always regard government intervention as oppressive but, instead, often welcomed it.

The Japanese government had reason to be anxious about the health, not only of its population in general, but specifically of the young men drafted to serve as soldiers. A January 1937 government journal canvassed six major cities to determine the state of the country's health. Out of 1,000 young men, Tokyo could only field about 255 with no health problems; Osaka was slightly higher with 264, while Nagoya, a less urban area, surprisingly came in at 373. What was noticeable, however, was that the report deemed more men unfit than fit for service. It is easy to understand why the military so fervently pushed for a health ministry to be created. Not only were the conscripts in poor health, they were small as well. The average height for a young man was 5 feet 3 inches, with an average weight of around 115 pounds. The most common health problems were lung and eye diseases, while endemic venereal diseases further sapped the population's well being.[97]

The government bureaucracy concerned itself equally with how the image of proper health and hygiene affected the country as a whole. Home Ministry Minister Yamamoto Tatsuo conveyed this anxiety, stating that "planning for the enrichment and diffusion of medical care relief, and dealing with the present emergency situation, especially on the level of preserving the health of the nation's subjects and on the level of relief is, I think, most crucial."[98] Health and hygiene became a vital topic for both public discussion and military programs. After decades of mounting pressure from the army and navy, the Japanese government finally, in July 1937, merged the various hygiene and health bureaus that had been under the jurisdiction of several ministries into one new Ministry of Health and Welfare.

This new ministry was completely devoted to the pressing issues of the physical welfare of the individual. The Health and Welfare Ministry included a Physical Strength Bureau and a Hygiene Bureau, which had jurisdiction over physical education and proper health education. The Ministry also had the responsibility for establishing city parks.[99] This combination of tasks demonstrates how closely associated urban planning and social health were within the sphere of the Japanese bureaucracy.

Mobilizing a large military to invade China stimulated Japanese government and military fears concerning the overall health of the population and most specifically the young men who would soon be on the battlefields. Once the July 1937 China Incident signaled the beginning of the major Japanese military offensive on the Chinese mainland, total war also brought the issue of health and empire to the forefront. A few weeks after the Incident, the Health and Welfare Ministry commenced six health awareness campaigns.[100]

Good Health as Propaganda—the Olympics

Japan's technological modernity also zoomed to the foreground with its participation in the Olympics. Sporting events played a prominent role in Japanese propaganda to portray Japan as the strong, modern leader of Asia. In early August 1936 both *Asahi shimbun* and *The New York Times* ran articles quoting Prime Minister Hirota Kōki, who stated that the choice of Tokyo for the Olympics should be "construed as the result of all countries of the world correctly understanding our nation."[101] Hirota's use of "understanding" simply implied that the world should recognize that Japan was the dominant force in Asia.

When news of Tokyo as the future site for the 1940 Olympics was broadcast, just as the 1936 Berlin Olympic Games opened, Japan went into a delirium. All the stores in Ginza, a posh shopping district in Tokyo, flew five-ring Olympic flags. Offices, department stores, and any building with a facade hung banners and took part in the celebration. Within forty-eight hours of the announcement a canned pineapple company, a chocolate manufacturer, and a sunscreen-lotion maker were already distributing advertisements employing the Olympic symbols.[102] One enterprising English school, firm in its belief that the 1940 Olympics would mean tens of thousands more foreign tourists, advertised its school as the place to "prepare for the Olympics."[103] An August 6, 1936, news article clarified that the Japanese Tourism Bureau predicted 80,000 foreign visitors and expected a budget of three million yen in order to deal with the demand.[104] The day before, a newspaper had demonstrated the latest hairstyle for women as none other than the "Olympic haircut," complete with five ringlets curling over the forehead.[105] The all-girl Takarazuka review quickly staged an Olympic Revue as did popular stage comedian Furukawa

Roppa.[106] Radio comedian Entan Enosuke even broadcast a comedy radio program titled, "I am an Olympic athlete."[107]

For the first two weeks of August 1936 anything relating to the Olympics caught the nation's attention. The interest in the Olympics was so intense that even in 1964, when Japan did actually host the Olympics, journalists clearly recalled the Olympic fever that had hit Japan almost thirty years earlier. Engineers and architects even used plans similar to those of 1940 to construct the stadiums and plan the pavilions in 1964. Trains and tourism also staged a repeat comeback. In 1964 Japan finally celebrated the first Olympics to be held in Asia, twenty-four years after it first won the honor. As Japan prepared to receive the world in 1964, in the hopes of gaining international recognition for the country's postwar rebirth, travelers rode the new bullet trains designed essentially from the wartime plans of the 1930s.

The 1940 Olympics never took place. Japan cancelled its Olympic plans in the middle of 1938 amidst worries over steel production and whether the government would be able to requisition from tightfisted military leaders the necessary funds. By the end of 1938 Japan's increased military presence in China demanded the country's entire concentration.

From the early 1930s Japan had streamlined and attempted to reorganize several key government agencies, such as the Cabinet Board of Information and the IRAA, to promote Japan's message of modernity at home and abroad. Domestically, intellectuals and professional propagandists had championed this effort and participated in studies and roundtables that focused on analyzing and producing quality propaganda. Internationally, Japan's propaganda efforts had led them to hire foreign journalists to broadcast its word abroad. Civilian and government efforts to win sponsorship of the Olympics, the promotion of Japan as a tourist destination, and the construction of a seeming technological impossibility of building a railway under the sea were major wartime undertakings. These projects testify that the Japanese were serious about promoting themselves as the most civilized, technologically superior, and strongest nation in Asia.

CHAPTER TWO

Defining the Limits of Society

One of Japan's most famous spies, Onoda Hirō, graduated from the Nakano School, the military's institute for espionage in the quiet western suburbs of Tokyo. School officials kept activities so secret that even townspeople living in the immediate vicinity had no idea what the buildings housed or that students there studied the "black arts." Sent to the Philippines in December 1944, Onoda fought there for thirty years. The army specifically commanded Onoda not to commit suicide because the imperial forces considered his mission of paramount importance to Japan's national security and ultimate victory. Army officers stipulated that even if it took three or five years military forces would eventually return and repatriate Onoda. In the meantime they ordered him to gather intelligence to be used to prepare the island for guerrilla warfare. After Japan's defeat, even though Onoda picked up news leaflets dropped by US planes, he believed they were counterpropaganda. He did not surrender and return to Japan until March 9, 1974.[1] A few years prior to Onoda's surrender, another Japanese soldier, Yokoi Shōichi, became a national hero after he emerged from the jungles of Guam twenty-six years after the end of World War Two. Japanese media broadcast nationally his first words upon arriving in Tokyo, "It is with much embarrassment that I return," a phrase that instantly became a popular saying.

Onoda and Yokoi are extreme examples of Japanese wartime perseverance, but their attitudes mark an interesting trend within the development of wartime Japanese propaganda. When these men and a few others returned to Japan decades after both sides had signed the surrender treaties, they did not face ridicule but celebration. The population, enthusiastic after hosting the 1964 Olympics and blessed with a burgeoning economy, held up Onoda and Yokoi as the epitome of the Japanese ability to persist in the face of adversity *(gan-baru)*, even in a losing situation. An eminent historian of Japan, Ivan Morris, understood this characteristic as belonging to a culture that championed a "nobility of failure." The ability to persist against dire odds intrigued the immediate postwar American research teams dispatched to calculate the Japanese response to the war's end. The US teams analyzed the Japanese psychological response toward domestic and Allied wartime propaganda and tried to establish a quotient correlating how public opinion varied with levels of bombing.[2]

The story of how Japan inculcated its population with the notion of destiny and modernity that raised soldiers like Onoda and Yokoi should begin with propaganda. Supporting the bureaucratic management already detailed was the physical reinforcement behind wartime propaganda. The police and the military played significant supporting roles in the construction and monitoring of wartime Japanese propaganda that over the period from 1931 to 1945 ultimately led to a society so galvanized by propaganda that it was able to change virtually overnight and accept defeat in 1945.

The propaganda stabilizing Japan's modern empire rested on a structure of collusion, and government rhetoric was not its only catalyst. The police, military, and governmental authorities worked to define and regulate the limits of acceptable behavior. The media and advertising industries assisted in visualizing those limits and created a concrete vision of what Japan's future utopia would look like. In this process the police wielded more than just batons. They served as surrogates for the propaganda and identified themselves as the vanguard in Japan's quest to build a new empire in Asia. A section of the Special Higher Police supervised foreigners residing in Japan and collected information on them. Other police divisions helped coordinate the ceremonies staged for soldiers departing from rural Japan. The police constantly took the pulse of the nation, like a doctor carefully keeping track of a needy patient.

The Special Higher Police

The police were indispensable to propaganda programs. The Tokkō Keisatsu, or Special Higher Police, were the central body that coordinated public safety from the prewar era and throughout the war. The Home Ministry, the main government department in charge of public order, formally established the Special Higher Police in August 1911, partly in response to a planned attempt on the Meiji emperor's life. This new division of police took responsibility for monitoring foreign elements residing in Japan, including Koreans, subversive thought, censorship, and other potential aspects of civic unrest. In 1920 the ministry strengthened these special forces because of a perceived threat from socialist groups and movements. Fear of Soviet influence also played a role. The Special Higher Police should not, however, be confused with the Nazi Gestapo. Japan's special higher police were often brutal, but they were not particularly secretive. The Japanese authorities regarded police suppression as an

important tool for social control, but it was not the only tool. Japanese officials also aggressively pressured dissidents to "convert," or change their allegiance. In Japanese they referred to this adjustment as *tenkō*. Many writers and
performers who had joined leftist causes in the 1920s and early 1930s realigned
their principles and toed the government line by the later 1930s. These were
rarely voluntary decisions. Police and judicial authorities cajoled, threatened,
and tortured many into submission.

The police played an unusually active role in preventing "dangerous
thoughts" through the mechanism of propaganda. Japanese police realized that
physical repression alone could not force dissidents to recant and reorient
themselves. The police's understanding of social mobilization mirrored the
understanding of the Japanese bureaucracy that to merely impose laws would
have little beneficial social impact. By the early 1930s the police understood the
role propaganda played in making society stable. Consequently, the police were
not interested in merely incarcerating dissidents, they wanted them to reform
their way of thinking. Propaganda became increasingly important because it
provided the vision of Japan's modern future to which all should pledge allegiance. The vision needed to be convincing because the authorities expected
the people to make sacrifices, but simultaneously wanted them to approve the
better future of the nation and empire.

To maintain a record of its surveys, keep track of what it had censored,
explain new policies, promote its own vision of what the "new" Japan should
look like, and inform other agencies of its efforts to keep the public in line,
Japanese police agencies published a myriad of in-house journals. Beginning
in the 1930s the Home Ministry's Police Bureau published the *Special Higher
Police Monthly Report, Foreign Activities Monthly, Foreign Activities Police
Report,* and the *Police Report on Publishing.* These periodicals addressed pend-
ing cases, new intelligence, and police concerns. On October 4, 1945, the American occupiers officially disbanded the Special Higher Police, but it remained
active unofficially for months afterward.[3] These changes will be discussed in
Chapter Six.

The creation of a police force to oversee foreign elements in Japan grew
from Japanese fears concerning the rise of Communism. Through brutal
repression and coercive tactics the Special Higher Police managed to crush
most nascent Communist cells by the mid-1930s. The "conversion" of two
leading Communist leaders, Sano Manabu and Nabeyama Sadachika, put the
final nail in the coffin of the socialist movement until after the war.

The fear of foreigners, however, also created several tangential problems
for those in the propaganda agencies in 1930s Japan. By the start of the war

with China in 1937, in the mind of the police "foreign" automatically meant subversive. The Japanese tourist industry, dependent on foreign travelers for good international commercial press about Japan, continually criticized police activities as counterproductive propaganda.[4]

Unlike regular police forces that seek to prevent physical crimes, the Special Higher Police continually attempted to gauge the public reception of foreign and domestic ideas or propaganda. Once the war with the United States exploded in December 1941, the police section that surveyed foreign activities grew even more vigilant. The police obsessed over potential spies or what they interpreted as a "hotbed of foreign enemies' machinations." The police considered the poor, the hungry, the unemployed, and Catholics as those most susceptible to foreign propaganda. In order to forestall potential dissent the police kept a keen watch and record of "trends and changes within the national psyche."[5]

The Special Higher Police were sometimes also called the "thought police" (shisō keisatsu) because they prosecuted crimes dealing with acts labeled "seditious." Their police manual openly declared that police duties bound them "to prevent and suppress social movements that attempted to disrupt the social order or place the nation at peril." Like the agencies that managed government-sponsored propaganda, the police realized that effective social control would not arise out of regulation alone. The "thought police" became a key node of force in the thought war against China, and later America because Japanese authorities defined thought as a weapon. The authorities charged that "the special higher police had to be victorious, standing as the vanguard, and fighting against the shapeless and formless bombs, the propaganda, that the enemy launched in this 'thought war.'"[6]

As the war with China turned into a larger war against the west in late 1941, the role of Japan's Special Higher Police expanded. In addition to stemming the flow into the country of detrimental foreign propaganda, the Special Higher Police assumed partial responsibility for prisoners of war (POWs) detained within Japan. These same duties required the Special Higher Police to manage the Chinese and Korean laborers working in Japan, and those who were later forced into slave labor. Japan captured tens of thousands of Allied POWs, but the Japanese military never housed many Chinese POWs. Japanese soldiers usually murdered them, or considered them "civilian spies," not worthy of military treatment. The infinitesimal number of Chinese prisoners who survived encounters with the Japanese military testifies to their harsh treatment at the hands of the Japanese.[7] Japanese wartime diaries, detailed in Chapter Five, also document this brutality.

The Kawaisō Incident: POWs and Propaganda

To the Japanese authorities successful management of POWs housed in Japan equaled effective domestic propaganda for three reasons. First, the Japanese authorities did not want Japanese on the home front sympathizing with the plight of POWs; fraternization was not an option. Since Japan's wartime propaganda sought to link the home front with the battlefront, compassion for POWs would threaten to break that bond. Japanese wartime propaganda needed armed Chinese and westerners to be seen as the despised enemy. Second, Japanese propaganda agencies employed Allied POWs for explicit propaganda purposes—in print, film, and radio. Third, authorities believed that the Japanese needed to be reminded constantly that becoming a POW disgraced the military's honor and one's family. Only westerners, who lacked *yamato damashii,* the Japanese spirit, surrendered. As part of an overall plan of propaganda, treating POWs poorly helped maintain a mental and physical divide between civilian and military Japanese and the prisoners with whom they had close contact. Imamura Shōhei depicted such an episode in his 1998 fictional film *Kanzō sensei.* In the film a small-town doctor in the south of Japan, Akagi, befriends an escaped Dutch POW. This relationship places the doctor in peril with the Japanese military, which is determined to pressure the local population into seeing the foreign soldier as the despised enemy.

POWs were not totally useless, however, to the Japanese wartime cause. Japanese propaganda agencies both in Japan and throughout the empire employed white Allied POWs in film and radio propaganda that was disseminated abroad. The Japanese realized that while POWs needed to be kept away from Japanese citizens and Japanese-controlled colonials, their image could be used simultaneously to display the vanquished white soldiers and to showcase the modern facilities the Japanese erected for such unfortunate westerners. Few examples of these items exist today, but *Calling Australia,* a wartime Japanese film showing the supposedly idyllic life of Australian POWs in camps that can only be described as palatial, seems to have fooled only the Japanese and Indonesians who produced the film.

Japanese wartime media castigated Japanese who did not sufficiently despise POWs. On December 4, 1942, Imperial General Headquarters Army Section Intelligence Officer Lieutenant Colonel Akiyama Kunio delivered a radio broadcast declaring that Japanese on the home front should not sympathize with POWs. The lieutenant's speech had been stimulated by an encounter he had on the street with a Japanese woman who felt that the foreign POWs "looked pitiful," *kawaisō.* Akiyama attacked the woman's reaction. He acidly

This article details the Kawaisō Incident. The headline reads "Eradicate America from your hearts." And the subtitle asks, "What's all this about feeling pity for an American POW?" The article then summarizes Akiyama's radio broadcast. *Asahi shimbun* (Tokyo), December 5, 1942.

remarked that "this lady is probably not the Japanese wife of a husband who has been sent to the front. And it goes without saying that she is not the mother of a dear child gunned down by automatic fire, at the hands of a barbaric American."[8] Mainstream Japanese newspapers like the *Asahi shimbun* immediately picked up Akiyama's broadcast and gave the story prominent attention.[9] Wartime propaganda asserted in no uncertain terms that emotions of sympathy should be reserved for Japanese soldiers only. The POW policy also drove home the unstated slogan "hate the enemy, do not pity him."

In other public lectures Akiyama also promoted the idea that Japanese women played a crucial role in the growth of the war. At a talk to a volunteer women's association, the Shining Brigade, Akiyama rhetorically asked, "What allows the Japanese soldier to persevere with all his might, bravely throwing caution to the winds in single-minded pursuit of the war?" It was, he said, only because soldiers knew that their homes were cared for and that their women were steadfast and true. The audience must have reacted quite favorably, because the third speaker of the day, one Dr. Tatsuno Takeshi, quipped that he felt quite guilty about his treatment of his wife, and wanted to hurry home to apologize.[10] Tatsuno said he had not realized that women were so instrumental to the war effort.

While POW propaganda projects never quite reached the scale military officials would have liked, officials did employ POWs for such purposes. Ikeda Norizane, head of the Bunka Camp, or "culture camp," in Tokyo testified in a postwar affidavit that in November 1943 he was transferred to work at the camp under Maj. Tsuneishi Shigetsugu. The Bunka Camp was a POW barracks in the middle of Tokyo where English-language propaganda radio broadcasts to the United States and Britain were produced. Tsuneishi worked out of Section Eight of the Imperial General Headquarters, which handled both foreign and domestic propaganda. When he began work, Ikeda interviewed dozens of Allied POWs, some of whom had broadcasting experience, and took fourteen of them to the special camp. Later their numbers grew. The first POW broadcast from Bunka Camp prisoners was transmitted on December 2, 1943. Major Tsuneishi, the highest-ranking military officer in charge of the camp, submitted testimony at the Tokyo War Crimes Trials that he had worked under direct orders from Lt. Gen. Arisue Seizō of General Staff Headquarters. Arisue headed Japanese military propaganda efforts and was supposed to have initiated the idea of using POWs for broadcasts.[11] As discussed in Chapter Six, Arisue also assisted in Japan's surrender meetings with Gen. Douglas MacArthur and had a hand in propaganda projects during the occupation.

Maj. Tsuneishi Shigetsugu's affidavit asserts that from the inception of the Bunka Camp in November 1943 to the end June 1945 he remained in charge.

The camp's primary mission was "to create antiwar sentiment within Allied Forces personnel and nations." After the war the broadcasts Allied soldiers made for Japan became grounds for several treason trials in Australia and the United States. Tsuneishi vociferously denied interrogating Allied solders at the camp or using torture to coerce POWs to broadcast radio propaganda for Japan.[12] His postwar testimony regarding his wartime actions, completed while he managed a coffee shop on Shikoku, is similar to Ikeda's. Both men wanted to paint a more humane portrait of themselves and hence described the camp more as a dormitory than the harsh internment center it actually was.[13]

One reason to use POWs for broadcasting English-language propaganda was that Japanese authorities grew worried over reports foreigners released once back in their countries of origin. This issue caused particular anguish in the case of newsmen repatriated during the coordinated exchange of diplomats and foreign nationals in the late summer of 1942. A top-secret document from June 1942 illuminates Japanese government fears regarding the anti-Japanese reporting of foreign newsmen after they returned home. An official conference analyzed the problem of how to prevent such anti-Japanese news reports once the newsmen left the area where Japan could censor their activities.[14] Japanese fears of what disgruntled repatriated newsmen would report was proved correct by what journalists like Theodore White, Joseph Newman, and others wrote immediately upon their return to the United States in 1942. The anxieties of Japanese officials concerning bad international press made all the more important the journalists Japan solicited to shape international public opinion towards Japan in a positive way (see Chapter One).

The Special Higher Police often botched their mission out of their very wariness of POW activities and manifest concern for potential subversion. The Japanese wartime police constantly saw threat and espionage where none existed. At the same time they often failed to observe such threats when it lay right under their noses. In the famous case of Japanese journalist Ozaki Hotsumi and his connection to Richard Sorge, a Communist spy, the police remained ignorant until tipped off by an insider.[15]

The police not only watched westerners, but also they kept a vigilant eye on Chinese and Koreans residing in Japan. Numerous Japanese authorities considered Koreans and Chinese residing in Japan as a palpable threat to a stable Japanese society. This interest in Koreans and Chinese had begun haltingly in 1910, with the High Treason Incident (Taigyaku Jiken) and the discovery that some elements of Japan's empire hated the emperor. After the great Kantō earthquake in 1923, the Special Higher Police took advantage of the chaos and moved to eradicate socialists, "troublesome Koreans," Japanese anarchists like Osugi Sakae, and others.[16] Korean involvement in a supposed plot to assassinate the emperor, hatched by Korean anarchist Pak Yeol and his Japanese female counterpart Kaneko Fumiko, fueled the authorities' belief that Koreans disrupted the social order in Japan. In a bid to dispatch any nascent move against the government in the aftermath of the debilitating earthquake, the government convicted Pak and Kaneko, though they were reprieved from a death sentence. In a rage against the government for its heavy hand of justice, Kaneko hanged herself nonetheless.

The police kept tabs on the general tenor of domestic public opinion and on what they felt could turn into a wide range of pan-Asian subversive activities as well. Six weeks after the China Incident on July 7, 1937, police investigated how Chinese nationals living in Japan responded to the incursion. Articles in the Japanese newspapers and radio news broadcasts reported that thousands of Chinese living in Japan wished to return home following the invasion of China. Police estimated that approximately 5,700 Chinese applied to return, yet this represented only one-fifth of the registered Chinese population living in Japan. An internal police document also detailed the significant fact that not all the Chinese wanted to flee home. Some donated money to the National Defense Charity and to the Japanese Imperial Forces Entertainment Brigades. It is not clear whether "volunteers" collected this money under duress, but the monies amassed demonstrates that sympathy for the Japanese cause may have existed in unlikely places. The police judged the Chinese donations to be a clever move because, Japanese authorities wrote, it demonstrated that the Chinese believed their best interests lay with Japan and that they believed they would be protected and treated well in Japan. However, the police also correctly estimated that sympathetic Chinese remained the minority, and that the new conflict in China would eventually cause great domestic problems between Chinese and Japanese in Japan.[17]

A similar report from a few weeks later noted that the Chinese working in restaurants and barbershops were still quiet, but as military activities on the mainland heated up, many returned home. In addition to sympathy for their homeland, those Chinese may also have been motivated by the fact that in those restaurants and barbershops clients had quickly dwindled to 50 to 70 percent of their original numbers.[18]

Pulse of the People

As much as the Special Higher Police feared a discontented minority population in Japan, they also scrutinized their own indigenous left wing and monitored its influence on public opinion. Religious groups also received much unwanted attention. Frequently, the Special Higher Police were overzealous;

they saw threats and potential unrest everywhere. For example, a twenty-six-year-old factory manager named Nobukuni Torao, from Shimane prefecture in southwestern Japan, encountered such police zeal. On August 1, 1937, Nobukuni had admonished several female workers employed at the Ishimi Rayon Factory for staying out late at night and going to the train yard to send off soldiers called to the front. Nobukuni criticized the young women for what he felt was "typical behavior," to be out frolicking late at night. He specifically reprimanded them for participating in the late-night railway-station ceremonies held for the soldiers' deployments, saying that attendance at such ceremonies was no reason to be out so late. This was not unusual, for prior to 1945 factory dormitories often treated young women as virtual prisoners and kept strict rules concerning curfew and guests. A few days later the Special Higher Police visited Nobukuni and warned him against such "anti-military behavior."[19]

Police coordinated, or at least helped with, the public spectacles and celebrations that sent soldiers off to fight. Japanese police files demonstrate that the Home Ministry held this activity in high regard as a mode of propaganda. Government officials happily noted how these rail-station celebrations to honor troops leaving for China positively influenced public perception of the war. On November 20, 1937, the governor of Shizuoka prefecture, Iinuma Kazumi, wrote to the vice minister of the Home Ministry, Hirose Hisadata, stating that such events had, until recently, been running swimmingly. Cheering crowds sent off and welcomed home imperial Japanese soldiers. In Iinuma's opinion, these ceremonies boosted the people's spirits, and arranging schedules ahead of time with the station head or leader of the town or village ensured a reception for the soldiers when trains arrived. There could, however, be a problem. "In cases where groups fail to assemble, or when instructions from the station chief are detained, or unusually secretive, the people's sincere welcome is stymied. This not only has a [negative] effect on the military's esprit de corps, but it creates problems for the railroad and people living in rural areas as well."[20]

The Japanese bureaucracy recognized that the people wished to be involved and that they were angry when they were not allowed to demonstrate their feelings about the war effort. Rural residents evidently cherished participating in send-offs at the local stations. The letter from the Shizuoka governor relates the story of one unnamed town where not everyone was notified about the arrival of a train of soldiers and the planned reception. When people in town later heard about the train's arrival, they voiced their resentment. They sent threatening letters to authorities and the media to make sure they would not be overlooked a second time. But when villagers were allowed to participate, they gushed emotional support for the war. In October 1937, one young woman, Okamoto Kanoko, who had participated in such a send-off wrote a letter to *The Shining Brigade's Magazine,* a women's association journal read both at home and abroad. She wrote, "when I see the parades of deploying soldiers and military officers, I feel that these Japanese men have already become gods. It's a glorious moment, and I feel now as if I am with them, bodies shimmering, in their determined movements across the fields of China."[21]

For the police to enforce appropriate rules they believed they had to measure accurately the public pulse, what they called the *minshin no dōkō.* The police were well aware of how quickly minor disturbances could escalate into major social upheaval. The police in-house manual cited a small 1918 rice riot that began in Toyama prefecture, a rural west-coast region, that spread within a very short time to the entire country. The manual stated that the police should keep seemingly insignificant local problems from developing into national disasters.[22]

To take the pulse of the nation, the police had many psychological and sociological tools at their disposal, one of which was the formal survey. In August 1938 the Home Ministry's Police Bureau sent a questionnaire to each prefecture to determine how the average Japanese felt about recent media regulations and how the publishing industry itself had reacted. People filled out the questionnaires and voluntarily mailed them back. The entire process necessitated little coercion.[23] Many contributors from Shikoku responded. Most wrote that they were grateful to newspapers for providing accurate reports of the war. They were also thankful that brave and daring reporters followed the military to gather news, risking life and limb. But not everyone's comments were so laudatory; some respondents criticized the papers and magazines. In general, however, popular support for reporters mirrored the support entertainers received when they returned from abroad and gave performances and lectures on the home front.[24]

By the mid 1930s police officers developed a new ethos concerning their work, even as they became aware that their prestige was diminishing in the eyes of the public. The police rationalized this as the result of political party control. The police felt that the political parties undercut effective police control and that the whims of the parties hampered effective implementation of national goals. By the late 1930s political parties became their enemy, and the police began to champion themselves as the "new bureaucrats" *(shinkanryō).* They redefined themselves as the emperor's police force and initiated a "police spiritual awakening movement." Kan Tarō, a Home Ministry official and motivating force behind this movement, penned several articles in the magazine *Policing Trends (Keisatsu shichō)* concerning the need to "imperialize" the police force.[25] The appeal found a strong following among the disaffected.[26]

The idea that Japanese police protected something greater than public safety—the country's honor—did not disappear upon Japan's surrender in 1945. A postwar history of the national police force, written in the 1960s, still echoed these wartime sentiments. At the end of the war the population was exhausted, and most Japanese faced an uncertain future with unemployment and rocketing inflation. Even so, the police's wartime condescending attitudes toward other Asians continued unchanged. According to the postwar police history, just after the war, crime rose significantly, mainly due to "third country nationals" (*daisan kokujin,* a derogatory term for Koreans, Chinese, and Taiwanese).[27] The police force also tried to take credit for the overall success of the occupation by concluding that it kept chaos at bay and Americans from intruding where they were not desired.[28]

Administration and the Media: Policies and Control

In its effort to create the proper social reception for propaganda during the war, the police worked in harmony with many other agencies. The police also co-opted numerous controls, such as censorship and media directives, to assist in regulating Japan's imperial society. These regulations and the images the media created helped define and strengthen notions of acceptable behavior for the masses. Pictures and advertising copy gave voice and vision to those notions, crystallizing them in the public mind.

Well before 1931, Japan had already severely constrained free speech and public debate. The Meiji constitution guaranteed a form of freedom of speech but only within the scope of the law as defined by the government. Moreover, Japanese authorities often drastically limited this acceptable range. The core of mass media laws governing wartime propaganda activities originated with the publication law of 1893 and the 1909 newspaper law. Regulations grew in number, with the parliament passing a dizzying array of media controls: the 1925 Peace Preservation Law, the Control of Subversive Documents Law of 1936, the Military Secrets Law (strengthened in 1937), the Press Industry Ordinance of 1943, the 1943 Publication Industry Ordinance, etc.[29] And these regulations existed only for civilians; military information campaigns fell under an entirely different structure and set of guidelines.

By the onset of large-scale war between China and Japan in August 1937, print media policy turned away from overt censorship and more towards propping up social support for the war. From the end of World War One the Home Ministry had held primary responsibility for regulating the print media. The government based its control on the dual principles of keeping social movements in check and preventing the disruption of social morals. Authorities censored the news, but more importantly they actively used the news to promote state purposes. Concentrating on using the media as a state tool, to unify public opinion, reflected a change in tactic.[30]

On October 15, 1937, fifty-four major publishing houses, including Iwanami Shoten, Kaizōsha, Chūō Kōronsha, Bungei Shunjū, and Kōdansha, formed the Publisher's Symposium. While the group was a voluntary, private organization, it held its monthly meeting in Home Ministry offices to discuss issues relating to the war and publishing. The Home Ministry also began to exert more direct pressure on magazine editorial policy and writing. At the end of April 1938, the Home Ministry separately invited the editorial staffs of *Housewife's Friend, Women's World, Women's Club, Women's Public Debate,* and *Women's Pictorial Report,* to meetings and consulted with them about prohibiting any articles that "went against the times" or exhibited signs of being "low-class stories."[31] The government differentiated its rules for newspapers and magazines, but similar measures applied. The publishing companies Bungei Shunjū and Gendai, along with several other general news magazines, were prominent in their assistance in mobilizing public support for the war. These magazine and publishing companies gave voice to popular calls for imperial expansion and often served as a surrogate for military propaganda.

Sex and Propaganda

The Home Ministry in particular scrutinized magazines for elements of debauchery that it felt would adversely affect society. Officials' anxiety over content matched their concern with commercial advertisements, which most bureaucrats judged, in general, to be socially deleterious. A 1938 Home Ministry plan for regulating advertisements in women's magazines highlights some of these peripheral issues related to censorship and wartime propaganda. What they regarded as licentious advertising in women's magazines incensed the authorities. Along with strengthening regulations against novels about sex and stories that could erode the morals of "virginal girls," authorities called for increasing controls of pictures published in popular magazines. Risqué article titles such as "Anxious Over Not Achieving Satisfaction," "The Differences between Virgins and Nonvirgins," "Methods for Dealing with Sexual Desire," "The New Wife's Secret Consultations on Hygiene," and other suggestive phraseology worried regulators that such consumerism would arouse unnecessary desire for sex.[32] Japanese authorities disapproved of a political and economic climate that they believed produced more and more women for the sex industry and more clients for the women.[33] Popular Japanese culture also reflected this discussion over the changing role and place of women in modern Japan, particularly the plight of working women who are separated from their families, as in Mizoguchi Kenji's 1936 film *Osaka Elegy*.

Well-known Japanese feminists also publicly called for the government to focus on women's sexuality as a topic of national concern. One of the first national meetings convened to discuss women's issues and the war featured Kōra Tomi as a speaker. Kōra, a power broker in prewar and wartime circles, obtained her doctorate abroad and returned to Japan in 1923 to teach at Kyushu Imperial University. She was the first female assistant professor to be hired at an imperial university. Kōra's speech centered on several issues, including the increasing harassment of women on public transportation. In some extreme instances, she noted, women had even had their kimonos cut by offenders. According to her assessment, the situation had deteriorated to the point that some suggested having "women only" cars, but Kōra felt this would hardly force men to alter their behavior. Her ire was also directed toward women. "For the surviving members of the families of the war dead," she noted angrily, "the issue of chastity has become an issue not only in the rural areas, but it is, in fact, a problem in urban areas as well, and that is a cause for concern."[34]

The police and authorities singled advertisements out for criticism not because they were puritans but because promoting chastity at home supported the war effort abroad. The police tolerated prostitution for men, even as they tried to get the population to deal with the increase in venereal disease. The male-dominated bureaucracy and police force maintained, however, that women needed to remain unsullied because the war needed women for the home front. The imperial military and the Japanese bureaucracy portrayed women as the backbone of Japanese society; mothers tended the home while the men glorified the nation abroad. Female sexual activity, encouraged in advertisements for sexual devices and ads for products designed to heighten sexual arousal, stood against that vision of home front chastity. No doubt Japanese officials and those technicians who worked on propaganda also wished to portray Japan as the antithesis of the supposedly sexually deviant and lascivious westerner. Wartime Japanese propaganda leaflets frequently played on this theme. In some Japanese propaganda broadsheets, white soldiers are shown raping native Pacific island women. Leaflets designed to leave Allied soldiers feeling nostalgic to return home often painted pictures of scantily clad women on one side, alluding to the supposed frequency of sexual activity to which Japanese assumed westerners were accustomed.[35]

Efforts to protect Japanese women on the home front from sexual activity sometimes contradicted social practice. The Japanese military apparently was interested in promoting the use of vibrators for women whose husbands were at the front, but once a model had been chosen and a factory established, authorities were at a loss over how to market the product to married women because the idea ran counter to their program to prohibit such advertising.[36]

Even though Japanese authorities worried that the moral backsliding of society would have dire military consequences, they also believed that sex assisted in mobilization. The Japanese military's massive effort to collect Korean, Chinese, Dutch, and Japanese women to serve as sexual slaves, known as "comfort women," at the battlefront is an example of such an ideology.[37] But sex at the home front was seen differently. The authorities judged advertisements dealing with sex-related topics capable of adversely influencing young Japanese women. Authorities even considered discussions of genital hair suspect. "Are you worried about the fact that you do not have hair where you should?" asked one advertisement held up as an undesirable example. Bureaucrats decried the ad as potentially harmful to social stability. "When I graduated from girl's school we went on a trip. For the first time, when my friends and I all went to bathe together, I realized that I was the only one who did not have hair where I should. I was so mortified."[38]

The authorities, and Japanese society in general, held advertising as a whole in low esteem, so it should come as no surprise that within a few years after the start of the war with China, ad executives jumped at the opportunity the war afforded to gain recognition for their trade and raise their professional prestige.

As the war progressed, the Home Ministry grieved over Japan's loss of morals and instituted a series of regulations designed to curtail what it viewed as a deluge of obscene advertising that disrupted society. Most companies cooperated but a minority used the time of crisis to profit.

Censors also targeted ads concerning men and masturbation. The message was clear—sex was fine but only if one followed certain conventions. The printed commercial "Boys with the evil habit of masturbating think about what you are doing," vexed the authorities. Officials cared little for the product being sold, with its "patented strong hoop method" that "naturally corrects the foreskin, nocturnal emission, premature ejaculation, and will help you purge the bad habit of masturbating."[39] It seems that the censors did not want their young soldiers-to-be masturbating, but even more importantly, they did not want them even hearing about masturbation. Sex by oneself was not proper; sex with a militarily regulated prostitute appeared to be regarded by Japanese officials as correct behavior.

The government's concern over establishing a morally stable home front, demonstrated by proper sexual conduct, paralleled their anguish over the contradictory goals of decreasing Japanese reliance on foreign material supplies and building a strong media to cultivate the court of public opinion. Initially the Japanese government faced both a recalcitrant advertising industry and a mulish newspaper industry. After several false starts, the Cabinet Board of Information finally drafted a plan to merge many of the regional papers. The plan itself seems to have been born out of the military's frustration at not being able to get its message out evenly across the country.[40]

On May 28, 1941, the papers banded together, more or less on their own initiative, to form the Japanese Newspaper League. This group and its various subcommittees debated the possibility and necessity of merging papers and limiting competition in order to increase "efficiency." It remains unclear whether the success during the war of getting each prefecture to consolidate all its newspapers into one should be attributed to the power of the military and Cabinet Board of Information, or whether the papers themselves took action as a way to stave off government intervention. Eventually, a new watered-down newspaper system was put in place. However, this action does show that the authorities did not have total control over the media, but had to negotiate. As with many other nongovernmental institutions, the media cooperated with the government in order to retain a modicum of power over its own destiny.[41]

Even during the war newspapers were not directly under the aegis of the government. Radio, however, was a different case. From its inception it had been in the government's domain, but radio censorship remained a subject of tense jurisdictional conflict among the Ministry of Telecommunications, which presided over jealously guarded technical aspects of broadcasting, the Home Ministry, and the imperial military, which wanted to control actual broadcast content.[42]

Although government agencies had agreed that propaganda policies and coordination would be located within the Cabinet Board of Information, actual propaganda activities often took place through a variety of other institutions, including the Foreign Ministry's Information Department, the Army Ministry's Newspaper Group (renamed in 1938 the Army Ministry's Information Section), and the Navy Ministry's Military Information Dissemination Section. The Imperial Armed Forces considered a separate media agency paramount to their success, so they reestablished the Imperial General Headquarters (Daihonei) on November 20, 1937. Headquarters housed two separate bureaus, one for the army and one for the navy, to deal with announcing news related to the military and war, both broadly defined.

A key element behind official propaganda plans was the concept of confinement. Throughout the war years, the window the average Japanese had to external information grew ever narrower. The same could be said about Soviet Russia and Nazi Germany, yet Stalin and Hitler continually met more opposi-

tion than occurred in Japan. The importance of the idea behind Japan's clo-
sure of foreign media was that in restricting the Japanese public's access to
outside information, the system simultaneously supported and encouraged
individuals with media skills. Writers might not have been able to write freely,
but they were frequently provided the opportunity to piggyback on the imperial budget and write about Japan's civilizing mission in Asia. The Japanese
army and navy drafted writers, cartoonists, musicians, and other artists to disseminate to the greatest extent possible this message meant to impress on
Japan's domestic population.[43]

Stemming the flow of outside information required that officials and the
police continually keep abreast of international developments. For that purpose the Special Higher Police served not only as a vehicle that supervised the
population, they also executed counterintelligence measures within Japan and
abroad. Katō Yūzaburō, a Home Ministry administrator, parroted Kan Tarō's
earlier remarks on the need to "renovate" the police force. In the police association's magazine, several months before total war with China, Katō pronounced that the only manner in which the police could achieve success in
aligning their duties with the larger national goals was to "eradicate extrem-
ism and caution against indecisive behavior."[44] Sections of the Special Higher
Police reported on the propaganda challenges faced by Japanese living abroad
and whether those messages wielded any influence. By 1942 the police blotter
outlined the efforts of Japanese who went over to the Chinese Communist
Party (CCP) side and then conducted counterpropaganda against their motherland. The Special Higher Police also systematically kept records on Asian
slave labor and POWs dragooned to toil and assist the dwindling Japanese
labor force at home. In the summer of 1943 police journals reprinted a translation of America's formal complaint about Japan's use of POWs as forced
labor and Japan's response.[45] To complicate matters, a Japanese taste for frat-
ernizing with POWs appeared hard to hinder even after repeated radio broadcasts and numerous reprimands. A March 1943 police article quantified the
continued exchanges between POWs working in Japanese factories and regular
Japanese laborers and noted that, unfortunately, Japanese continued to trade
with the POWs and sometimes sympathized with them.[46] The police asserted
they had to be continually vigilant in preventing escapes because many POWs
worked near or in residential areas.[47]

Nonetheless, even with all their efforts to maintain a cultural gulf between
Japan and the Allies, Japanese propaganda forces sometimes failed to achieve
their goals. In contrast, ironically, they often were more successful at alienating
other Asians. As Japan moved through the 1930s, a growing distrust of non-
Japanese fed government paranoia and heightened the Special Higher Police's

constant surveillance of aliens residing in Japan. Furtive attempts to establish a bureau that fed native-language propaganda to Allied forces, and the establishment of the Bunka Camp and its staff of POW English-language broadcasters, demonstrate that the Japanese understood what they should do to mobilize, but the cacophony of civilian and military officials often prevented these ideas from being translated into effective outcomes. Nonetheless, the message that the Japanese heard—that Asians should unite under the modern leadership of Japan—had great value for many throughout the empire and was promoted by the spies in the Nakano School, the publishers who banded together to promote prowar materials, the public intellectuals who spoke at large gatherings to applaud support for the war, and the various levels of police, who felt it their duty to guide and persuade the home populations in correct behavior during the war.

CHAPTER THREE

Advertising as Propaganda

I t is easy to understand why Japanese civilian and military officials denigrated advertising and deemed the industry vulgar. The society at large emitted a collective groan when it confronted examples of the excesses of advertising products, such as certain feminine hygiene aids and devices for impeding sexual curiosity in young men. However, the government was in a quandary because it desperately needed professionals to aid in the production of wartime propaganda. Propaganda products, *senden seihin,* did not just create themselves. Government and civilian propaganda agencies required talent to draft, write, produce, and print the myriad propaganda items for imperial consumption, both within Japan and more importantly abroad.

For their part, advertising executives and the industry in general recognized they had a window of opportunity to join with the government, jump on the war bandwagon, and raise their professional prestige. Opportunism and the desire to increase profits merged nicely with patriotic fever. Small-scale advertising companies, not the military or the government, often produced the propaganda in government advertisements, tourism posters, and related items. These producers often wrote or reworked the propaganda that gave the Japanese the idea that Japan was modern, efficient, healthy, and thus deserved to lead Asia. For the first time and based on initiatives developed during the Sino-Japanese war and the Russo-Japanese war, mobilization combined with promotion of consumer products. Japanese living in the most remote rural town in northeastern Japan could own part of the empire, buy a ticket on the Ajia train through Manchuria, go touring, and participate in modern Japan. Consumer appetites supported the nation's imperial quest by making commerce and war a significant part of popular culture.

Society for the Study of Media Technology

Consumer tastes filtered into the public consciousness in part because advertisers applied their techniques to wartime propaganda. Propaganda technicians banded together in voluntary associations to supplement what they saw as a deficient bureaucratic propaganda product. Companies were not the only institutes to sign up for propaganda work. In major cities like Osaka and Tokyo voluntary research groups assembled to work in association with the Cabinet Board of Information and the Imperial Rule Assistance Association, producing posters for dissemination and exhibitions. One active group, the Hōdō Gijutsu Kenkyūkai, or Society for the Study of Media Technology, began on February 28, 1940. The group developed under the leadership of Yamana Ayao, Imaizumi Takeji, Arai Seiichirō, Saitō Tarō, and others. The bylaws, printed some months later, enunciated that the association wanted to "unify the country and people" and promote research into propaganda technology for activities within Japan and abroad.[1] In an advertising trade journal, Imaizumi waxed eloquent, explaining that the only way for Japan to succeed in the war with China was for the country to adopt a more totalitarian ideology, which he understood as the coalescence of personal goals and national aspirations.[2] The Society for the Study of Media Technology held its first meeting at a restaurant in the swank Marunouchi section of Tokyo. Professional propagandist and government consultant Koyama Eizō joined first as a member and later became chair of the volunteer organization in early 1944. At its height the group had enrolled around fifty members, and it did not disband until a month after Japan's surrender in 1945. Many of the members were also active participants in another voluntary association, the Puresuaruto group, centered in the Kansai region. Puresuaruto, an Esperanto word, means the "aesthetics of publication." According to the fifth issue of their magazine, subscribers and writers aimed to collect all sorts of propaganda materials ranging from posters, pamphlets, labels, magazine covers, billboards, etc., from Japan and throughout the empire and analyze them as media creations.[3]

Propaganda was also good business for the companies that employed all of these professionals. The Morinaga Advertising Agency, where several founding members of the Society for the Study of Media Technology worked, created a product tie-in with the propaganda disseminated for the popular song "The Patriotic March." The march sang of "leading the people of the four oceans" and "establishing a just peace" throughout the world. The tune did not originate within government circles; officials had sponsored a song contest and the winner had produced these motivating lyrics.[4]

The fact that the Society for the Study of Media Technology professionals voluntarily banded together on their own free time, while still maintaining full-time jobs, demonstrates a salient point.[5] The profit motive did not wholly drive the advertisers' move to raise the status of their profession. These technicians openly announced that the government lacked the adequate technical expertise to produce effective propaganda. An article by one of the association's founding members, Arai Seiichirō, printed in the magazine *Japanese Pro-*

paganda Culture Association, suggested that professional advertisers wished to help the government promote the aims of the war and at the same time "cleanse themselves," after having been steeped in the lowly work of commercial advertising.[6]

Yamana Ayao and Arai Seiichirō both graduated in 1932 from the economics department at Keiō University, an elite institute in Tokyo. Both also later worked at the Morinaga Advertising Agency. Yoneyama Keizō, another prominent professional propaganda theorist and government consultant, was a professor of media studies at Keiō. Yamana and Arai may have taken Yoneyama's classes, and they certainly came into contact through association meetings. Imaizumi Takeji studied commerce at Meiji University and entered the Morinaga agency about a year before Arai. Although Japanese society held advertising in low regard, the profession was slowly managing to shed its stigma and advertising was even attracting college graduates as an acceptable career. By the early 1930s advertising research groups had sprouted at prestigious Japanese universities such as Waseda, Keiō, Rikkyō, Meiji, and elsewhere. Even though a significant portion of the ad men studied at Keiō University, Waseda also remained a force. The school also published a journal, *Waseda Journal of Advertising Research (Waseda kōkokugaku kenkyū).* The university did not produce an association like Yamana's, but the journal did print the results of academic conferences held on themes concerning the war in China and advertising. During one of these public roundtables an executive from Columbia Records asked the other participants, "in this time of stronger economic regulations, it has been said that advertising is no longer needed. What do the rest of you think?" Many of those who responded had a difficult time hiding their pessimism concerning the future of advertising. However, most agreed that advertising would remain, but would have to transform the way it looked and change what it offered. Many at the conference concluded that if advertising did not adapt to the times, wartime inflation and declining spendable income would threaten the profession with extinction.[7]

Media vs. Propaganda

Prior to the Society for the Study of Media Technology, propaganda intrigued few outside of the bureaucratic sphere. Koyama Eizō, Yoneyama Keizō, and related military researchers produced copious theoretical material, but their enthusiasm had not yet spilled over into the mainstream civilian population. The research group that Yamana and others founded expanded the Japanese practice of propaganda—how to create it and, more importantly, how to gauge its effects. In many ways, though, these men were disingenuous about

their work. The technicians easily switched from creating company ads to creating propaganda for the government, all the while blurring the distinctions
of their work under the rubric of "media." Many advertisers began to incorporate product placement into the national consciousness via the propaganda
and specifically labeled their activities as related to *hōdō,* or media. In an internal report for the association, Imaizumi explained that his group had made a
conscious decision to use the term "media" instead of "propaganda." He and
other advertising professionals felt, at least by early 1940, that the term "propaganda" called forth images of manipulation, mind control, and deceit. Imaizumi's group determined that this negative conceptualization of propaganda
did not mesh with the ideas that Japan wished to promote internationally,
including the fact that the members of the Japanese empire were a "people
united as one."[8]

The association's first manifesto demonstrates that Yamana, Arai, and
others were acutely aware of the subjectivity that photographers and writers
put into their work and how that affected the final product. These men knew
that the war with China altered how the media represented events of national
importance. Generally speaking, "news" meant notifying people about actual
events, even if personal biases skewed the presentation of facts, but Japan's
invasion of China changed that dynamic. "Now we believe that it [news] has
come to mean more, it stands for informing the people about the national
will," the advertisers proclaimed.[9] By the time the group altered its definition
of propaganda to media, its members no longer thought of media merely as
information within a social or objective context. By the late 1930s news and
advertising represented national ideology and patriotic rationale. Information
could not exist on a neutral plane but had to project an image that the state
wanted transmitted to the people.[10] When these private research groups
formed, they wished to repackage their material in ways that would *specifically*
assist in the government's project of mobilizing society for war. This model had
not existed before. The advertising association felt that earlier theorists had
conceived of propaganda only in terms of content but had ignored the technical side, including layout. The group wanted to raise awareness that everything about presentation fulfilled an equally important function in the propaganda equation.

Layout technicians, graphic artists, and draftsmen complained that professional propagandists, mainly theorists, impeded the development of effective
propaganda because they looked down on the technicians whom they regarded
as unskilled clerks. The technicians, in turn, despised those writing the actual
propaganda because they thought the theorists messages were clumsy and ill-
conceived. To alleviate this tension and massage relations, Yamana and Arai's

group published a monthly journal called *Media Technology Research (Hōdō gijutsu kenkyū).* The group pleaded its case that unless producers of propaganda paid serious attention to artistic layout, the resulting work would be ineffective. During the war, most propaganda workers felt that the work suffered because the Japanese national propaganda agencies failed to be brought into a coherent structure and operate under a coherent policy. The fact that many countries, both Axis and Allied, also faced this problem never dawned on them.

The Society for the Study of Media Technology yearned for public recognition. Members contacted the Cabinet Board of Information, which emphatically told them to organize. Arai Seiichirō served as the liaison with the Board since he had the longest professional experience. At the society's opening ceremonies, the Cabinet Board of Information sent a representative. In February 1941 the group's first posters were displayed at an exhibition entitled "Pacific News Exhibition" at the Shiseido Gallery in Ginza. The exhibit examined the conflict between the "past history of white aggression" and the "inevitability of Japan's southern advance" as the conclusion of immutable historical forces. At this point Japan had not yet opened hostilities with the United States or Britain. After the initial success of the exhibit in Tokyo, the Cabinet Board of Information purchased the show from the media group and took it for a tour around the country.[11] The society proposed a second exhibition to the Cabinet Board of Information, this one to display posters that visually represented propaganda slogans. Many members complained, however, that the war slogans were too abstract and the project too disorganized to yield decent results.

In February 1942, only two months after the attack on Pearl Harbor, advertising writers officially established the Japanese Propaganda Culture Association under the government umbrella organization, the IRAA. This propaganda association announced its mandate to employ professional advertising for national propaganda and to raise money for the study of propaganda by collecting funds from advertising agencies. Fundraising and subcontracting work kept this group busy at the opening of war with the United States. Later they changed their name to the Japan Propaganda Association and hosted lecture meetings with Hayashi Kenichi and Koyama Eizō as speakers.[12]

The media technology association's efforts to promote technically brilliant propaganda did not lessen as war with the Allies intensified and spread across the Pacific. In 1943 the organization published an edited volume on the need for good propaganda, especially in view of the expanded Japanese empire. The group now defined propaganda as a vehicle that fused nations, races, and the people together. Imakura Kitarō wrote a chapter on the true meaning of the "craft of creating media." Indefatigable Koyama Eizō composed the section on problems related to competition among propaganda agencies. Imaizumi Takeji focused forty pages on skills that gave the propaganda form and function, and his colleague Okubo Kazuo discussed how editing influenced the outcome of propaganda. Yamana Ayao concentrated on his favorite topic, propaganda art. Hayashi Kenichi looked at reportage photography and propaganda, while Arai Seiichirō attacked the written word and propaganda.[13] The men did not design their book to be a bestseller, but the intricacies into which they delved lay bare their devotion and support for the war.

Propaganda Companies and Their Magazines

Yamana and his fellow advertisers also worked on a variety of print magazines in association with the Eastern Way Company (Tōhō). Okada Sōzō, who until the start of the war had been a famous actor for Shōchiku pictures under the name Yamanouchi Hikaru, served as the first director of the Eastern Way Company. Okada's grandfather was an Englishman, and as a consequence, Okada had traveled abroad extensively during the 1920s and 1930s, studying film and photography in Germany and the Soviet Union. Soviet propaganda magazines and methods from the 1930s left their mark on Okada and heavily influenced the type of photojournalistic propaganda that Japan would later try to promote abroad. The subsequent company director, Hayashi Tatsuo, spent his childhood in Seattle because his father had been a diplomat. Hayashi graduated from Kyoto Imperial University where he studied philosophy and worked on art magazines in his spare time.

The origins of the Eastern Way Company, established in 1939, are shrouded in ambiguity because wartime records were either burnt or intentionally lost. However, some of the puzzle can be reconstructed. The general consensus is that the army's intelligence bureau created the publisher as a subcontractor to produce Japanese propaganda for foreign audiences. Civilians who worked on propaganda and military management could not agree on a budget large enough to launch the company so the initial business arrangement rested on an oral agreement that the various military propaganda agencies would purchase back the magazine as it rolled off the presses. The Eastern Way Company also received money from large commercial conglomerates— Mitsui, Mitsubishi, and Sumitomo—who commonly worked as contractors for the military. Eastern Way produced pictorial magazines specifically targeted to foreign readers. The firm's internal documents state that the primary focus centered on "proclaiming to the Chinese and other nations the Japanese empire's true form in this time of extreme international change."[14]

Ironically, even though the Eastern Way Company operated essentially under the jurisdiction of the Ministry of Foreign Affairs and the military, numerous artists who worked there had belonged to Communist cells or were still under the watchful eye of the Special Higher Police. Eastern Way had to employ a wide variety of people with varied linguistic and technical abilities for the international propaganda work and such propaganda work did not stop with technical expertise. Mikami Isao, who had graduated with a degree in English literature from Ohio State University, taught English at Meijigakuin University during the war. Near the end of 1943 he received a call from Eastern Way regarding work on English translations. By late 1943, university classes were barely in session since many of Mikami's students had been mobilized to work at the Yokohama Mitsubishi factories. Because professors also "voluntarily" labored for a week once a month, alternating with other faculty, free time abounded. Mikami reminisced that most of the people working at Eastern Way were self-proclaimed leftists with varying degrees of international experience. He enjoyed working there and deemed the experience interesting and enjoyable.[15]

The Eastern Way Company produced a range of propaganda materials for the government and military, but the oversized, glossy broadsheet *FRONT* stood out, with its photomontages and high production values. Loosely styled on America's *Life* magazine, and designed to promote Japan's image abroad, *FRONT* was eventually translated into fifteen languages. The staff attempted to visualize graphically the image of Japan's war in Asia. Editors did not want to document the war but rather aimed to record the evolution of the war by utilizing recent advances in propaganda technology. With an advanced understanding of print media, gained by the research of "media technologists," Japanese propagandists now paid attention to background, foreground, color, layout, font, and montage.

The Eastern Way Company had created a magazine that propagated the idea that the war was worth fighting. *FRONT* did not overemphasize the "necessity of war," or its "inevitability," two expressions found frequently in military slogans. Instead, the magazine portrayed regular soldiers in daily action, albeit in a stylized photographic reproduction. Readers quickly became accustomed to images of war. They became something so ordinary that for the public the shock of the actual harshness of the war slowly lessened.[16] Emperor worship appeared only infrequently as a theme. In contrast to American visual reproductions of the war, which emphasized heroes and stupendous feats, the Japanese magazine emphasized the war as mundane, relentlessly reminding the average imperial Japanese subject that the war continued and required personal involvement. In a sense the magazine also affirmed that the war was greater than the individual. From 1942 to 1945 the Eastern Way Company labored to produce special issues on the Imperial Navy, the Imperial Army, Manchukuo, northern China, the Philippines, India, wartime Tokyo, wartime art, and so forth, and they shipped the volumes abroad. However, in their haste to compete internationally with the propaganda products the Chinese and Allies produced, the Japanese publisher encountered an unforeseen difficulty. Even though editors, graphic artists, and writers spent sleepless weeks creating a splashy magazine that would pique the interest of the newly conquered regions and convince them of Japan's technical greatness, the magazine editors and their military partners neglected to pay attention to just how they were going to distribute the final product. The magazine, larger in size than a standard magazine and heavier due to the quality of paper and ink employed, could not easily be dropped from an airplane because it could potentially harm its intended targets. Even the Japanese military seemed to recognize that heavy glossy magazines falling from the sky did not make for good propaganda. Eventually, the company decided on land and sea routes, but overseas shipping lanes were slow and as the war escalated it grew more difficult to guarantee shipments.

At the end of the war the *FRONT* staff quickly burned as much evidence of their work as they could, privately wondering when the Allies would come to arrest them. Employees started feeling better once they heard that the Allied Command had released a statement to the effect that "the creation of propaganda is a natural byproduct of war. Those who worked on such activities will not be considered war criminals."[17] Many of the Eastern Way staff quickly regrouped during the occupation as the Culture Publishing Company (Bunka Shuppansha) and even printed several books for the Allies.

FRONT was not the first private Japanese magazine to catch the bureaucracy's eye or aim to attract an overseas audience. Internationally renowned Japanese photographer Natori Yōnosuke's photomontage magazine *Nippon* actually predated *FRONT*. The Ministry of Foreign Affairs later acquired *Nippon*, originally a privately published magazine. Yamana Ayao and others worked on the first issue. While studying photojournalism in Germany from 1928 to 1932, Natori met and married a German woman. For a period he worked in Germany and later he worked abroad as a photographer for the *Berliner illustrite zeitung*, (Berlin illustrated news).[18] In 1933 Natori founded *Nihon kōbō (Japan's Atelier)*, but it lasted only a year. In 1937, at the Paris Expo, the group, which also called itself Nihon Kōbō, worked on a full-length wall photo at the behest of the Rail Ministry's national tourism bureau.[19] Natori later reestablished *Nihon kōbō* and worked on other periodicals designed to introduce Japanese culture abroad. In his second *Nihon Kōbō* effort, staff members again included Yamana Ayao, and Kono Takashi, a noted designer from the Shōchiku film company.[20] Natori and his colleagues later split, and one group formed a sister organization for graphic design in Ginza, called Central Atelier (Chūō Kōbō). Central Atelier later formed part of the publisher that became the Eastern Way Company, the publisher that produced *FRONT.* Eastern Way's popularity and its fine propaganda products helped it to gain clients such as the International Tourism Bureau and the Ministry of Foreign Affairs.

The advertising writers who formed the voluntary technical media research organizations, and those who worked at the Eastern Way Company, producing subcontracted propaganda work for government leaflets and posters, also participated in propaganda activities that helped lay the groundwork for Japan's massive 2,600th year imperial anniversary celebrations. According to wartime national rhetoric, 1940 was the 2,600th year anniversary of the founding of the Japanese imperial line. To celebrate, the government and private businesses staged a multitude of exhibitions exalting Japan's history and its national glory. Shinjuku's Isetan department store held an event called "Our New Heavenly Land." The Takashimaya store near Nihonbashi produced an exhibition entitled "Our Imperial Military." The Ginza Matsuya shop managed an event entitled "Our Spirit," while the Mitsukoshi store across the way from the Takashimaya store held one called "Our Ancestors." Both Matsuzakaya stores in Ueno and Ginza staged an exhibit labeled "Our Life," and Nihonbashi's Shirogiya store operated one called "Our Land." In total, approximately five million people attended the events at all of the stores. Similar events were also held in outlying areas.[21]

Advertising copywriters who volunteered to study and produce wartime propaganda created most of the copy used in the events held in department stores and other businesses. Artists and advertisers did this in part because they felt they were helping the war effort, but it also made good business sense. Yamana Ayao's postwar memoir, *War and Propaganda Technicians (Sensō to senden gijutsusha),* reprints several of the group's more popular visual efforts.[22] Activities did not stop with posters and magazines. Miyazaki Takashi, editor of the trade journal *Advertising World (Kōkokukai),* probably coined the popular wartime slogan "Luxury is the Enemy" used to urge Japanese to consume less, buy war bonds and economize.[23] In the postwar era Yamana Ayao, Arai Seiichirō, and photographers Horino Masao, Watanabe Yoshio, and Kanamaru Shigene became giants in the world of Japanese advertising.

Because the government continually exhorted the population to rein in its consumption during the war, department stores had to find a place for themselves in Japan's new order. It was for this reason that stores began to sponsor war-related exhibitions, if only to prove that business, too, played a significant role in supporting the war. Opening an exhibition concerning some aspect of the war helped maximize profits in a tight economy because customers who attended these events would invariably purchase items. Even with all the new savings and frugality propaganda, a viable Japanese consumer economy continued to exist during the war. People continued to spend.

The leaders of Japanese advertising significantly aided in the government's efforts to mobilize domestic and foreign populations. Advertising executives, copywriters, designers, and photographers joined the war effort for a variety of reasons. More importantly, their participation demonstrates that wartime propaganda initiatives and programs developed from a range of sources. The government and military were not the only players. The more interesting question to examine, however, is how after the war these individuals seamlessly continued their employment, using many of the same techniques and working for many of the same companies.[24]

The Japanese government did not serve as the sole architect and developer of its own propaganda. It often left the creation up to the voluntary associations that petitioned the government for subcontract work. Contrary to assertions about measures hostile to business during the war, Japanese government and military officials often linked hands with business leaders and executives to produce propaganda for the war effort.

The Imperial Japanese Military and Advertising

The Imperial Japanese military operated its own propaganda agencies, separate from the civilian government. It conducted massive leaflet and poster campaigns throughout China and Asia. Nor did it neglect movies and radio as tools for mobilizing non-Japanese support for its aims on the Chinese continent.[25] Research elsewhere has ably described many of these campaigns, so I will focus solely on military propaganda as it related to civilian operations. Even though civilian and military propaganda agencies existed in separate spheres, their efforts were often interrelated.

Mabuchi Itsuo is a key figure in the link between military and civilian propaganda operations in China and Japan. His role also demonstrates the military's need for cooperation from the civilian sector. His participation at the juncture of these two worlds helps highlight the environment that gave birth to military propaganda efforts. Mabuchi single-handedly managed to launch the career of several wartime literary giants, while at the same time accomplishing what many propagandists desired but few achieved—unifying the home front with the battlefront. Mabuchi Itsuo served in various capacities as a commander in the intelligence section in Shanghai and central China from July 1937 until December 1940. For the first ten months of 1941, Mabuchi operated as a captain in the Army Ministry's Information Section and coordinated the Imperial General Headquarters' Army Information Division. Near the end of the war the army shifted Mabuchi from his intelligence position in China and stationed him in Indonesia to assist in propaganda efforts. There he won the trust of many locals and provided arms and ammunition to the independence movement in Indonesia.[26]

A newspaper article detailing how Japanese children's "comfort letters" to soldiers demonstrates the unity of home front and battlefront. *Asahi shimbun* (Tokyo), October 8, 1941.

Mabuchi was instrumental in supporting famed journalist Hino Ashihei's writing in China. Hino had been a popular prewar writer who later won a prestigious Japanese literary award, the Akutagawa award, for his story *A Tale of Excrement (Funnyōtan)*. In September 1937 the army drafted Hino, and he sailed to Hangzhou, China. Soon after Hino's mobilization, the famous literary critic Kobayashi Hideo traveled across the Sea of Japan to deliver the Akutagawa award to Hino. With Mabuchi in attendance, the military staged a ceremony near Hangzhou to fete Hino's honor. The prize was a literary award created by Kikuchi Kan and sponsored by the Bungei Shunjū publishing company.[27] While a soldier in China, Hino penned articles on the war that were serialized in the magazine *Kaizō* and in 1938 were published as a collection that became the bestseller, *Wheat and Soldiers (Mugi to heitai)*.[28] The book had immense appeal for Japanese readers, sold 1.2 million copies, and catapulted Hino Ashihei to fame throughout the Japanese empire. In the same manner that the magazine *FRONT* depicted the war, *Wheat and Soldiers* carefully detailed the difficulty Japanese soldiers faced in China. At the outset of the war the book had a profound impact on the home island's popular opinion. It elicited sympathy for the average Japanese infantry soldier in China, by portraying the rigors of war. In addition, the book contained numerous photographs of soldiers, "usually pictured marching on foot, carrying packs. The soldiers at rest are exhausted, but able to laugh together. Other visual elements, like the propaganda cartoons Hino distributed to the Chinese civilians and soldiers, reproductions of Chinese signs and banners, work to emphasize the book's authority and immediacy."[29]

The Japanese military, and Mabuchi in particular, realized the stupendous propaganda value of Hino's work, so in April 1938 he was transferred to work as an embedded journalist, accompanying Japanese infantry platoons fighting in the Chinese countryside. Hino's later works on similar themes—*Earth and Soldiers (Tsuchi to heitai)* and *Flowers and Soldiers (Hana to heitai)*—also became wartime bestsellers. His constant use of the term *heitai*, a word similar to the American term GI, brought to life average Japanese soldiers as "simple, dedicated, fundamentally decent men who fight on the front lines, slogging through mud, seeking shelter in trenches and foxholes. . . ."[30] These images of the hard-working, realistically human Japanese soldier also drew public acclaim in Japanese films of the late 1930s.

Following the Shanghai bombings and the 1937 Nanjing atrocities, Mabuchi and his company remained active in Hangzhou. They even published a newspaper, the *Hangzhou Newspaper*. Famed for its natural beauty Hangzhou was a popular spot for tourists and army visitors alike. The Hangzhou battalion frequently hosted celebrity visitors from Japan, such as famed entertainers Nishimura Rakuten, Entatsu, Misu Wakana, Kanda Rōyama, and others.[31] These visits are detailed in Chapter Four.

As was true for many Japanese military men active in the propaganda field, Mabuchi's efforts did not cease when the war ended. As mentioned earlier, even after Japan's surrender Mabuchi worked with the Indonesian independence forces. He felt that if Indonesian independence was not successful, Japan would not have realized its wartime goals. Mabuchi and others like him firmly believed that if the power relations in Asia remained unchanged after the war, Japan's war would have been in vain. Part of this group's attachment to wartime Japanese propaganda lay in their belief that Japan's modernizing goal in Asia was to help Asians in occupied areas and colonies become independent. According to this propaganda logic, even if Japan lost the war to the United States, Japan had nonetheless achieved, in a sense, its war goals and certainly the aim of its propaganda.[32] In other words, the military could fail but the propaganda could still retain value.

Mabuchi's insistence on promoting the literature of war, combined with the Japanese military's general dissatisfaction over fleeting victories in China, prompted the Cabinet Board of Information to put out a general appeal for writers to join the war effort. On August 22, 1938, the Cabinet Board of Information called writers in for consultation at the prime minister's house. The letter of invitation was signed by Kikuchi Kan, journalist, novelist, and editor of the highly influential magazine *Bungei Shunjū*. Kikuchi stood at the head of the line promoting writers in support of the war effort. At first not many authors appeared interested, but once they learned of the high salary (the equivalent of two months' salary for a university graduate), many more began to take an active interest.[33] Eventually, about twenty-two writers signed onto the project, as part of a group called the Writers' Military Attachment, or more commonly, the "Pen Platoon."[34] Since both branches of the military wanted civilian writers, the army chose a group of fourteen. The navy settled for eight. On September 3, 1938, the *Tokyo Daily Newspaper (Tokyo nichi nichi shimbun)* celebrated the writers' inauguration, and the members flew off in military planes to various destinations across Asia. They filed reports to news agencies from all the hot spots on the continent and the rest of Southeast Asia.[35] In addition to their regular salaries from the military, these writers also profited by selling their reports to popular journals, newspapers, and magazines around the Japanese empire. At the same time they managed to raise their literary profiles.[36]

In a pattern that would become increasing familiar for many Japanese touring China, sponsors underwrote many public meetings and media events thematically based on these writers' military attachment reports and stories.

Once they returned to the home islands these writers' platoons later transformed into a whole variety of platoons such as music platoons, poetry platoons, and the record platoon.[37] Most of the reporters or authors who followed the military ate the same poor food and lived under the same terrible conditions as regular soldiers. Mabuchi Itsuo felt that this sort of reporting duty was necessary for excellent propaganda and ultimately helped to forge a bond between the military and civilian society. He, too, labeled the war a thought war in his own book on war propaganda published in 1941.[38]

Many of these early Pen Platoon writers found themselves formally drafted into the military once again after the war with the West exploded in December 1941. Ozaki Shirō, who had first traveled to China as an embedded writer, suddenly became a member of what became known as the PK Butai, a propaganda company modeled on the Nazi Propaganda Kompanien der Wehrmach.[39] Germany had learned the harsh lessons of World War One that social mobilization and propaganda were one key to victory. The Japanese also realized that the intelligentsia also had to be mobilized, along with photographers, novelists, poets, cameramen, journalists, cartoonists, Catholic priests, and others.[40] The writers, now formally working as military men, not only published articles in the major presses but also continued to write their own books concerning their experiences in the Philippines, Burma, Indonesia, Indochina, and other locales. At times personal diaries also made it into magazines.[41] While the conditions described often mirrored the hardship detailed by Hino Ashihei, many writers lived a different life on the island nations of the Pacific. Well-known journalist Ōya Sōichi described his two years of service as part of the military propaganda corps in Southeast Asia as the "highlight" of his life, "the main event" as he put it.[42]

But not every soldier experienced an idyllic and pleasant war. Mizuki Shigeru, drafted during the war and later a famous cartoonist, exposed some of the horrible conditions many soldiers and writers experienced in the military. In an essay he wrote after the war he described the volatile and often grotesque situation.

> When I first entered the Tottori battalion as a soldier the platoon sergeant said, "In the military there is no time for taking a crap and no time for pissing. So, if you want to take a dump, either wake up early or do it while you are asleep! While training, it is forbidden to piss or shit."
>
> Of course if you had to go during battle you'd probably be in a tight spot. One day, as usual, I awoke early before role call and made my way to the latrine to take a crap. I hadn't gone for 2 or 3 days so it was a big one. At that moment I heard the trumpet for roll call. I thought I should cut off the flow, so I put all the strength

I could muster into my sphincter but the package was as tough as iron and I couldn't squeeze it off. I thought about taking a piece of paper and kind of trapping it and wiping it away, but there was only one piece of paper so it was out of the question. In the end I figured I just had to push it out, so red in the face in an all-out effort I managed to evacuate my bowels. The problem was the speed of evacuation—it did not follow military regulation. The pace was about 2 centimeters per minute. I resigned myself to nature's regulations.

It took five minutes. In a rush, I ran to the roll call square and there was a big commotion. It appeared that a soldier had gone AWOL, and soldiers were being repeatedly required to sound off. I slid into the ranks, and our platoon's numbers matched up, but being the military it didn't quiet things down any. After being called to the commander's office, there was the platoon sergeant with a tight expression on his face. "Why were you late to roll call," he yelled. I explained about the shit in excruciating detail. I thought I shouldn't just do this verbally, so I included action and hand gestures to demonstrate the shape and such of the shit. "Don't fuck with me," the platoon sergeant said, and then I was beaten.[43]

The harsh reality in which artists like Mizuki Shigeru and others served as soldiers in the war in China frequently impeded the creation of influential propaganda. In addition, multiple propaganda agencies and competing realms of jurisdiction plagued the efficacy of Japanese military propaganda. Various military offices, called *sendenbu,* coordinated straight propaganda activities, media platoons called *hōdōbu,* and the special forces, the *tokumukikan,* all supposedly worked in coordination. However, at times they were clearly in opposition.[44] In some areas, considered particularly susceptible to outside influence, pacification platoons or *senbuhan* were also created. Descriptions of many of these platoon activities were openly published in the popular Japanese press, and personal accounts from soldiers frequently found their way into the mainstream media.[45]

As the war escalated, military propaganda agencies became easily as complex as civilian propaganda agencies. One officer who worked in the Army Ministry's newspaper group sketched the fractious nature of the organization. The army had started the newspaper agency to assist reporters working within the Army Ministry. At the start the agency was used mainly as a center that put materials together for the army and then offered them as prepared text to newspapers and other publishing companies. By late November 1937, as Japan bogged down in China, the military recognized it needed to enhance public support for the imperial project and issued an order to reestablish the Imperial General Headquarters (Daihonei).

The Japanese government and military had previously instituted the

Imperial General Headquarters during the first Sino-Japanese war in 1894–1895, and then again during the Russo-Japanese war a decade later. The Daihonei created separate army and navy information divisions, a split that exacerbated an already severely divided propaganda strategy and also mirrored the continuing tension between the military branches. The headquarters was supposed to act as an authoritarian aid in the management of war in a fashion parallel to the Cabinet and the Diet and, like them, under the aegis of the emperor.[46] Among its other roles, the Imperial General Headquarters Army Information Division continually broadcast news of the war and items concerning military decrees. By contrast, the Army Ministry's newspaper group worked on announcements regarding political-military matters and features concerning other legal issues.[47] Both the Imperial General Headquarters and the military branches also sponsored reporters to go abroad, report on Japan's overseas war, and send their dispatches back home. Not only did the Japanese public voraciously devour these stories, but once repatriated, the reporters' personal stories and writings also fed an insatiable literate public, eager to read books by those who had had firsthand experience fighting or traveling on the fringes of the empire. To be sure, most of these volumes presented a positive image of Japan's efforts and the war in general, even if at times the authors also described the hardship of their experiences.[48]

A feeling of malaise often gripped the civilians and military officers attached to propaganda activities. There was a pervasive belief that the Japanese race were genetically incapable of creating effective propaganda, even though Japanese propaganda projects and campaigns abounded. At one point the military went so far as to publish a book entitled *Paper Bullets (Shidan)* to demonstrate that contrary to popular stereotypes, the Japanese did produce effective propaganda. Opening remarks in the book came from China Expedition Army Military Intelligence Section Chief Iwasaki Harushige. Iwasaki noted that the average Japanese believed Japanese did not excel at propaganda but "recent teams and our experts have disproved that notion." He announced that this book offered a true demonstration of Japan's experiences. Iwasaki felt the work showed how to improve the propaganda in the thought war, which would help to conquer the enemy in Chongqing and the United States.[49] The Japanese reading public already knew Iwasaki. He had written a chapter in a 1937 volume Asahi Shimbun had published entitled *Returning from the China Incident Front.*[50]

Commentary from disparate competing sources, such as Iwasaki as a military man and Arai Seiichirō as an advertiser, helped to construct a social identity within Japanese society during the war. Government bureaucrats and the military played key roles in illuminating trajectories for the population to follow, but the paths they urged were not the only choice. The government needed the active participation of the media industry in order to produce effective propaganda. Passive acquiescence, the kind that writer Nagai Kafū spoke of when he criticized the war in his diaries, did not provide enough stimulus to galvanize a society to maintain the level of popular support necessary to continue a war with China. Ideas concerning empire and nation appealed to the wartime Japanese, but for advertisers and others who produced the propaganda so did the ability to make a living by rallying behind the war effort.

One significant facet of wartime advertising copy and police interest in social propaganda is the absence of the emperor. To be sure, emperor worship existed. Soldiers on the field made mention of his name, and orders were given in his name. But the posters, pamphlets, glossy magazines, travel brochures, and frugality slogans produced en masse for the propaganda assault usually focused on images of a sleek and modern Japan triumphantly striding toward the future. *FRONT* magazine definitely attempted to promote this image. Japan stood at the forefront of Asia in this vision of the future. Japan's urban centers of Tokyo, Dalian (on the Liaodong peninsula), and Xinjing (the new capital of the puppet kingdom of Manchukuo), were apparent; the emperor remained absent. In ways quite different from the cult of personality that developed around Hitler, Mussolini, and Stalin, the image of the emperor is not what sold wartime propaganda. Through military, bureaucratic, and civilian agencies Japanese wartime propaganda instead presented images of a clean and modern Japan to mobilize society.

CHAPTER FOUR

A Funny Thing Happened to Me on the Way to the Front

On the surface nothing about Japan in World War Two seems humorous. Images of stern-faced soldiers marching in formation dominate our memory. On the Japanese home front, pictures of young, determined women in cotton trousers hoisting bamboo spears, preparing themselves for the ultimate invasion of the home islands, reflect our perception of wartime Japan. Historians have presented the war as a monolith of government suppression, an evil conspiracy of military men denying the people freedom and forcing Japan into battle against western Allies that the Japanese armed forces knew to be militarily superior. Postwar Japanese intellectuals speaking for the masses found the wartime anything but lighthearted. In his wartime diary Nagai Kafū complained that the whole exercise of the war hampered access to entertainment. In an essay written soon after the surrender, the renowned folklorist Yanagita Kunio similarly deprecated the wartime products of Japanese entertainment. Journalist Kiyosawa Kiyoshi's diary was notable for its title, *A Diary of Darkness*, and many Japanese commonly refer to this entire period as the "dark valley." [1]

Western commentators on wartime Japanese culture held similar views. The Allied command research teams designated to study the Japanese psyche for counterpropaganda activities concluded that most Japanese were humorless, that they did not readily laugh.[2] These US military agencies theorized that the war had forced humor out of Japan, and the Americans estimated that this lack of humor would increase the effectiveness of wartime US propaganda. Near the end of the war the US military was even hopeful that such desperation might lead more Japanese to surrender.[3]

> While this humorlessness sustains and makes possible Japanese fanaticism in victory, it may well prove a drawback in defeat. The emotional range of the Japanese is violent, from exultation to the blackest despair. A sense of humor has served as a shock-absorber to individuals and to other nations in tiding them over grim times. Of all modern peoples, this quality is most conspicuously absent in the Japanese.[4]

Although Japan's Fifteen-Year War is usually depicted as grim and without humor, entertainment played a surprisingly major role in Japan's successful mobilization of the country. Entertainment, especially comedy, had deep and intricate ties with wartime propaganda. This chapter examines the use of humor and entertainment in Japanese propaganda from 1931 to 1945.

Japanese comedic entertainment was both a package for wartime propaganda and part of the message itself. This presentation of war goals helped both distribute propaganda to a wider audience and reformulate the war and the propaganda as a consumer product of entertainment. Wartime entertainment as propaganda can be divided into three periods. The first period begins with the Manchurian Incident in September 1931 and ends with the China Incident of July 1937. But even before the early 1930s, comedy had shifted focus from traditional stories about Edo (as Tokyo was called pre 1868) life and stubborn samurai to new material concerning contemporary Tokyo residents. By the time the Japanese military landed on the Chinese continent, routines that dealt with the military had exploded onto the scene. Entertainment companies saw opportunities to piggyback on popular support for the Manchurian war and began to send out their own bands to entertain troops abroad. As comedy and amusement venues proliferated throughout the 1930s, the authorities—including politicians, police, and the educated elite—moved toward promoting entertainment that was wholesome and good, *kenzen,* for the "public health."

The second period covers the time from the China Incident in July 1937 to the outbreak of war with the United States in December 1941. During this time heavier government censorship and social pressure served to bring about a renewed interest in more routines concerning Chinese and Japanese soldiers. New careers and new acts based on such routines abounded. Groups of popular performers journeyed abroad more frequently as imperial entertainment brigades, or *imon butai.* On their return, these performers lectured the public about the war at a variety of media events. This type of press coverage increased dramatically, reaching its peak during 1941 with the opening of hostilities across the Pacific.

The last period begins at the start of the Pacific War and ends with Japan's surrender in August 1945. By 1941 comedy was moving almost in tandem with national policy, and so it continued until the end of the war. As late as May 1945 entertainment companies still sent performers abroad to entertain the troops. Surrender did not appear to be an option for those in the field of amusement. Yet following the end of the war and the landing of the Allies in Japan, many of the agents of wartime comedy continued in a business-as-usual fashion. They felt no need to reflect on their wartime activities. Ironically, some even banked on their former wartime popularity. Unlike many countries—France, China, Germany—where new governments and the populations at large held performers somewhat responsible for their actions during the war, there was scant discussion of entertainers' culpability in Japan.[5] Examining the role of entertainment in the war extends our understanding of the popular culture's contribution to the war and to the process of social mobilization.

Japanese wartime comedy, although often censored by the government, arose independently within the private sector. Desire among providers of entertainment in the private sector to participate in promotion of the war effort gained credibility when their efforts mirrored government-sponsored propaganda. Examining the work of comedians can demonstrate how popular perceptions concerning the meaning of the war changed as they filtered down to the public through these entertainers.[6]

Japan was not the only nation in which comedic entertainment mobilized itself for the war effort. For seven years the Nazis produced a satirical magazine called *Die Brennessel* (The stinging nettle). As did Japanese wartime comedy, Nazi satire mocked its colonized and occupied regions as backward and uncivilized.[7] The comedy routines of both the Japanese and the Nazis frequently encouraged support for the government's plans and policies in pursuit of empire. Anti-Semitism, a mainstay of Nazi propaganda and humor, also appeared in Japanese war comedy, even though Japan lacked any domestic Jewish population. The most telling similarity between Nazi and Japanese comedy efforts is that both complained vociferously that the non-Axis media spread lies and deceit concerning the causes of the war. The Japanese may have been more successful in utilizing comedy as a means of mobilization than the Nazis, but in both regimes comedy arose as a champion of the state. The 1936 German film *Lucky Kids* testifies to the fact that the movie "was an anomaly only insofar as it was a German comedy that pleased German audiences—including Hitler. . . ."[8] Japanese imperial subjects continued to purchase comedy albums and consume comedy products throughout the war.

Entertainers in the Soviet Union also promoted comedy as an agent of national salvation. As was true in Japan, Russian comedy proved more popular on stage in live performance than in the movies. Comedy in film form employed anti-Nazi satire, though the overall number of these films was small. *Estrada,* a Russian version of vaudeville, flourished during the war, especially near the front lines, with scores of performance platoons entertaining Soviet troops.[9]

Although the importance of comedy at the front for the Soviet Union paralleled its importance for Japan, what happened to Russian comedy after the war does not resemble the Japanese case at all. In Russia many of those who eagerly entertained the Soviet soldiers were Jewish and they met with a cruel fate after the war. In contrast, Japanese comedians who had supported the war project continued to work in the mainstream and met little criticism or difficulty in the postwar era.[10]

The Calm before the Storm

In the city of Tokyo that rose from the ashes of the Kantō earthquake, entertainment was a major component of daily life. By the 1930s entertainment in Tokyo took a variety of forms. Cinema attendance increased through the decade, as did construction of new teahouses, dance halls, and other amusement ventures.[11] The threat of impropriety at the dance-hall performances so scandalized the authorities that they urged the adoption of explicit laws to prohibit expansion of this type of entertainment. A 1930 police law clamping down on dancers and revues stipulated that performers could not expose the lower half of the body or underwear, or display any part below the nipple (one is left to wonder whether the nipple itself was permissible). A performer could show one leg but only below the crotch. No dances that made the performer swing her hips suggestively, "like the Hawaiian dances," were permitted.[12]

Comedy performances, such as *rakugo* and *manzai*, also grew in number and variety throughout the 1920s and 1930s. In *rakugo* a lone performer sits in the middle of the stage on a cushion and recites a humorous story for anywhere from ten to thirty minutes.[13] One might say the performer is a stand-up comedian who's sitting down. Performers employ various voices and gestures to portray the various characters in their routines. Until the end of the nineteenth century most of their stories were based on traditional Edo culture and dealt with drinking, visiting the red-light district, and arguments among blockheaded samurai. But following the Meiji Restoration in 1868, the old traditional life in Tokyo began to fade away. By the late 1920s *rakugo* performers who wanted to maintain an audience had begun actively including new routines that had more in common with city life of the early twentieth century.

Although *rakugo* remained popular, the new Japanese comedic tastes and styles of the 1920s grew into another form called *manzai*.[14] *Manzai* performers are comparable to the genre made popular by the well-known American comedy duo Bud Abbott and Lou Costello, and pairs like them flourished with the advance of radio technology. In *manzai* two people, two men or a man and a woman, stand on stage with a microphone between them and banter back and forth. As with many forms of spoken Japanese comedy, the routines depend heavily on slapstick comedy, word play on terms that sound the same but are written with different characters, and generally low-brow, but funny stories. *Manzai* grew in popularity as the number of city dwellers rose, and it represented the new urban consumer class taste of the 1930s. *Manzai* routines centered on daily life and contemporary issues, while most *rakugo* still maintained its traditional character in language and format. Unlike *rakugo,* where to this day the performers wear a kimono and sit on stage in a kneeling position, *manzai* performers stood and were clothed in western suits. No music accompanied their performance, and they spoke modern colloquial Japanese. In both *rakugo* and *manzai* the punch line, or *ochi,* was often less important than the flow of the story. The performer's ability to speak in distinctly different voices and accents also remained a cherished performance skill.[15]

The lax popular mood of the late 1920s gave way to a sharper-tongued and at least superficially more conservative government administration in regards to entertainment by the early 1930s. Amusement was all well and good for the masses, but it had to be amusement with a purpose, something that would promote the "public health." As Tokyo rebuilt itself, so did the Japanese military. After a lackluster performance in the 1920s, the Japanese army and navy commanded a stronger presence in 1930s Japan. Japanese military life was tough, dirty, extraordinarily demanding, and sometimes comical. As in western nations, routines dealing with military life naturally caught the public's attention.

One of the first performers to take advantage of this new comedic potential and launch a new genre of *rakugo* dealing with military matters was Yanagiya Kingorō and his *Heitai rakugo* (Soldier's *rakugo*). Yanagiya Kingorō, born in 1901, the same year as the Shōwa emperor, had been a performer from an early age. Drafted into the military, he spent time in Korea as a soldier in the early Taishō period. Once demobilized, he returned to the stage where he capitalized on his military experiences, building a solid career on roles dealing with the ironies and vagaries of being an imperial Japanese soldier. His most famous routine, "Rakugoka no heitai" (Comedian soldier), depicted a young soldier unsure of himself, face to face with a gruff officer.

The routine opens with the soldier, Yamashita, returning to barracks after a long day of training. As he is about to polish his shoes, the lights-out trumpet sounds. In order to keep himself awake while stowing his gear the soldier starts singing a little ditty mocking the military.

> Non-com officers are a pain in the boot
> Corporals are an annoying buncha fruits
> Ranking officers are short on dough
> Cute new recruits are just here for the show!
> Doo-dah, doo-dah . . .

(An officer walking by overhears the singing and barges in, screaming.)
OFFICER: WHAT THE . . . ? WHO ARE YOU?
(The officer continues to yell his questions to the new enlisted man.)
YAMASHITA: *(Barraged with questions, stammers.)* I am myself. I . . . mean, it's me.
OFFICER: SOUND OFF!
YAMASHITA: Imperial Army, infantry soldier, private first class, Yamashita Keitarō. Sir. *(Startled, Yamashita slurs his words.)*
OFFICER: Yamashita Kettarō? SAY IT AGAIN! CLEARLY THIS TIME.
YAMASHITA: Imperial Army, infantry soldier, private first class . . .
OFFICER: *(Sneers and yells incredulously.)* YOU'RE A PRIVATE FIRST CLASS?
YAMASHITA: Imperial Army, infantry soldier, private first class. Yamashita Kettarō . . . *(His voice begins to fail.)*
OFFICER: REPEAT!
YAMASHITA: Imperial Army, infantry soldier, private first class. Yamashita Ke . . .
OFFICER: ALL THE WAY, DAMMIT. AGAIN!
YAMASHITA: Imperial Army, infantry soldier, private first class. Yamashita Keitarō. *(Yamashita manages to get it all out, but he is breathing hard now and not quite sure of his own name or rank.)*
OFFICER: AGAIN!
YAMASHITA: Imperial Navy . . .
OFFICER: NAVY? I DON'T SEE ANY GODDAMN SAILORS?
YAMASHITA: Oh, gosh. Ahh . . . Imperial . . . uh . . . Arm . . .[16]

For readers who do not find this routine particularly funny it is important to remember that wartime Japanese humor used the background of the military because it was an experience common to its listeners. Mocking the army or at least the difficult relations between officers and enlisted men was not unique to Japan. Wartime American comedy also played on these tensions. In a scene similar to what Kingorō created for Japanese spectators, Danny Kaye portrays an enlisted man who is suddenly caught in his colonel's quarters in the middle of the night with a female stowaway. He tries to conceal her in his coveralls while pretending to be a Scotsman to deceive the colonel.

COLONEL: Who are you?
PRIVATE: Me?
COLONEL: Well, who are you?
PRIVATE: *(Affecting a Scottish accent.)* Uh, Pvt. McTavish, sir!
COLONEL: Get up! Come out of there! Well, what's going on here?

PRIVATE: It's a broad Bri'cht, moon'licht Nicht nicht! Very bricht and very moon'licht!

COLONEL: On your feet!

PRIVATE: It's a wee bit of a mistake, Colonel. I was lookin' for me bagpipes and I mistook a bit of your quarters for a wee bit of my quarters, sir. Sorry, sir!

COLONEL: McTavish, you're under arrest!

PRIVATE: Aye, sir! Uh, I was lookin' for me bagpipes, sir. *(In gibberish.)* Uh, ubecka bricka, bree, surr-a-gurr-a whrr . . . brrrr!

COLONEL: You're drunk! Report to the ship's brig!

PRIVATE: Aye, sir! Pvt. McTavish places himself under arrest. *(Saluting, then screaming and pointing behind the colonel.)* Eaaagghh! 'Twas a wee bit of a moose, sir!

COLONEL: Wha—?

PRIVATE: But 'tis a bonnie nicht, and a bonnie nicht to yeh, sir! *(Half speaking in gibberish.)* Arurrah richt an gotta me midd'l bagpipes! *(Pretending to play bagpipes unwittingly reveals the woman.)* La la-la-la-la-la-la, la, la, la . . .

COLONEL: There are two of them—Corporal of the guards![17]

As an innovator of *rakugo* routines that dealt with more modern Japanese experiences of the twentieth century, Kingorō is remembered in the annals of *rakugo* as a father of the modern form and his routines continue to be popular. Kingorō's performances bridged the gap between old and new as Japanese entertainment matured amid an atmosphere of government concern and public demand. As Kingorō's career took off through the early 1930s, major entertainment talent agencies like Yoshimoto Kōgyō (Yoshimoto Entertainment Company) and film companies like Tōhō and Shōchiku branched out from film and traditional forms of comedy. These companies profited from the expanding repertoire of amusements that the urban dwellers now demanded and, more importantly, could afford.

Manzai and *rakugo* performers traveled around the country and grew immensely popular primarily due to the efforts of Yoshimoto Kōgyō, the main talent agency before, during, and after the war. Originally established in late Meiji as a small vaudeville *(yosegei)* stage, the Yoshimoto complex grew to massive proportions by early Shōwa to command dozens of performance venues in Osaka, Tokyo, and areas in between. In the early 1930s the company even launched a short-lived, yet fairly successful magazine of the same name, *Yoshimoto*, devoted to entertainment. Yoshimoto is important in wartime comedy studies since it is the company that created several of the more popular *manzai* duos and was the agent for more than a handful of influential *rakugo* stars. The Yoshimoto agency created the two biggest names in 1930s *manzai*, Hanabishi Achako, popularly know as Achako, and Yokoyama Entatsu, known as Entatsu. The company also helped to popularize the idea of sending entertainment brigades, known as *imon butai*, abroad to amuse imperial Japanese troops.

Entatsu was born in 1896. His father had been a doctor in the military, and Entatsu had graduated from middle school. He floated around Manchuria working odd jobs and even performed abroad as far away as the United States. Achako was born a year later, in 1897, and eventually graduated from high school. The Yoshimoto agency scouted both these performers and placed them together starting in May 1930. Entatsu and Achako wrote some of their own material, but comedy writer Akita Minoru wrote most of it. Akita, an intellectual, had attended Tokyo Imperial University and briefly studied Chinese philosophy.[18] Akita had political aspirations and was also a lapsed Communist, which makes his liaison with the military-supporting Yoshimoto Company all the more interesting.[19] Like many writers Akita had previously participated in the proletarian literature and Communist movements of the early 1930s. He later switched allegiance *(tenkō)*, although this change may have been due to police pressure and the fear that many leftists felt at that time. Or, as one Japanese historian implies, perhaps Akita discerned that the newly emerging urban population was changing. Previously, a rougher crowd had frequented the entertainment districts, but the newer consumers were more sophisticated, and Akita felt he could launch a productive career among them.[20] Faced with mounting social and political pressure in the 1930s, writers of proletarian literature often "converted" to support the government's positions. Akita's appearance on the comedy writing scene signaled a clear break with previous comedy writers because most Japanese considered *manzai* and *rakugo* to be pursuits for the lower classes, not a decent career for an intellectual, let alone a young man educated at an imperial university.

From the Manchurian Incident (1931) to the China Incident (1937)

Although the Yoshimoto Company's fortunes continued to rise through the 1920s, the war of the 1930s brought even greater success. The Yoshimoto Company's most popular performers in the early 1930s led the drive to support the Japanese military's actions abroad. In December 1931, only a few months after the Japanese army instigated fighting in Manchuria,[21] the Yoshimoto Company combined its resources with the Asahi newspaper group to send Achako, Entatsu, Kanda Sanyō, and a host of other popular entertainers to Manchuria as part of an entertainment platoon, an *imon butai*, to amuse the imperial troops stationed there.[22] Even though the Japanese armed forces did not provide financial assistance, the Japanese military officially sanctioned the tour and often provided transport for the entertainment troops as they traveled through sometimes hostile areas. The group traveled to Xinjing (later the new capital of Manchuria, now Changchun), Hōten (now Shenyang), as well as other areas in Liaoning province and surrounding regions. They returned to Japan on February 25, 1932.[23] Yoshimoto unilaterally decided to celebrate the founding of Manchukuo, the puppet state that the Japanese army had carved out of Manchuria. On March 1, 1932, the agency mobilized its performance halls in Osaka, Kobe, Nagoya, and Tokyo to celebrate the occasion. Yoshimoto frequently had one of its star performers, Yanagiya Kingorō, perform his popular routine *Comedian Soldier* at similar venues.[24] Yoshimoto performances on the Chinese continent for the imperial forces appear to have been performed for free, but back in Japan the company made great profits by getting free publicity for its tours and raising the profile of its more popular stars. Shows at home continued, as before, to be profit-making ventures.

In November 1933 the Yoshimoto agency again joined forces with a news agency and sent another platoon of performers to China to entertain imperial troops. Achako and Entatsu also participated.[25] Their smash hit *Sōkeisen* (The Waseda-Keiō University baseball showdown), a comedy skit about the popular yearly baseball battle between two rival Tokyo universities, had just been produced live on radio, and they were household names at this point.

In February 1934 Yanagiya Kingorō traveled by himself on a one-man entertainment itinerary to amuse troops in Harbin, Jilin, and the surrounding areas. When he returned on March 18, the Yoshimoto Company staged an enormous event at Tokyo's Hibiya Public Hall called *Manshū o kataru yoru* (Evening chats about Manchuria). The Yoshimoto Company was not disappointed with the publicity. The beverage company Calpis sponsored the event. Other performers, such as Entatsu, Achako, and Ishida Ichimatsu, were invited to headline. For about ten days after that event, starting on March 21, there were similar events at Shinjuku's famous *rakugo* hall Suehirotei and the Kagurazaka Performance Hall, with a performance called *Kingorō's Experiences in Manchuria*.[26] On April 20, 1934, Columbia Records released an album entitled *Kingorō no kōgun imonshi* (Kingorō's Imperial Army entertainment mission) that made these events available to the wider public.[27] Entertainment brigades for the Japanese troops stationed in China had an influence back on the home islands. Domestic audiences were eager to hear about performer's travels and keen to pay to attend performances that reenacted these journeys and experiences.

The Japanese government was not adverse to such promotion, and the

Yoshimoto Company's activities drew a range of commentators. In fact, scholars in government agencies and think tanks had earlier suggested that the country needed an entertainment policy to align amusement with national goals. A prominent prewar social anthropologist and government consultant on entertainment and education matters, Gonda Yasunosuke, frequently commented in the popular press and in government research papers on the need for government entertainment policies. In the May 1935 issue of *Chūō kōron,* Gonda wrote that *minshū goraku* (popular entertainment) was disintegrating and that the time had come to prepare for *kokumin goraku* (national entertainment).[28] Gonda meant that the time had come for the nation to think about entertainment not as an individual pursuit of amusement but as a means of uniting groups, and ultimately the nation, toward a common goal. He was a prolific writer as well as a special member to the National Recreation Association, which helped promote new trends in physical education and amusement. Gonda also acted as a consultant for the Ministry of Education and the city government of Tokyo. Due to his experience and work as a consultant for educational matters, Gonda's writings were highly influential. His works helped shape how other intellectuals and the government viewed popular amusements.

Gonda's influential ideas on entertainment did not develop in a vacuum. Japanese officials had long been toying with ideas about how to prod entertainment toward social suasion campaigns. A 1934 book on police ethics concerning *fūzoku,* or public morals, detailed how the government conceived of entertainment, its ability to influence the social climate, and its necessity. Due "to the manner in which today's society is organized, the lifestyle of the masses is exceedingly monotonous, uninteresting, and dull. More and more, daily life is itself at the point where there is nothing fun to do anymore. As such, entertainment is not merely a diversion or a way to kill time. It is, in fact, an indispensable element of living."[29]

To build public support on this "indispensable element of living," Japanese government and military authorities eagerly banked on the popularity of certain stars. Through popular acclaim for his soldier's *rakugo* act and accounts of his travels abroad, Kingorō had become a national icon. In the public mind his image was so tightly linked with the military that the Japanese Imperial Navy asked him to publish a book on the navy. Kingorō kindly obliged and published *Kaigun banbanzai* (A million cheers for the navy). It was later turned into a 1935 movie titled *Ore wa suihei* (I'm a sailor). Interestingly, a problem developed on the movie set due to Kingorō's baldness—he had been balding since his early twenties due to improper medical care while he was an enlisted man. The navy felt that having a bald sailor on screen would harm its image, so the military authorities asked the producers not to show Kingorō's head. Obviously, this created a huge problem for the director since it would be impossible to have a headless leading man. In the end the director filmed Kingorō always wearing a hat, even while sleeping.[30]

Kingorō's skits dealing with the military did not please everyone in Japan at that time. In his autobiography Kingorō mentions that occasionally he received messages from the *kenpeitai* (military police), asking him to refrain from performing his military-related skits. He thought this was strange. Since there was no actual law preventing him from performing, Kingorō went to the military police station for illumination. The muddled response did not provide any explanation, and officers of the military police, who always had seats reserved in the wings of theaters for censorship purposes, would come and glare at him during performances.[31] Unlike Gestapo actions in Nazi Germany, however, harassment of Kingorō and other performers rarely surpassed this level of discomfort.

Many popular wartime comedy routines by Kingorō and other entertainers were pressed on records. Contemporary Japanese historical accounts appear to have neglected the fact that numerous comedy albums were readily available to the public during the war. Columbia Records' official history plainly states that "due to national policies, virtually all entertainment albums were requisitioned for military entertainment and it became gradually more and more difficult to produce records for the national market."[32] In fact, records as a medium of entertainment developed into a massively popular form during the 1930s. From 1926 to 1937 the number of records sold shot up five times from 2 million to 10 million.[33] Records were also sent to the front as entertainment for the troops and used in comforting recuperating soldiers. The government was not the only provider. One women's group in Iwate prefecture in northern Japan purchased twenty record players for use at hospitals caring for wounded soldiers. In the capital, Morioka, the same women's group pressed people to donate old records or those they no longer needed to hospitals at the front so soldiers could enjoy music and comedy.[34]

The authorities' reactions to specific comedy records can be charted through an analysis of police archives. Until August 1, 1934, records eluded overt government censorship, but starting on that date the Home Ministry began to censor records, since the disks were beginning to proliferate in massive numbers. Even before the police implemented actual censorship of records, however, they had concerned themselves with routines they felt harmful to the social order. At this early stage they seem to have been primarily concerned with stories of sexual escapades and ribaldry. On March 14, 1934, they found suspect several albums put out by the Regal Record Company and performed by Entatsu and Achako. The authorities specifically censored Entatsu and Achako with the charges of "disturbing the military order, and blasphemy against the Yasukuni shrine."[35] (Yasukuni is a shrine dedicated to fallen soldiers.) Two albums pressed by Polydor Records, *Stories of the Pleasure Quarters* and *More Stories of the Pleasure Quarters,* performed by Yanagiya Mikimatsu, also garnered undesired attention.[36] Police prohibited their sale and the broadcast of those that had already been sold.

Comedy's influence spilled over into print media. In May 1934 the popular magazine *Hinode* printed a special issue on new *rakugo* sketches so readers who had no access to live performances or radio could read and enjoy the new routines.[37] Other popular mass magazines, such as *King* and *Eloquence,* along with newspapers, followed suit with periodic publications of new routines and news about the performers.[38]

Through print media and popular live performances entertainers from the Yoshimoto Company continued to support Japanese military actions in China through the 1930s. In January 1936 Yoshimoto brokered a deal with a record company and began to let its performers press records on their own. In November 1936 the company formed an alliance with Tōhō films against its competitor Shōchiku films. And by 1938 the Yoshimoto agency had 278 *manzai* performers under exclusive contract with its offices. By the time of the China Incident, the Japanese entertainment world eagerly backed the imperial Japanese military.

The China Incident and the Rising Importance of Entertainment

The insistence on entertaining imperial troops as well as the home audience —promoted simultaneously by the Japanese authorities and the Yoshimoto Company—strengthened following Japan's wholesale military invasion into China in July 1937. The government now seemed committed to keeping the citizenry amused, within what the authorities defined as the boundaries of good taste. Government actions demonstrated that supporting an environment of "healthy entertainment" helped unify the Japanese population. Private entertainment companies, like Yoshimoto, not only continued to send performers abroad to entertain, but when these performers returned, their press conferences and lectures served equally as domestic propaganda for the war. In addition, participation in wartime entertainment helped increase a star's own popularity and the company's profitability as well.

As the war with China escalated, the Japanese government grew more concerned with maintaining popular support for its policies abroad, and more anxious about popular dissatisfaction. Entertainment policy became a key ingredient in the government plan to sway public opinion in its favor. Recently opened police archives demonstrate the authorities' concern with public amusements on the eve of the China Incident. The police were convinced that entertainment could influence the masses' support for the war. The Home Ministry, which was in charge of the police, held meetings in November 1937 dealing with the necessity to organize entertainment as a tool for social mobilization. The ministry concluded, "As can be seen recently in drama, musical revues, *manzai, rakugo, kamishibai* (children's plays performed with cardboard cutouts), and other diversions, amusements for the masses are debasing themselves to the lowest common denominator. The actual quality of entertainment is plummeting toward the crude, and social morals are not being heeded. Moreover, while it is true that many of the diversions are treating the China Incident, the content is usually unpolished. . . ." The police believed that even if the performance managed to arouse feelings of support for Japan's aims, the amateurish productions could undermine later efforts to mobilize the public. The Japanese government desired to push entertainment into that arena that Gonda Yasunosuke had detailed in his essay—entertainment needed to be a public space where national unity could coalesce under the guise of amusement. To accomplish that goal, the ministry decided the following at that meeting. "We need to get entertainers and others to mobilize as employees, to aggressively and in an entertaining fashion use the performing arts and cooperate to help conquer the difficulties Japan currently faces. . . ."[39] Ironically, the government was behind the times; performers and entertainment companies had already mobilized their venues for the war effort.

While entertainment agencies mobilized the stage, the Japanese government continued to struggle with policies and research designed to further control amusements during the war. Several years into the war with China but before the outbreak of the Pacific War, Gonda Yasunosuke expanded on the status of "amusement" under Prime Minister Konoe's New Order, or Shintaisei, a program supposedly designed to renovate Japan and help it achieve its wartime goals. Previously, Gonda had explained in a government social research magazine that amusement was a personal thing. How one amused oneself was left up to the individual. Companies offering entertainment services existed for profit. In contrast, Gonda asserted, the new system no longer focused on the individual as the center of the equation. Gonda hoped that the new "entertainment" would be for society as a whole, a unified system bringing everyone together and replacing the old goal of individual happiness.[40] In a related article written only a few months earlier, Gonda outlined why the study of entertainment was important. He stated that the type of amusements Japanese found entertaining was a barometer of people's lifestyle attitudes, or *seikatsu taido.*[41] Gonda felt that if the public consumed entertainment that favored the war, it followed that the masses would support the war aims. It was therefore necessary to determine which forms of entertainment supporting the war the population regarded as amusing and then employ those forms as vehicles for propaganda.

Following the China Incident and into 1938 the Japanese government increased its scrutiny of the performance world and devised new methods to coerce its cooperation. In December 1938 a new system was implemented for registering and licensing all performers including *rakugo, manzai,* and singers. In January 1939 a temporary system of censorship for comedic scenarios was created as well. On April 1, 1940, the government admonished performers who "made a display of their eccentricity" by having strange stage names and requested that they change their names. This regulation applied to those with foreign-sounding names as well as those with outlandish names.[42]

As they strained to control entertainment the authorities continued to pay close attention to the record industry, identifying it as a source to help motivate support for the war. In the forward to an early 1940s book on record censorship, House of Peers member Kyōgoku Takatoshi discussed the importance of records in influencing public opinion and repeated the overarching philosophy of the elites. "Records, which are but one weapon of the thought war, an element of total war, play an important role in the development of the nation's psyche, as a form of relaxation for our valiant soldiers at the front as well as helping to form wholesome entertainment for imperial subjects at the home front. . . ."[43]

On January 13, 1938, six months after the China Incident, the Yoshimoto Company again teamed up with the Asahi newspaper group to assemble an entertainment platoon to amuse the imperial troops in China. There were two groups, each consisting of approximately twenty performers. The troupes now had an official name, the Warawashitai (We want to make you laugh brigades).[44] The troupe that traveled to North China included Yanagiya Kingorō, Achako, Chitoseya Imao, Yanagiya Mikimatsu, Kyōyama Wakamaru, and others. Kingorō mentioned that before the group was sent off, they prayed at a local shrine. When the Shinto priest of the shrine read off the travelers' names, he prefixed each with an honorific "O." Since the names of the performers were mostly stage names of their own creation, it made for some comical names, and everyone in the group began giggling during what was supposed to be a solemn occasion.[45] The second group, which journeyed to central China, included Ishida Ichimatsu, Sugiura Enosuke, Misu Wakana, Tamamatsu Ichirō, Entatsu, Kanda Rōyama, and others.

The first group had a grand send-off from Tokyo's largest public hall, the Hibiya Public Hall, on January 13, 1938, followed by a similar event at the Osaka Asahi Hall the next evening. Both groups took off from southern Japan and crossed to China by boat, where they arrived within days of one another. When they returned home after more than a month of touring, the Yoshimoto Company hosted one of its typical media events for them. At this press conference not only did the amusement brigades discuss their experiences and impressions of China, but they also reenacted some of their actual performances to the delight of eager audiences. Press conferences for their triumphant return were held in Shimonoseki, Osaka, Kyoto, Nagoya, and later at several performance halls including the Yūrakuza in Tokyo and the Takarazuka Gekijō in Yokohama.

Their appeal must have been enormous since this combination of press conferences and performances continued until April. The first press conference was pressed into a record and sold in stores. A script version also made it into popular magazines. Yoshimoto and the Asahi newspaper companies, which had paid the performers' salaries and transport costs, donated proceeds of the record and magazine sales to the war effort, or so they claimed publicly.[46] Exact profits from such tours are impossible to determine, but these tours certainly sold plenty of products upon their return and made Yoshimoto's stars popular performers throughout the country and the entire Japanese empire. In March 1938 Yanagiya Kingorō released an album entitled *The Warawashitai's Laughing Battlefield Report*.[47]

When Warawashitai performers returned to Japan, they frequently wrote about their experiences in China for release to the general public. Many of these works reflect a Japanese wartime feeling of superiority over the Chinese, while others report glowingly of Japan's actions on the mainland. Soon after their return from the first Warawashitai tour in early 1938, Ishida Ichimatsu and Kyōyama Wakamaru composed a humorous yet informative booklet about their tour entitled *Warawashitai's Field Diary: The Imperial Army's Entertainment Brigade Travels*. While they do recount some of the performers' actual experiences, other comments are demonstrably far from the truth. When the crew lands in Tianjin, the authors note that the city that was once the pride of Chiang Kai Shek had easily been captured by the Japanese, with no civilian casualties.[48] The performers also describe how the Chinese hurl insults like "fuck your mother!" at Japanese travelers and soldiers going up river because, the authors write, Chiang Kai Shek convinced his people that the Japanese are to be feared and despised. For a while the performers travel to different areas, but after they regroup, the authors relate that Yanagiya Kingorō described how he saw battle scenes with piles of Chinese corpses lying about, some partially eaten by wild animals. Consistent with their feelings of superiority to the Chinese, the authors write that in no matter what battle the Japanese always clear their dead away, while the Chinese leave them to beasts and the elements.[49] Extreme circumstances may have made this the case in some situations, but it was more often the case that the Chinese removed their dead and treated their wounded as well. Private entertainment troupes who published versions of the war doubled as unofficial propaganda and bolstered condescending attitudes toward the Chinese. As was true of other accounts written by performers, Ishida and Kyōyama commented on the hospitality and fine behavior of the Japanese imperial soldiers as well as on their own bravery in performing almost in the heat of battle, so close that they could hear the bombs exploding.

Other comedians who did not tour for long periods took to scribbling shorter comedic essays. One example is Sanyūteikinba, who wrote an article called "Sights around Northern China," which came complete with an illustration of the author-comedian himself astride a bomb in the sky overlooking the mainland.[50] In a related article Sanyūteikinba wrote that the Japanese army's success and continuous victory had impressed the world and domestic Japanese to such a degree that children were now playing *senso gokko* (pretend war). Based on this observation, he composed a new routine, called *senso gokko,* which appeared in the January 1938 issue of the popular mass magazine *King.*

Because of their hardships and tenacity, along with the fact that their routines were popular and amusing, the Warawashitai experience catapulted the careers of many performers to great fame, especially Misu Wakana and her partner Tamamatsu Ichirō. They were one of the most popular wartime *manzai* duos, mostly because Misu Wakana had an uncanny ability to mimic accents from all over Japan, imitating regional differences, and her husband Ichirō played a good straight man to her biting commentary.[51] Wakana first met Ichirō when she was still a teenager in Tokyo, but her family had betrothed her to another and she was forced to return to the countryside. Unable to bear life under such circumstances, she fled that marriage and returned to the performing world of Osaka. There she unexpectedly ran into Ichirō again, and they set off together to Qingdao, China, where Wakana worked for a short time as a dancer. They were eventually scouted by the Yoshimoto agency and signed on as performers. Since they had not been a *manzai* duo for very long, some suspect that the Yoshimoto Company signed them because the troupe had few attractive younger women, a necessity for groups entertaining soldiers. But their success ended abruptly when Misu Wakana died from an overdose of amphetamines soon after Japan's surrender.

In addition to the Yoshimoto Company, a multitude of Japanese companies mobilized popular performers to support the war effort. Entertainment troupes completely unrelated to the Yoshimoto Company discussed their experiences in a variety of magazines. Azabu Shin wrote about his time in China performing for the imperial troops as part of an entertainment brigade sent by the King Record Company (a subsidiary of Kōdansha) and the army. Azabu discussed the hardship that soldiers faced in the field but the quiet fortitude with which they carried out their mission. The people back at home, he respectfully wrote, should be proud of their armed forces in China.[52]

Entertainment businesses competed to send talent abroad to amuse Japanese imperial troops, and the Yoshimoto agency sponsored a second Warawashitai tour of China in November and December of 1938 when it sent three groups to South, Central, and North China. When these groups returned in early 1939, they too held press conferences around the country to similar applause.

The Yoshimoto-sponsored Warawashitai tours made ample use of the media to inform the reading and paying public about what was going on in China and, perhaps more to the point, what the Yoshimoto agency was doing about it. The magazine *Shūkan asahi* (a subsidiary of the Asahi newspaper group which had cosponsored the tour) ran a photomontage and roundtable discussion with the performers of the January 1939 Warawashitai tour. As in the other articles, the performers discussed their own hardships, the endurance of the Japanese soldiers, and their pleasure at being so well received.[53]

Besides publishing several books of their experiences as part of the entertainment troupes in China, Misu Wakana and Ichirō pressed a record in 1940, after the second Warawashitai tour, called *Wakana and Ichirō's Collection of Greatest Manzai Routines*. One skit, "We want to make you laugh: Part One," starts out discussing how successful the Japanese are and how they are assured of total victory. As in their other skits, they would half-heartedly try to explain Chinese culture while at the same time make fun of it. The second popular skit, "We want to make you laugh: Part Two," takes a familiar tune but changes the words to be funny. To the tune of a well-known song entitled, "The Imperial Army's Great Victory," the duo opened this skit with these lyrics:

> On the day these *manzai* performers departed Japan
> their tongues flapped so much they ran out of juice
> during their dramatic performances,

Magazine article on "Warawashitai Victory Souvenir Stories." In addition to caricatures of well-known performers shown at the table, this article also contained numerous photographs of the popular stars on these entertainment visits to China. *Shūkan asahi*, May 1939, p. 21.

but now these tongues have scaled the Great Wall of
China and are here to make you laugh,
The make you laugh brigade![54]

In another skit, called "Shina benritai" (Chinese troops are convenient), performed during the same tour, Wakana and Ichirō opened with a song mocking the Chinese Nationalist Army sung to the tune of "The Tokyo Marching Song." The song was the theme song for the popular 1929 film based on a Kikuchi Kan novel of the same name. The Japanese public adored the film as well as its title song in part due to the story but also because of director Mizoguchi Kenji's cinematography. The original tune is a peppy but overall sad melody describing unrequited love in modern Tokyo. The two comedians kept the tune but substituted slightly different lyrics along the same rhyme scheme to parody the Guomindang (KMT; Chinese Nationalist) forces.

> Once upon a time dear General Chiang
> Putting on a mask of bravado, who gives a dang
> Spreading lies against Japan, every day every place
> Now he's crying himself a river as he faces his disgrace.
>
> Shall he ask for help from Russia, or flee to Great Britain
> Or to Hong Kong will he soon be forgotten
> The voices of the 400 million cursing his name
> Even the moon's glare not hiding his shame.[55]

The same skit continues to denigrate the Chinese lack of military prowess. The duo remark that Chinese soldiers are only interested in what a platoon can pay them and, if they do not like the conditions in one troop, they will just leave and find another.

ICHIRŌ: That's a pitiful song, isn't it? I heard that basically as long as you have money, you can hire Chinese soldiers. All sorts will show up.
WAKANA: Yeah, as soon as they got nothing to eat, they start signing up to enlist.
ICHIRŌ: Oh, really?
WAKANA: And if they don't like the monthly wages in one platoon, they just hotfoot it over to another.
ICHIRŌ: So they live kind of a migratory life and all, huh.
WAKANA: They are only out to rip y'off.
ICHIRŌ: But don't they have to have a physical checkup or something?
WAKANA: Naw, there is no need.

ICHIRŌ: Oh, there isn't any?

WAKANA: It's very simple, you see. As long as you have a body, you can get in.

ICHIRŌ: That's pretty convenient, isn't it.

WAKANA: Yep, that's why they call Chinese troops, troops of convenience, *benritai.*

ICHIRŌ: Don't you mean *benitai?*

Benitai were Chinese troops who wore civilian clothes and went into the Japanese-controlled areas to spy. The Japanese military frequently complained in the press and its own propaganda about the Chinese lack of fair play in the war. The supposed Chinese use of civilians in military matters irritated the Japanese.[56] *Benri* is the Japanese term for convenience, so the joke is that Chinese soldiers displayed no loyalty, conveniently hopping from platoon to platoon. Readers should note that while these performers made fun of stereotyped images of the Chinese to entertain the public, Japanese military documents reveal that the military took a much more serious view of the potential for the Chinese to wage war against Japan.[57]

Soldiers also clamored to see stars perform their most popular routines, the ones that made them stars before their tours. Along with their immensely popular routine about baseball, Achako and Entatsu also performed a skit that delighted audiences in the early 1930s. As with much Japanese comedy, the humor centered on word play, homonyms, and banter between the straight man and the funny man. One popular routine, "Ears," which they performed in China and at home, turned on numerous plays on words that started out with a classic misunderstanding.

ENTATSU: I heard that you weren't doing so well.

ACHAKO: Yeah, well . . .

ENTATSU: Are you all better?

ACHAKO: Yeah, thanks for asking.

ENTATSU: Good to hear.

ACHAKO: To tell you the truth, I was out of it for about a month.

ENTATSU: What exactly did you have?

ACHAKO: Well . . . you see. It seems there was something blocking my ear.

ENTATSU: Oh, well, that's not good.

ACHAKO: Yep.

ENTATSU: So, um, did you take an enema?

ACHAKO: Huh?

ENTATSU: An enema?

ACHAKO: WHAT?!? For an inflammation of the ear, what kind of help can an enema do?

ENTATSU: Well, when my rear is all blocked up, nothing better than an enema to clear the problem.

ACHAKO: Who said anything about "rear"?

ENTATSU: You did. Didn't you say you were blocked in your rear?

ACHAKO: No, I am completely regular.

ENTATSU: Oh, so what's the problem?

ACHAKO: Well, to tell the truth, sometimes I am a bit too regular . . .

ENTATSU: That won't do either.

ACHAKO: What have you got me saying! I had an inflammation problem with my EAR.

ENTATSU: Inflammation of the ear?

ACHAKO: The inner ear to be exact.

ENTATSU: That's pretty serious.[58]

In their 1941 film *Buck Privates,* Bud Abbott and Lou Costello performed a comparable routine that had audiences laughing at the time. It should also be noticed that in addition to the similarities of using the military as background, misunderstandings based on word play featured prominently in both US and Japanese wartime comedy. This scene from their movie shows Abbott and Costello running away from the police and into a movie theater to avoid detection. They do not realize that the movie theater has been turned into a local military recruitment center.

ABBOTT: Get in line. We'll hide in the movies.

COSTELLO: Yeah, and when we get in, we'll stay a long time!

ABBOTT: All right, get a couple of tickets!

COSTELLO: What's the hurry? We got ridda that dumb cop! *(To the receptionist man.)* How much to get in?

RECEPTIONIST: Nothing. We're gonna give you $21.

COSTELLO: Oh, bank night! Giving any dishes away?

RECEPTIONIST: No, tin pans. Go on, step inside.

ABBOTT: Well, come on or we won't get a seat.

COSTELLO: Hey usher *(To another soldier.),* what picture's playing?

SOLDIER: You're in the army now.

COSTELLO: Good, I've never seen that picture.

(Announcement.) "Calling Dr. Coldwater, Calling Dr. Coldwater . . ."

ABBOTT: What's this "calling Dr. Coldwater?"

COSTELLO: Must be a double feature.

ABBOTT: I guess so.

SOLDIER: Draftee?

COSTELLO: Not a bit. *(To Abbott.)* Do you feel it?

ABBOTT: No.

COSTELLO: I feel very comfortable in here.

SOLDIER: Right over there.

ABBOTT: Hey, come on, let's register before the drawing starts.

COSTELLO: Think you're gonna win, huh?

SOLDIER: Step right up, boys. Sign right here, please.

COSTELLO: "Please?" Boy, what polite ushers!

ABBOTT: Quiet!

SOLDIER: And let me have your signature right there, please.

COSTELLO: I'd be delighted and I hope I win.

SOLDIER: Well, congratulations, men. We're glad to have you in the army!

ABBOTT & COSTELLO: Thanks! *(Beat.)* What!!??

ABBOTT: Army!?

COSTELLO: *(To Abbott.)* You win! Gangway!![59]

Japanese audiences continued to enjoy wartime comedic performances so much that by the time of the third Warawashitai trip on April 28, 1940, additional entertainment brigades were added and performers visited Japanese troops in North, South, and Central China. Misu Wakana and Ichirō became huge stars due to these trips, and when they performed upon their return, people flocked in droves to attend. Several routines that received enthusiastic responses from the soldiers in China were later sold by Victor Records.

The Yoshimoto Company's efforts were not wasted on the domestic audience, which understood very well the meaning of sending entertainment platoons to the troops in China. In the December 1938 issue of the magazine *Hōsō*, the chief of the Scientific Labor Research Institute, Dr. Teruoka Yoshitō, wrote that in this time of crisis, humor was obligatory for workers and soldiers alike. The work of *rakugo* performers and others performing at the front was necessary, he declared, and would help the country and production.[60]

Government-paid scholars were not the only analysts who saw entertainers as real soldiers fighting at the front. Not all entertainment performances were funny, and sometimes the performers met with tragedy. One female *manzai* entertainer, Hanazono Aiko, wife and performing partner of the famous Katsura Kingo, was killed by a guerrilla attack as her truck traveled through an unstable area in China. For her sacrifice in the name of the imperial nation she was enshrined at Yasukuni National Shrine when her remains were returned to Japan.[61] Entertainment performances were considered important enough that Hanazono's body was stored for the remainder of the tour, and Katsura and the rest of the troop continued on to finish the tour in its entirety. When the performers arrived back in Tokyo by train, there was a massive homecoming event for their return and the wife of then Army Minister Tōjō Hideki participated in the official public ceremony conducted for Hanazono's funeral.[62]

A book published during the war, the *Textbook of National Entertainment Arts,* added melodrama to the original incident. In an effort to show that performers supported the military and assisted in the war effort, Hanazono is credited with asking her husband Katsura to kill her since she did not want to wind up in the hands of the Chinese.[63] The author, Yamachi Kunio, added his own validation concerning the activities of the Warawashitai. "Hanazono did her part for the country, and she died while splendidly carrying out her mission to provide comfort to the imperial troops." [64]

Comedy troops provided a moral guide to wartime Japanese society and prompted many to devote personal time to the war effort. In her book published in 1941, *Mother of the Firing Lines,* the author Hagi Shūgetsu recounts how she was on her way to Europe in September 1937 and was in Monji in the south of Japan when she saw boats coming in with wounded soldiers. Hagi cancelled her vacation plans and instead set off to travel around China for three years. Her book recounts those experiences and the commander of the Military Propaganda Corps in China, Mabuchi Itsuo, wrote the forward for her story. Hagi provides the reader with more than just anecdotes about the "dastardly" Chinese soldiers and how they employ children to ambush Japanese troops.[65] The book is also partly a travel journal as Hagi describes some of the Buddhist statues she had time to visit in Datong, in northern China.[66] In many ways it reads like the Warawashitai accounts of China, for like the *manzai* stars and *rakugo* performers, Hagi consistently reminded the home audiences about the important work of the Japanese Imperial Army in China. Hagi's goal was to impress upon Japanese at the home front the need to support soldiers on the battlefields. She was also critical of the Chinese, and thus implicitly supportive of the Japanese efforts there. She claimed that the Chinese had a tendency to steal, implying that the Japanese did not. Hagi's sorrow over the supposed low moral standards of the Chinese parallels the wartime comedians' scornful attitudes toward the Chinese in print and on stage.[67]

Manzai and *rakugo* performers continued to perform throughout the war, and many even made careers for themselves by doing so. But the *rakugo* performers also decided at this time to determine what would be acceptable material by unilaterally banding together and grading their *rakugo* routines. In what appears to be a preemptive move on their side to avoid displeasing the authorities with sexual innuendoes, *rakugo* associations banned fifty-three of their own traditional routines without any prompting from a government agency. Routines that dealt with sexually transmitted diseases, prostitutes, drinking, and similar topics were buried during a ceremony at the Honpō Temple in Asakusa, Tokyo, on October 13, 1941.[68]

On the eve of the Pacific War, debates concerning entertainment and amusement proliferated in the popular press. In July 1941 the magazine *Itaria* held a roundtable discussion with prominent members of the entertainment industry, including composer Yamada Kōsaku, film critic Tsumura Hideo, the Ministry of Education's Physical Education Section Chief Kitasawa Kiyoshi, and others. In great earnest they discussed exactly what type of specific entertainment policy the country needed. A similar article in the same issue, by Sugiyama Heisuke, discussed the urgency of cutting down on the amount of money people spent on amusement each week and at the same time raising the "spiritual" level of the entertainment offered during this time of need.[69]

Even after ten years of mobilizing entertainment to work in congruence with state goals, by the end of 1941 many continued to push for more. In an article published in December 1941—although it was probably written before the outbreak of war with the United States—the prominent prewar intellectual Nakajima Kenzō clamored for a more concrete government policy toward entertainment. Nakajima considered amusement directed at national mobilization to be a top priority. He believed the authorities gave individuals and private companies too much leeway and needed to guide the development of amusements that would methodically and prudently lead the masses to continued support for the war aims. "Entertainment for the nation is an absolute. After careful planning and consideration, the establishment of a solid entertainment policy is of the utmost importance," Nakajima explained.[70] Nakajima's declarations concerning the social importance of entertainment were reflected in the behavior of other groups. As the war with China escalated, even sports in Japan took on new meaning. It was not seen as ridiculous to compare the bat used by a baseball player with the sword wielded by a samurai, which was therefore to be treated with appropriate respect. After hitting the ball during a game, players no longer threw their bats and ran to first base. Instead, they lovingly placed the bat on the field and then ran. Catchers, too, removed all protective gear but their mask in order not to play with an unfair advantage and to prove that they had the mettle and spirit to help with the war effort.[71]

The Pacific War and Entertainment

In the days and months following the attack on Pearl Harbor in December 1941, the Japanese were far from depressed. On the contrary, the country was elated over its gains. The decade had proven Japan successful in its military endeavors and the quick victories at Pearl Harbor, Singapore, and later the Philippines only reaffirmed Japan's belief in its own superiority. If soldiers and civilians alike had been excited to hear Kingorō years before, astounding applause followed when the attractive and talented Misu Wakana and her partner Tamamatsu Ichirō performed one of their smash hits from a 1942 routine called "Charging into the Jungle." Following commencement of hostilities with the west, Japan's performers added the new *bête noire* of the United States to their list of characters to mock in their routines.[72]

The Yoshimoto Company's Warawashitai tours seemingly ended with the advent of the Pacific War, but other companies, perhaps spurred by Yoshimoto's successful example, established similar troupes. Comedy continued to flourish even after the attack on Pearl Harbor. One popular sketch that mocked early US military "prowess" was called "The Pacific Sumo War" and was performed by the Lucky Seven team. The sketch remains humorous while alluding to all the slogans for keeping the home front in support of the war, such as staying prudent and thrifty.

The following translates part of a much longer routine. It is important to note that in sumo matches, the opposing sides are from the west and east, like corners for a boxing match.

LUCKY: *(In announcer style.)* Ladies and gentlemen. Here we are in the 13,000-meter-high Sumo Stadium in the sky. This is our last match of the evening in this summer sumo tournament for the world's fighter planes. In the east, from the Rising Sun stable, the ace of the Axis, Hayabusa (falcon). His opponent from the west, the Allied Yokozuna[73] Boeing B-17...

SEVEN: That's pretty good. Let me give it a shot. Let me take charge of the announcements for their entrance into the ring.

LUCKY: Ring announcements . . . okay go for it.

SEVEN: In the west Boeing B-17, the fortress of the sky, with a height of 72 feet 7 inches and weighing in at 52, 518 pounds and 3 ounces.

LUCKY: Yes, that's right. Boeing B-17, fortress of the sky, is originally from Yankee prefecture, in the country of the Jews, from a pirate village. His first appearance in the ring was March 1941, and his specialty is fleeing into the mists of the clouds.

SEVEN: In the east corner Hayabusa, from the Rising Sun stable. His height and weight remain—classified as top secret.

LUCKY: Yes, Hayabusa from the Rising Sun stable. He is originally from Toyoashiharamizuho (an ancient name for Japan) and his first appearance in the ring is also—classified as top secret. His specialty is blitzkrieg warfare every single day of the week.

SEVEN: Our referee for today is Zeppelin . . . *(Mimicking an echo.)* Our referee for today is Zeppelin.

LUCKY: The two opponents enter the ring . . . Hayabusa of the east is ready for his first volley of attacks; his opponent, the fortress of the sky, is arrogantly poised looking like the cat that ate the canary . . . Boeing is now leaving the ring for more gasoline. His opponent Hayabusa is readying his machine gun and waiting for his enemy to regain the ring.

SEVEN: Ladies and gentlemen, your attention please. We would like to announce the results of the rest of today's matches.

LUCKY: First off, the American Hurricane vs. the German Messerschmitt, Messerschmitt wins with a knockdown. In the second match, the American Douglas versus the German Junker, the German victorious with a wing-clipping take down. In the North American vs. German Heinkel, the German again the champion (due to the American having a broken engine). In the last match, Curtis Hawk vs. the Italian Marchetti, the Hawk had its propellers broken and loses.

SEVEN: The results of today's matches leave the Axis armies with 175 points, the Allied armies with zero.

LUCKY: Okay, our two opponents are done warming up in the ring and they are ready to face off. The referee Zeppelin moves to the center of the ring and they go at it.

SEVEN: Ladies and gentlemen, we have the following announcement to make. Mr. Roosevelt of the Washington White House. Your house is on fire and burning down. Please go home immediately.

LUCKY: Hey, cut that out. Back to the action in the ring . . . and Boeing is slapping around his opponent. He's slapping him with the force of his 4,800-horsepower Wright cyclone engine—that's some fierce punching power. But the Rising Sun's Hayabusa is smiling and just shrugging it off. Wait, Hayabusa is coming right back at him with a vicious return. He's hitting his opponent with huge bombs, ohh!! . . . Ladies and gentlemen, this is truly a monumental battle. Both sides are really fired up. Wait, Hayabusa is inching closer toward his opponent . . . Boeing is beginning a big turn to the left. Oh, Hayabusa . . .[74]

The sketch goes on to detail Hayabusa's stupendous flying technique and, of course, it describes how Hayabusa routs the American Boeing.

Records of such popular skits continued to be routinely available throughout the war. In June 1942 one company, Teichiku, pressed an album called *Meijinkai,* which had performances on it by Tokugawa Musei, a famous *benshi*[75] turned performer, Misu Wakana, her partner Ichirō, and others. A year later Teichiku pressed a second version. Statistics specific to sales of these comedy records are unavailable, but Japanese wartime consumers purchased many records throughout the war, even though by 1943 records were almost triple their prewar price.[76]

In the summer of 1942 the Japanese navy was partially crippled at Midway, and nonetheless the public clamor for entertainment continued to grow. But what kind of amusement had the blessings of the government authorities? What they denominated as good amusement were activities that were "healthy" and that would lead the people through a war envisioned as a long and drawn-out battle.

Wartime comedy both reflected popular attitudes and strengthened resolve during the war. This is most obvious in a book entitled *Great Manzai Routines for the Decisive Battle,* published in 1943. In it is a routine by Kōriyama Kazuo called "Comparing Japanese and American Mothers." The skit informs us that Japanese mothers are superlative because they raise their sons to be the source of the Japanese race's greatness. US mothers, on the other hand, worry about their sons and put nice white flags in their service bags so that if the enemy catches them . . . well you know. And they tell them to take care.

In this same routine the performers mock how American mothers are so happy when they hear that their sons have been taken prisoner and have not died in battle. As a contrast, the performers quote a letter from an actual Japanese mother. Japanese mothers, the skit points out, openly write that they are happy to have raised sons who are courageous enough to die gloriously in battle, shouting the emperor's name as they go down, like falling cherry blossoms.[77]

Japanese domestic support of the war effort required that the battlefront be linked to the home front, demonstrated by a series of articles on records and war issued in late 1943. The problem was that those on the home front could not see the face of the enemy. What's more, one author said, people on the home front "cannot see the enemy's airplanes. The enemy's bombs are not raining down. Since the enemy is not yet a visible threat, it is difficult to inculcate hatred against him." In order to rectify this problem people had to hate the enemy, the article explained, and understand why they should.[78] During the Pacific War, as before, the Japanese authorities felt that albums played an important role in raising the population's morale and supporting the war, and this included entertainment records. Records helped keep the domestic population in line.

Entertainment troupes continued to be sent to China even after the war with the United States took a turn for the worse. Shibusawa Hideo, son of famed industrialist Shibusawa Eiichi, wrote about his travels and experiences as part of a Tōhō company entertainment brigade journey through China. In March 1943 his troupe of fifty-five people went to Shanghai to celebrate the third anniversary of the Japanese puppet Chinese government in Nanjing. Part of that group toured Central China to entertain the Japanese Imperial troops. At the same time the Tōhō troupe also entertained a portion of the puppet government's Chinese troops and gave performances to Wang Jingwei and the Chinese masses. The entertainers also performed in a Chinese mainland film. Shibusawa assured his readers that his book would provide them with a clear image of what the entertainment troupes were doing and how they assisted in the "cultural development" in China.[79] Shibusawa clearly saw his troupes as more than mere entertainment, since on more than one occasion he called the dancers in the group not just entertainment performers but *bunka shisetsu,* or cultural ambassadors.[80]

Shibusawa's account helps us understand that Japanese entertainment in China was far from a politically unmotivated activity. The chroniclers of *manzai* performer Hanazono Aiko's life highlighted her presence on the mainland as a soldier helping out the war effort. Shibusawa's performers and performers in other companies knew that entertaining on the mainland was neither easy nor always safe, but most were convinced that their presence made a difference to the Japanese war effort and so they persevered. Theaters in China were frequently the focus of anti-Japanese and anti-Nationalist party terrorism. On May 27, 1943, a time bomb went off on the second floor of the Shanghai Theater and wounded over a dozen people. The Tōhō show had performed there earlier in the month. The next day a bomb exploded inside a grand local department store, the Daxin Gongsi. Threats to physical safety were so commonplace that when some of the performers from Shibusawa's troupe went to see a movie in the beginning of June, they remarked that a message flashed on the screen for all patrons to "please check under your seats."[81]

Shibusawa tells us that Japanese soldiers were not the only ones viewing the Japanese entertainment brigade shows. Chinese children in areas where the troops were stationed would come to watch. Because the people behind the stage would pass out candy and smile at the kids watching from behind the scenes, Shibusawa wrote, "Thus you could say propaganda operations also took place behind the stage."[82]

The Tōhō group that Shibusawa led attended a performance by a Japanese military information platoon, a *hōdōhan*, who were practicing a play to perform for Chinese villagers. The play was titled *Dadao yingmei*, or *Down with Britain and America!* Shibusawa spoke with one of the Japanese Imperial Army commanders in that town who remarked that to show only straight propaganda plays in the local theater would eventually have a deleterious effect. It was necessary to show comedies and lighthearted fare as well. The important goal, the commander asserted, was to concentrate on *minshin haaku*, maintaining a grasp over the hearts and minds of the people.[83]

Comedy Performers and the End of the War

As a Japanese triumph became more elusive, the country needed to increase mobilization, tolerate decreasing standards of living, and rationalize the fact of fewer military victories. In March 1944, mirroring military rhetoric, the entertainment industry adopted kessen, or "final battle" standards: movies were to be kept within one hour and forty minutes, stage performances within two hours and thirty minutes. The number of theaters also declined during the last few years of the war, but a few stalwarts remained and performers continued to amuse.

Even the March 1945 fire bombing of Tokyo, which killed an estimated 100,000 Japanese, did not deter elite entertainers from continuing their profession and demonstrating their support for the war. As late as May 1945 two well-known *rakugo* performers, Kokonteishinshō and Sanyūteienshō, traveled to Manchuria to delight the imperial troops. At this time Shinshō was fifty-seven and Enshō about forty-seven. Shinshō was already a famous *rakugo* performer who loved the red-light districts and loved Japanese liquor even more. It is said like a true resident of Tokyo he never let the sun shine on his day's earnings and changed his name sixteen times in a bid to evade creditors. He is considered a major figure in *rakugo* of that era. Enshō also reigned as one of the great names in *rakugo*, and he was president of the Rakugo Association from 1965–1972. He helped postwar *rakugo* attain new heights of popularity. He is supposed to have memorized close to three hundred stories, an unheard of number. In 1974 he performed for the imperial court, something that would have been inconceivable even a few decades earlier.

The two signed two-month contracts and were off. Shinshō joked in his autobiography, *In Praise of Poverty*, that when the war got worse and the Allies began dropping bombs, the worst part was the lack of decent alcohol.[84] The two also figured they were going to be drafted so they might as well make the best of it. They journeyed from Niigata in western Japan to Korea by boat and after an unpleasant crossing traveled northwest by train to Xinjing, Manchukuo's capital. They went throughout Manchuria entertaining troops, but when their contract was finished, there were no return boats for transport. They fled to Dalian when the Soviets announced they were entering the war. Everyone was trying to flee, the trains were jam-packed, and Dalian was crawling with Japanese, both civilian and military. Shinshō wrote that he could not quite believe it when he heard that Japan had surrendered. In confusion and uncertainty surrounding the time of surrender, rumors abounded: "The emperor committed ritual suicide; the crown prince is being taken to America and held hostage for twenty-five years; in Tokyo all the young women have been raped by Americans and there are no more virgins left; etc."[85] Shinshō and Enshō did not return to Japan until January 1947.

Yanagiya Kingorō's younger brother, Sekisekitei Momotarō, a big moneymaker for Tōhō entertainment, departed for Manchuria in 1944. When his troop engaged with the Soviets at the border, he escaped injury but he also got separated from his platoon. Eventually he found his fellow soldiers and, as he jocularly recalled, asked them, "Hey, how did so few of you capture so many Soviet POWs?" It was only then that he realized that it was his platoon that was captured and that he was among the POWs. He also returned home in 1947.[86]

Given the dual nature of wartime entertainment—as a form of amusement for the Japanese and vehicle for propaganda—questions dealing with how the propaganda and comedy were received by the society at large remain unanswered. However, this chapter offers an overall picture, a beginning from which to analyze how popular, nongovernmental culture came to terms with its participation in the war and its effect on wartime Japanese society. Comedy contributed to national mobilization. The Yoshimoto Company is an example of the force nongovernmental initiatives exerted in the creation of *imon butai*, entertainment brigades, and marshalling popular support for the war. These *imon butai* demonstrate the formal and informal cooperation that existed among the entertainment industry, the military, and the civilian government. This exchange reveals a picture of greater complexity concerning how the Japanese public mobilized for war. Authorities did not always have to push the population toward war; at times the people adopted the very slogans of the war into their own lives and promoted it as their business.

During the 1920s the Japanese elite worried about the effects of increasing urbanization and the ensuing destabilization of traditional social relations. In response, the Ministry of Education and the Home Ministry launched various movements to urge urban and rural residents to fly the national flag and to believe in the sanctity of the local Shinto shrines—in short, to be good national patriots. The Japanese government believed its first priority "was to instill at the level of daily living, ideas about nationhood." [87] The militarization of comedy was successful in this regard, since it helped national goals soak down into the very fabric of daily entertainment and amusement.

Part of the problem in dealing with wartime entertainment is the bias with which it is regarded by postwar generations. This is true not only of comedy, but of stage drama as well. Hatta Motō, a well-known postwar drama critic and professor, wrote that wartime authorities pandered to the masses in order to get the population to follow the government's lead. This produced, Hatta felt, a vulgarization of popular drama.[88] Of course, such an approach allows the postwar generation to eradicate its responsibility and make a clean break with wartime entertainment, even though a majority of the performers remained popular in the postwar era and performed many of the same routines, minus, of course, some egregious wartime references.

Wartime comedy was a pillar of support for wartime propaganda, and it also maintained a strong popular following. It was a mainstay that served to tie the home front to the battlefront. Furthermore, entertainment propaganda served to popularize Japanese wartime attitudes about China and the war's aims as the battlefield grew to include Southeast Asia and America. During a period of economic privation, the Japanese spent money on comedy products that voiced support for war aims. Unlike Nazi Germany, which faced difficulty maintaining state-produced humor, the private entertainment industry in Japan actually used the war as a means to stay in business. Not only did Japanese comedy and entertainment businesses stay open throughout the war, but afterwards they also did not purge the performers who had supported the war, as was the case in postwar Soviet Union. Moreover, the very structures that supported the war remained wholly intact after the surrender. The Yoshimoto Company is still the premier comedic force in the Japanese entertainment industry and has recently taken steps to enter other Asian markets, including Taiwan, mainland China, and Southeast Asia. World War Two launched numerous careers and brought fame and fortune to many others who continued to be popular after the war.

The difficulty with discovering the line between propaganda and comedy in wartime Japan parallels recent studies on Nazi cinema that address "the problem of how to distinguish propaganda from entertainment, because the

German film industry was at once heavily regulated and heavily profit-oriented."[89] The fact that Japanese wartime comedy persisted throughout the war and remained a vibrant, dynamic product reveals that Japan's Fifteen-Year War was not an entirely "dark valley," but a much more complex period in which a multiplicity of values interacted to help the war effort.[90] How comedy developed in such a tragic environment helps us to understand more comprehensively the inner workings of Japanese society at war.[91]

CHAPTER FIVE

The Japanese Propaganda Struggle on the Chinese Mainland

apanese infantryman Shinotsuka Yoshio did not personally participate in the vivisections and bestial bacterial tests that the now-infamous Unit 731, located outside of Harbin in North Manchuria, conducted on its Chinese victims. However, Shinotsuka did attend the gruesome experiments, visually recording the proceedings as a medical sketch artist. During an interview conducted fifty years after the war with a popular Japanese magazine, this former imperial Japanese soldier's eyes glistened with tears as he recalled his crimes. Decades removed from life as a soldier in Manchukuo, Shinotsuka could no longer fathom the horrors he committed as a member of the Japanese imperial armed forces.

After the surrender of the Japanese in 1945, Shinotsuka's superiors told him that whatever he did, he should not submit himself to the Soviets. Shinotsuka missed his chance to escape back to Japan and fell in with the Chinese Communists, who provided him with assistance and guaranteed him safety. The Chinese Communist Party (CCP) did not shoot or beat him even though technically this Japanese soldier was a war criminal. As Shinotsuka explained, "The liberation army soldiers were very kind. They aided me in my time of need, and during that time I came to understand the severity of my crimes."[1] In 1951 Communist officials were still detaining Shinotsuka and in 1952 they placed him in prison. He was released in June 1956 and returned to Japan that summer.

This Japanese POW's story exemplifies a common, immediate postwar phenomenon of Japanese soldiers surrendering to the Chinese Communists in order to protect themselves. Shinotsuka recognized that he had committed serious crimes, yet he did not fear surrendering to the CCP after Japan's defeat. Considering all the training that Japanese soldiers received before deployment, coupled with the fact that Japanese military manuals explicitly forbade surrender and reading enemy propaganda, it may strike the reader as odd that an imperial Japanese soldier would want to give himself up to the Chinese Communists. The Chinese, Communist and otherwise, were quite aware of the indoctrination Japanese soldiers underwent. A Chinese translation of the Japanese military booklet *What Every Soldier Should Know* detailed in plain language that each Japanese soldier existed to serve the emperor and should be readily prepared to sacrifice himself.[2] Shinotsuka Yoshio's testimony and that of others about turning themselves in to the CCP after the surrender lends credibility to the assertion that Japanese soldiers believed they would receive good treatment from the Chinese Communist Army if they surrendered. The fact that Shinotsuka trusted that he would be safe is evidence that the CCP propaganda, which guaranteed Japanese soldiers' safety, did not entirely fall on deaf ears.

Japanese Propaganda Abroad: Competition for Adherents

Japan had mobilized its population to an extent unattainable in Nazi Germany, Fascist Italy, or Franco's Spain. In Germany, where Nazis faced discontent and attempted political coups, intellectuals and antifascists fled the country throughout the war. In Japan few went into exile. In the face of this obvious propaganda success in the domestic sphere the subsequent question remains: what response did Japanese propaganda elicit among peoples throughout the empire and the rest of Asia? The quick response is, of course, that the Japanese created several problems that continually detracted from effective propaganda. First, due to consistently poor control of behavior of troops in the imperial armed forces, atrocities were rampant.[3] Second, bureaucratic and racist arrogance rendered it difficult for Japanese to sympathize or even empathize with the very Asians they claimed to be liberating. The result was the construction of a tiered society that often failed because it did not offer imperial subjects a reason to fight or to support the empire.

But this rationale does not really provide an adequate explanation. The British and French empires, as well as that of the United States in the Philippines, all constructed tiered societies in their empires. In fact, when the United States wrested the Philippines away from Spain just before the turn of the twentieth century, American troops killed an estimated 200,000 Filipinos.[4] Moreover, Japanese propaganda abroad did not always fail. In fact, many groups on the Chinese continent took it quite seriously. Contrary to the popular perception that Japanese propaganda failed because it did not respond to local needs, wartime Japanese Foreign Ministry documents suggest that Japanese propaganda within China influenced both a response from the Chinese and the development and growth of propaganda back on Japan's home islands.

Japanese propaganda on the Chinese mainland and at home affected both Japanese and Chinese, and Japanese propaganda on the mainland also interacted with Chinese-produced propaganda. This resulted in both the Chinese and Japanese struggling to win the hearts and minds of the whole population in China—Chinese (Nationalist and Communist) and Japanese. In China, the Chinese Nationalists and Communists continually monitored each other and the Japanese for breaks in everyone's propaganda defenses. In marked contrast to the bravado displayed in public announcements and more specifically in the radio messages broadcast by the Japanese Imperial General Headquarters, the Japanese government and military were keenly aware of, and concerned about, the threat Chinese propaganda posed to their wartime aims because of its effect on the Japanese—both military and civilian—and the counter effects on the whole Chinese population.

Japanese Propaganda in China

To truly understand how Japanese propaganda developed during Japan's Fifteen-Year War requires an analysis of how Japanese military and civilian plans and programs operated in the international arena. Japan started out as a fledgling empire soon after the Meiji Restoration, and a few decades later acquired Taiwan and Korea. Throughout the first two decades of the twentieth century, it obtained railway and land leases in North China, which were followed by annexation of several Pacific islands after World War One. By 1938 Japan was a nation poised on the threshold of establishing its Greater East Asian Co-prosperity Sphere.

The Japanese did not design propaganda merely for themselves. Imperial Japanese propaganda had two aims. First, wartime propaganda served to coax the domestic Japanese population to think of itself as the leader of Asia, and second, propaganda urged the Chinese to feel that the Japanese would help them achieve the goal of liberation from western imperialism. At the same time parallel propaganda operations aimed at the United States focused on American duplicity in its treatment of Black Americans and other minorities. From the outset, the Japanese conceived of their propaganda as internationally oriented.

Evidence suggests that problems on the Chinese mainland influenced the development of Japanese domestic propaganda. On the mainland Japanese propaganda had to compete alongside Chinese and later American propaganda. The struggle for the "hearts and minds of the people" should be viewed as a competition among three distinct parties—the Chinese Communist Party (CCP), the Chinese Nationalists (KMT), and the Japanese. In addition, Wang Jingwei's collaborationist group stationed in Nanjing in 1940, an often-neglected player in the propaganda war, drove a wedge into KMT activities and can even be considered a fourth propaganda center. Each group competed for power and an audience on the mainland.[5]

The existence of this range of propaganda in wartime China is important for several reasons. A discussion of the Chinese response to Japanese propaganda on the mainland, and the Japanese countermoves to that response, forces us to take wartime Japanese propaganda seriously. The Chinese were worried enough about the impact and influence of Japanese propaganda to make concerted efforts to block its influence wherever possible. Understanding that Japanese, Chinese, and American propaganda interacted on the mainland should force us to reconsider Japan's wartime impact on China and on relations between the KMT and the CCP.

The Chinese also did not develop propaganda unilaterally, but through interaction among the CCP, the KMT, and the Japanese propaganda activities. Rural China saw and heard a barrage of messages. The Chinese were not competing solely for the hearts and minds of their own citizens, nor were they competing with one voice and message. The Japanese faced competition from the KMT and the CCP not only with regard to the Chinese but also with regard to their own troops.

Overall, KMT propaganda toward the Japanese seems to have been less effective than that of the Communists. CCP propaganda appeared so powerful that it obliged the Japanese military to analyze very specifically its potential influence on Japanese soldiers. Later American propaganda did not worry the Japanese in anything like the same fashion. CCP propaganda also came to wield more influence in turning Japanese soldiers and then using them for propaganda purposes. The achievements of the Chinese Communist propaganda aimed at the Japanese military proved so nimble that it stunned US authorities. Communist success may explain, in part, what prompted a US delegation to visit Yenan, China, in the summer of 1944 because American military authorities mandated the group study Chinese wartime propaganda methods against the Japanese.

The competition between Japanese and Chinese propaganda influenced the outcome of China's war of resistance and subsequent civil war. The propaganda rivalry among the disparate groups involved should force us to reevaluate one historian's claim that "[w]hat provoked the anti-Japanese movement was neither discussions made by the Chinese Communist leadership or the agitation of Communist agents among the students; it was Japanese aggression."[6] Research completed for this volume demonstrates that what mattered most in China was the manufacture of public opinion and not simply military prowess. By the start of 1938 Chinese and Japanese leaders could no longer afford to ignore the opinion of the masses.

What happened on the mainland should change our preconceptions that the escalating propaganda war occurred between clearly delineated opposing

Anti-Japanese leaflet produced by the Chinese. The caption and visual assert that the military clique and traitorous elements within Chinese commerce are suckling at the breast that is Japan. Manshū Nippōsha, ed., *Jikyoku oyobi hainichi posutā shashinchō*, p. 54. The caption in Chinese claims the leaflet was produced in Shanghai, around the time of the Manchurian Incident in September 1931.

sides—the Japanese and the Chinese. This chapter describes the efforts made by the Japanese and the Chinese to gain trust on the mainland. It particularly highlights the CCP's policy regarding Japanese POWs and its propaganda aimed at the Japanese military. A later section deals with the KMT and how the struggle between Chinese propaganda and Japanese propaganda on the mainland involved the United States.

Japanese Propaganda at the Local Level in China

Japanese civilian and military propaganda agencies engaged in a constant struggle to win the allegiance of the Chinese. The military distributed posters of the Japanese army pleasantly hosting Chinese soldiers who had surrendered. In June 1939 the Japanese military dropped Chinese-language propaganda leaflets that cited Confucian principles on Chinese civilians. Basic Confucian ideology held that when leaders failed their people morally, the dynasty toppled, having lost "the mandate of heaven," and new leadership took over. The imperial Japanese military also attempted to bolster its support among the Chinese by offering rewards to Chinese citizens who reported broken power lines or train lines.[7] The personal diaries of Japanese soldiers who fought on the mainland reveal that most often these posters and leaflets were blatant fabrications. The Japanese military routinely slaughtered surrendering Chinese soldiers.

Japanese propaganda photos from July 1939, published in Chinese-language magazines published by the Japanese, showed Chinese POWs having fun in Japanese-supervised POW camps.[8] Japanese propaganda sought to undermine enemy military morale and beliefs, to push the Chinese to clamor for peace, and to weaken their desire to fight. To urge Chinese to think twice about the cost of war on their families, photos and picture leaflets showed women crying, worrying about their men.[9] By October 1939 the Japanese produced leaflets that played to the rising power of Chinese nationalism. Broadsheets mockingly posed the question, "Hey China, do you want to be a pawn of the Soviets?"[10]

The Japanese military carpeted villages in China and Manchukuo with handbills and leaflets. Large, brightly colored posters extolled the virtues of the new imperial Manchukuo nation and the peace Japan had allegedly brought to Asia. The Japanese military enjoyed depicting itself as the force that had ousted warlord rule from China and established a more stable and ordered Chinese society. Some of these posters may have been effective, though this is difficult to calculate. This does not mean that the Japanese neglected their research. In fact, detailed discussions concerning color, layout, slogans, and construction crowded the government-sponsored journals that published propaganda research, including the Manchukuo State Department Information Bureau's *Pacification Monthly Report.*

Just as the IRAA lectures had charted the popular response to propaganda on the Japanese home islands, Japanese overseers in Manchukuo sent out questionnaires concerning the efficacy of the posters that dotted the entire countryside. Although officials considered the rate of return poor, their investigations quantified that Japanese propaganda posters were most frequently pasted to the sides of police stations, public notice boards in shopping areas, schools, and local businesses.[11] Japanese propaganda efforts in China also took note of the research produced by home-front propaganda organizations like the Society for the Study of Media Technology. Articles complained that Japanese propaganda efforts in Manchukuo were disorganized and dissatisfying, and such criticism received press and bureaucratic attention on the home islands. The authors of such criticism called for redoubled efforts, saying that propaganda

Japanese color poster that celebrates the prosperity and bright future of Manchukuo. The Chinese writing says, "Everyone lives in peace. Young and old are happily singing 'Manchukuo! Banzai! Banzai! Ban Banzai!'" The flags are all the new Manchukuo flag. In the far upper left, Japanese soldiers are "purging" various bandits. Kenseishiryōshitsu, Manshūkoku nihongun sendenbutsu [1310, 5], National Diet Library, Tokyo.

the Chinese masses did not understand had the reverse effect and counteracted any progress Japan made.[12]

Japanese-produced posters in China covered a wide variety of subjects; they were not limited to extolling the virtues of Japanese rule. Some concentrated on creating popular distaste against the Communists. In one color handbill a young woman can be seen bending over a pretty flower bush. She does not see the large snake behind the bush labeled "Communism." In the upper right-hand corner a little boy is drawn running toward the woman shouting, "Wait! Wait! The flowers look pretty but behind them there is still a poisonous snake." The implication is that while Communism seems appealing, in actuality it will destroy China. Not all posters were so blatant or poorly conceived. One poster came with the caption "China will not be safe until it eradicates harmful pests." This poster depicts a man spraying a pesticide over his fields from tanks attached to his back. The characters for defending against the Communists are written on the tanks and the bucket beside him.[13]

Japanese color propaganda poster printed in Chinese. A Japanese soldier shakes hands with a happy Manchukuo peasant. On the top right, the soldier says, "Come, my brothers. Change the bad and install the good, for peace and prosperity." The peasant on the left responds, "Older Brother, what you are saying is right. We must correct the past and carefully listen to officials' orders." Kenseishiryōshitsu, Manshū nihongun sendenbutsu [1310, 5], National Diet Library, Tokyo.

Japanese poster from Manchukuo written in Chinese. The top right extols the virtues of the new nation of "Manzhou," which is "following the Imperial Way and creating harmony among the races." Kenseishiryōshitsu, Manshūkoku nihongun sendenbutsu [1310, 6], National Diet Library, Tokyo.

Japanese color leaflet aimed at less literate Chinese. The buckets are labeled "Defend against Communism." The caption reads, "Only with the removal of harmful insects will China be safe." The two men are pictured pouring chemicals into a bucket and tank to spray the foliage. The implication is that Communism is like a swarm of pests. Kenseishiryōshitsu, Nihongun sanpu bira [shū, 1236], National Diet Library, Tokyo.

(Facing page)

Japanese color propaganda poster. In the top panel where a skeleton embraces a pagoda and people are being killed, it says, on the far right, that the military clique is corrupt and the good people are wallowing in misery. "Barbarian peoples" are also coming across the Great Wall and harassing the masses. The flag shown flying is the KMT party flag. The middle panel shows order and happiness restored. People are rebuilding, as soldiers and peasants kick the invaders back across the wall. On the right, the panel reads that the people are rising up and establishing an ideal nation. The flag flying on the pagoda is now the new Manchukuo flag. In the bottom panel the once-miserable people now "Live happily and prosperously. Manchukuo Ban Banzai!" The writing on the pagoda says the "Great Manchukuo Nation." The Manchukuo flags fly above it, and the sun shines on the right side of the panel. On the left, all is dark and the sun weeps. At the bottom left, Zhang Xueliang, son of assassinated Manchurian warlord Zhang Zuolin, holds his sweaty head down in regret and shame. Kenseishiryōshitsu, Manshūkoku nihongun sendenbutsu [1310, 12], National Diet Library, Tokyo.

The Japanese military command in North China took careful note of the Chinese propaganda aimed at its own forces.[14] An April 1939 top-secret imperial Japanese military report concerning "Communist thought propaganda aimed at our forces and how to defend against it" detailed their worst fears. The report admitted that although the Japanese military had accumulated impressive victories, in terms of the "thought war" with China, success was far from complete. Imperial Japanese forces singled out the Communist army as being most successful at recruiting local Chinese populations against the Japanese. Japanese military analysts responded that Japanese propaganda was not simply for defensive purposes, but should assume an active policy of weeding out the influence of Chinese propaganda by promoting "pro-Japanese ideology."[15] The Japanese even charted how the Chinese were adept at using Japanese POWs to write Japanese-language propaganda aimed at the Japanese military, and they judged these Chinese propaganda activities as highly skilled.[16]

This top-secret Japanese military report detailed exactly how CCP propaganda strove to break apart the Japanese forces—through written materials like leaflets and posters, radio and letter campaigns, rumors, and direct advertising. The CCP even taught its lower ranks basic Japanese slogans and how to use them at the front lines.[17] A 1940 article from *Pacification Monthly Report* disparaged Japan's "disdain" for oral propaganda and its sycophantic worship of the "holy trinity" of propaganda media—radio, film, and newspapers. Print propaganda might work in countries with high levels of literacy, but in "our country" (meaning Manchukuo), the Japanese authors wrote, rural illiteracy ran as high as 80 percent, making the need for aural propaganda much more significant.[18] More importantly, the CCP implemented a policy of treating Japanese POWs well, thereby hoping to encourage Japanese soldiers to flee to their side. Preferential CCP treatment of Japanese POWs compelled the Japanese military to admire Chinese Communist propaganda.

> The method that the CCP has been employing with oral slogans has been extremely skillful. The CCP's propaganda is starting to have a broad impact on our military. Last December in the Biyang county of Henan province, we obtained a book that had been published by the Communist Eighth Route Army's political section, entitled *How to conduct demoralization campaigns*. This book is an extremely well-planned and effective tool for conducting psychological operations against the Japanese military.[19]

A Japanese summary of this captured Chinese document described the Chinese plan to undermine the morale of the Japanese Imperial Army. The guidebook reasoned that a majority of Japanese soldiers were peasants or came from rural areas. Newly enlisted soldiers continuously fed the ranks, but they lacked the more rigorous mental training and experience on the battlefield that veterans had slowly acquired. The Chinese analysts, therefore, assumed that new Japanese draftees would be more susceptible to Chinese propaganda. As a countermeasure, Japanese officers frequently employed scare tactics to frighten their own soldiers, teaching them that if the Chinese captured them they would be executed.[20] Since the Japanese routinely slaughtered captured Chinese POWs, it was not hard for green Japanese soldiers to believe that the opposite would also be true.

The Chinese report emphasized the need to care for injured Japanese soldiers and to treat POWs well. Chinese propaganda teams fervently read the diaries of captured Japanese soldiers, and these diaries often revealed the soldiers to be quite concerned about their homes and families, as well as what would happen to their families when they died.[21] The KMT and the Communists frequently translated and published these captured Japanese soldiers' diaries as propaganda but also as a form of literature for the Chinese masses.[22]

Japanese authorities, in turn, analyzed the effect Chinese propaganda exerted on the Japanese military. At first, they concluded that Japanese soldiers were immune to Chinese propaganda and that Chinese propaganda only antagonized Japanese soldiers. Once soldiers had been stationed in one area for a long time, however, and victories become less frequent, the Japanese analysis admitted that Japanese soldiers naturally began yearning for their home villages and families. Demonstrating a cryptic reluctance to speak outright, the Japanese military report also averred that the CCP was adept at understanding hierarchical inequalities within the Japanese armed forces. "The influence of their propaganda is not something we can take lightly," the Japanese analysts at headquarters wrote.[23] The North China Japanese Imperial Army Headquarters was not the only military agency to notice the impact Chinese propaganda had on Japanese soldiers. Central military offices on the Japanese home islands routinely censored soldiers' letters home from the front and in doing so discovered numerous instances in which Chinese propaganda was judged to have had harmful effects.[24]

In an astonishingly frank admission, the report warned that "if the military does not take adequate moves in response, or in a sense change its policy of complacency, not only will the Japanese military spirit continue to worsen, but we risk an extremely undesirable outcome. This Chinese propaganda is truly something we need to worry about."[25] Civilian propaganda advisors working for the Manchurian Film Company, a Japanese-sponsored company and often the agent of Japanese film propaganda aimed at the Chinese, also held Chinese propaganda in high esteem. Quoting liberally from the Japanese military intelligence attaché Mabuchi Itsuo, one film company employee reasoned that the Chinese were adept at propaganda because their 4,000-year-long chaotic history under despotic leaders had left them morally groundless. In a revealing moment the author noted that "even while the Chinese continually meet with crushing defeat on the military front, in the propaganda war they are able to trick the people into thinking that they are victorious and they have a curious ability to use other countries in the means to that end."[26]

In the initial weeks of the war in early July 1937, the Japanese believed they were capable of quickly subduing the Chinese. But several months of fierce fighting in Shanghai and the acquisition of Nanjing in December 1937 only after fierce battles changed their minds. After the fall of Hankou and Wuhan, the Japanese advanced no further and remained bogged down in China for the remainder of the war.

During this time the magazine *Nihon hyōron* (Japan review) reprinted important Chinese speeches and articles concerning China's propaganda toward Japan. In June 1939 the magazine published a speech that Zhou Enlai had delivered in China and retitled it "The New Stage in the War of Resistance against Japan and Japan's New Policies."[27] By early 1938 the Japanese military recognized that circumstances had changed and officials switched from emphasizing a military victory in China to strengthening their policy of an economic and intelligence war against the Chinese. In line with this shift, in April 1939 officials in the South Manchuria Railway Company reorganized a research division that focused on domestic Chinese issues. Ozaki Hotsumi and others soon joined the office. Ozaki's office soon began pumping out reports analyzing the ability of China to wage a war of resistance. He later leaked classified reports to Richard Sorge, a spy for the Soviets.[28]

The conclusion of the Japanese report on Communist propaganda specifically underscored the CCP policy of treating Japanese POWs well. But once again demonstrating the Japanese military's inability to deal with problems flexibly, officers rigidly responded by reaffirming to Japanese soldiers that to become a POW was a disgrace. The military also emphasized reeducating military men concerning the crime of leaving their units. Japanese soldiers who had been captured but then somehow managed to return to their platoons knew they would be interrogated and usually executed, depending on the circumstances.[29] Reeducation of decommissioned soldiers required they not speak badly of the military once they went home. Once repatriated, the military counseled them to avoid talking about their experiences abroad in a way that would damage the nation's belief in the supremacy of the Japanese military.[30] This prohibition on "blasphemy" on the part of repatriated soldiers was a subtle form of propaganda that additionally helped to link the battlefront with the home front even after military service was completed. Soldiers were encouraged to take the battle home, but only in a form that would provide a positive image for those waiting back on the home front.

The average Japanese soldier's belief in the war stemmed from many different sources, and they did not surrender for a variety of reasons. Training and culture were only two criteria, and Japan was hardly the only country that dogmatically indoctrinated its troops in this fashion. The Soviet Union also forbade its soldiers to become prisoners and even stopped payment to families of those who had been taken.[31] The primary motivation behind any given soldier's refusal to surrender probably had little to do with emperor worship. The divergence in military cultural strategy between the United States and Japan primarily concerned the soldiers' views regarding life and death. At the moment of enlistment, Japanese soldiers were already resigned to die in battle, while the goal for US military men was to return safely home.[32] This idea is encapsulated in the famous remark attributed to Gen. George S. Patton: "The object of war is not to die for your country, but to make the other bastard die for his." The comedy routine in Chapter Four that mocked the distinction between how Japanese and American mothers treat their sons going off to war demonstrates the pervasive Japanese social pressure creating this mindset. At the same time Japanese soldiers also feared for their families at home. Troops knew very well that if they were taken alive and the news leaked out, it would be hard for their families to avoid harassment in their own villages.[33]

Faced with such conflicting feelings toward platoon and family, Japanese soldier's diaries frequently meditated on their confrontations with Chinese propaganda. One soldier, Kuwajima Setsurō, sent to the Shandong region in early 1942, recounted how Japanese soldiers were taught to think of captured Chinese as not worthy of consideration, thus making it psychologically more difficult for them to surrender to either the CCP or KMT. Early on a platoon leader had commanded Kuwajima and other soldiers, "You guys watch how we slice the heads off the Chinese Eighth Route Army prisoners." Sixteen Chinese prisoners were marched out in front of Kuwajima's troop and sat in front of a pit. The sergeant wielding a samurai sword stood slightly behind them, smoking a cigarette. With a swing of the long weapon, the sergeant tried to lop the first POW's head off, but had to take another swing to complete the execution. The blood spurted up a full two meters, Kuwajima wrote.[34]

In his recollections as a second-year infantry soldier Kuwajima remembered his encounters with Chinese propaganda. Night patrols of Japanese POWs who worked for the CCP and called themselves members of the Japanese Anti-War League plagued his platoon, Kuwajima said. Late one night Kuwajima was on sentry duty in northeast China when a broadcast suddenly cut through the silence of the night and blasted his battalion. The memory seems to have remained extraordinarily vivid for the author:

> Hey, sentries from the XX division. Good evening everyone. Hope that you are all doing well. My name is Ensign Yamamoto and I am from the 18th Division. Presently I am with the Japanese Anti-War League, assigned to the Eighth Route Army. Tonight we came to this village to deliver our message to you. Thank you in advance for your consideration.[35]

The announcement came clearly over a loudspeaker in the dead of night, but because it was pitch black Kuwajima could not see where the voices originated. The voice continued, "Soldiers, you are fighting in the bitter cold for your country, but you are being misled. Actually only commanding officers benefit from the war with their medals, while the military and financial conglomerates only get wealthier. Hey guys, don't you want to stop this senseless war and surrender to the Eighth Route Army?" Kuwajima wrote that the Chinese army knew the Japanese army did not venture out at night, and the Chinese took advantage of this fact to launch their propaganda activities after sunset. A few weeks after his initial encounter, a CCP propaganda platoon again visited Kuwajima's area and proclaimed to the Japanese soldiers, "You think you are fighting a holy war, but in fact you are forcing people out of their homes and killing them. This is a war of aggression." The voice explained that if the Japanese soldiers surrendered they would be treated well, given food and shelter the same as everyone else—meaning that even officers would receive similar treatment. The propaganda also appealed to the soldiers' homesickness by asking, "Don't you want to go home and see your family?"[36]

Several months later, yet another Chinese propaganda platoon staffed with Japanese attempted to induce members of Kuwajima's platoon to surrender. This time the message concerned the Allies' conquest of Italy. The messages announced that the Japanese had lost at Tarawa island in the Pacific and that the surrender of the home islands was just a matter of time. At the end of the announcements, the group sang several popular Japanese songs. Two of the songs, Kuwajima distinctly recalled, were "The Tree-Lined Street of Life" and "Tokyo Rhapsody." Kuwajima admitted that these songs struck a chord with him. Nonetheless, he remained untempted and neither he nor his platoon mates ever surrendered to the Chinese.

Sometimes the antiwar Japanese POW groups working for the CCP sent care packages to the Japanese troops. One platoon received chicken meat. Worried that the meat had been poisoned, Japanese soldiers made the Chinese porters who carried water for the Japanese platoons test to see whether it was safe. It was.[37] Wartime Japanese soldier's diaries suggest that the CCP Eighth Route Army propaganda was not always effective, but that the Communists had grasped a few basics about the inequities of Japanese military life.[38] As the interview with former soldier Shinotsuka Yoshio revealed, the CCP's message got across. Communist propaganda may not have motivated Japanese soldiers to surrender en masse but they did listen.

CCP Propaganda Policy and Its Impact

The Chinese Communist Party's Eighth Route Army and New Fourth Army had a most unusual *fulu youyu zhengce* or "treat POWs well policy."[39] Japanese soldiers were used to poor treatment and beatings in their own platoons, so the CCP's generous policy caused some consternation. Japanese military repatriates affirm that near the end of the war there were rumors among Japanese troops that if the situation deteriorated to the point of starvation, surrendering to the Chinese Communists guaranteed nourishment and good treatment. Japanese soldiers were savvy enough to realize that not all Communists were alike. In Manchuria, near the end of the war, Japanese military and civilians alike studiously avoided, insofar as possible, surrendering to the Soviets.[40] Most preferred the Chinese or the Americans. (This seemed to be the case among German soldiers at the end of World War Two as well.)

On September 25, 1937, early in the war against Japan, the CCP and Eighth Route Army issued two proclamations. The first announced that Japanese soldiers were farmers and laborers just like the Chinese and that if the Japanese relinquished their arms the CCP would return the soldiers immediately back home. Or if they wanted to work with the Chinese they could. The second message, issued in the name of the commander of the Chinese Communist forces, Gen. Zhu De, stated that the Chinese and Japanese were friends. The CCP welcomed Japanese soldiers to come over to the Chinese side and work for the Chinese war effort.[41]

The initial CCP policy to protect Japanese POWs is well known, but this policy subtly shifted a year later, on October 22, 1938. As Canton fell and China faced the loss of the city of Wuhan in December, the new CCP policy now considered using Japanese POWs for explicit propaganda purposes. CCP leaders wanted Japanese POWs to speak in front of Chinese living near areas controlled by the Japanese, to demonstrate publicly that the CCP did not slaughter Japanese POWs. At the same time the CCP tried to gain Japanese adherents to stand as examples for the Chinese masses concerning the party's benevolence. While the CCP mastered many of the propaganda techniques against Japanese soldiers, allowing it to gain a following of Japanese POWs, many of its tactics had been borrowed from the Soviet propaganda education centers in Jiangxi province and transported to Shaanxi where the Chinese Red army made its headquarters against Japan.[42]

Kagawa Takashi, a Japanese soldier who became a POW of the CCP in the late 1930s, stated that at least within his military circles Japanese soldiers knew that the CCP did not murder Japanese POWs. The CCP was aware that if Japanese POWs used their real names after they were caught, their families back in Japan would suffer. The Communists thus encouraged Japanese POWs to create false new identities.[43] In this fashion their families in Japan would receive death benefits instead of being bullied for their son's failures. Japanese POWs captured by the United States employed similar tactics to avoid detection. Upon capture or surrender, many of them would exclaim that they felt "reborn."[44]

The CCP and the KMT faced continual difficulties in implementing the practice of treating Japanese POWs humanely. At one point during the war of resistance against Japan, the Nationalist government repeatedly broadcast that it had captured large numbers of Japanese soldiers in its victorious battles. Unfortunately, however, no POWs arrived at Wuhan as promised. When pressed by international news agencies to produce the supposed prisoners (who had been killed in the interim), the KMT was forced to borrow several dozen POWs from the CCP's Eighth Route Army to keep the massacre from being uncovered.[45]

Usually under CCP command Japanese POWs were well cared for, fed, provided with a little spending money, and given literature in Chinese to read.[46] At Yenan, the Chinese Communist base camp in remote western Shaanxi province, Kagawa and other POWs started working and studying at the Japanese Labor School. Japanese POWs attended classes in politics, economics, and social studies, but mostly they focused on politics and Chinese language study. On the home islands the Japanese, at least officials and military intelligence officers, recognized exactly what was going on in Yenan. Japanese intelligence reports outlined the CCP's cultural propaganda activities and detailed the Lu Xun School for the Performing Arts and how it produced graduates who wrote anti-Japanese war literature.[47]

The establishment of a school in Yenan to reeducate Japanese POWs probably grew out of the combined Japanese-Chinese effort of two men, Wang Xuewen and Nosaka Sanzō, who claimed credit for managing the institution. CCP Eighth Route Army political section officer Wang Xuewen officially administered the school. Wang had traveled to Japan in 1910 and studied economics at Kyoto Imperial University. He completed a Chinese translation of Karl Marx's *Das Kapital* and entered the Chinese Communist Party in 1927.[48]

Nosaka Sanzō also played an influential role in the school's day-to-day operations. Nosaka was an important Japanese Communist who had fled to Moscow before the war and then in March 1940 journeyed to Yenan, the base camp for the Chinese Communists.[49] While the Chinese Communists treated the Japanese well and the project may have been a true collaboration, the Chinese did not really have much use for the Japanese POWs. The Japanese may have initiated the school to demonstrate how they could be helpful to the Chinese war effort.

Japanese POWs in China were not numerous, but they were active in propaganda activities. From 1937–1944 the Eighth Route Army housed approximately 2,400 Japanese POWs.[50] The actual activities that the troops conducted included leaflet production, broadcasting megaphone propaganda announcements, sending packages, letters, etc. The numbers of POWs rose sharply in the last year of the war, and by the end of the war the CCP's New Fourth Army and Eighth Route Army held a combined total of 6,959 Japanese POWs.[51] This number was virtually a third more Japanese POWs than the United States housed domestically, even at the peak of its POW camp assignments in June 1945. Just before the end of the war more than 666 POW camps dotted the American landscape, providing shelter to 340,000 German POWs, other Axis internees, and around 5,000 Japanese soldiers.[52] While the total number of Japanese soldiers who worked for the Chinese remained less than 1 percent of the total force in China, their activities did not go unnoticed. *The Special Higher Police Monthly Report* in a March 1944 article detailed precisely what activities the Japanese antiwar leagues carried out in China. Gen. Zhu De, speaking at the Communist Party's seventh annual meeting, openly congratulated Nosaka Sanzō and the Japanese working on the anti-Japan war propaganda. In return, the Japanese Anti-war League thanked the CCP for delivering them from the "clutches" of the Japanese Imperial Army.[53]

Nosaka Sanzō's influence on Chinese-sponsored Japanese-language propaganda aimed at the Japanese military appears to have been fairly extensive. In October 1942 he printed a draft of his propaganda plan for Chinese-sponsored anti-Japan propaganda.[54] In his strategy Nosaka admitted that propaganda implemented by the antiwar Japanese groups, the Awakening Alliance and the Anti-War League among others, was plentiful, but in terms of raw efficiency it fell short. Nosaka explained that for propaganda to be effective the Communists first needed to scrutinize the Japanese soldier. Research and analysis groups needed to decipher the needs and motivations of the Japanese soldier, and Nosaka suggested opening study groups to delve into these questions.

Nosaka's plans paid close attention to detail. Chinese-sponsored Japanese-language propaganda should offer Japanese soldiers precise means, Nosaka declared, to present their grievances to their superiors.[55] Dissension could be sown by appealing to the ties soldiers had to their hometowns or by appealing to the soldiers' sense of futility concerning the goals of the war. Nosaka also reminded his colleagues that their propaganda needed to underscore the fact that Japanese POWs would be treated like brothers and friends.[56]

The approach of Nosaka and the Chinese Communists stood in contrast to that of US Gen. Douglas MacArthur's head of psychological operations, Brig. Gen. Bonner Fellers, who placed a premium on propaganda operations as something linked to military victory. Fellers felt that propaganda could only follow a military victory. Had the CCP followed a similar philosophy, their propaganda might never have been heard. When Nosaka Sanzō exhorted his compatriots to think about propaganda in the fall of 1942, defeat of the Japanese was not a forgone conclusion.

Nosaka reminded the Japanese POW staff that wrote and often rewrote the Japanese-language propaganda material, "You were once Japanese soldiers, so try and remember what it was like, and use those feelings and emotions when you write. Think how a soldier would react." Nosaka also instructed the writers to use accurate materials and not to rely on rumors.[57] In addition, he and the other Chinese propaganda troop leaders urged their groups to use cartoons and pictures as much as possible.[58] The Japanese Communist's attention to detail was relentless. The group wanted to produce portable propaganda, something that could be stuffed in the pocket as a soldier carried his rifle. As a rule, Nosaka continued, propaganda leaflets should be fewer than 500 Japanese characters long and should focus on a central theme.[59]

Nosaka's blueprint even had pointers for wall slogans. Do not write long slogans, he suggested; make them short and brief to stress the horrid nature of war and get the soldiers to reflect. Nosaka felt that earlier propaganda slogans had been so complicated they required additional explanations. As an example, he noted the wall slogan "The Japanese soldier is not the enemy." "Why is the Japanese soldier not the enemy," Nosaka asked? This slogan requires a sister slogan—"because the imperial army military clique is the enemy." Without it, the first slogan makes no sense.[60]

Nosaka's plan mandated putting up slogans only in areas that did not have slogans directed at the Chinese people. It makes no sense, he explained, to have a poster demanding "Defeat Japanese Imperialism" on a wall right near another poster that says "Let's Stop the War." Antiwar platoon members were told not to write on the walls of Chinese houses, since those actions could have dire implications for the people who lived inside. In contrast to earlier CCP leadership directives, Nosaka explained to Chinese leaders that yelling Japanese-language antiwar propaganda slogans at Japanese soldiers had little effect. Even when they were surrounded completely, Nosaka believed, this method rarely caused the Japanese soldiers to surrender.[61]

To research the enemy, Nosaka and his crew took care to analyze current events in Japan and China, which they did by stocking Japanese newspapers, magazines, journals, and diaries that were purchased or seized on the battlefield.[62] The first few hours or days after a Japanese soldier surrendered were considered the most crucial, Nosaka felt, because then the subject would be scared and psychologically disoriented. Knowledge of contemporary Japanese culture was considered the best means of identifying with the newcomer and assisting him to acclimate.[63] When American officers from the Office of War Information (OWI) and the Office of Strategic Services (OSS) met with Nosaka in Yenan, they were impressed with his efficient intelligence-gathering network. Copies of the *Asahi shimbun* arrived in Yenan only a week and a half after they had been published in Japan.[64] The Americans even set up a microfilming laboratory in the caves near Nosaka's office in order to copy his extensive collection of intelligence concerning Japan.[65]

The CCP's propaganda did not end with the Japanese surrender in August 1945; nor did Japanese wartime propaganda (see Chapter Six). The Communist Party not merely sought the destruction of the Japanese military, but also wished to help Japan to revolutionize. Kuwajima Setsurō wrote that after the surrender, in 1946 while decommissioned Japanese soldiers were milling around mainland camps waiting to go home, the propaganda platoon of the Eighth Route Army visited at night with megaphones. The United States wanted to disarm Japan and repatriate everyone as soon as possible, but the Chinese Communists wanted to obtain the weapons the Japanese were supposed to surrender. In the immediate, chaotic weeks and months after Japan's surrender on the mainland, the CCP announced that Japanese soldiers should not believe Gen. Chiang Kai Shek, leader of the KMT. This CCP propaganda was a specific ploy that played on the ambiguity surrounding the Japanese surrender. While the Japanese acceptance of the Potsdam surrender was duly noted and broadcast around the empire, to whom the Japanese should surrender in China was not always entirely clear. "Believe us," the CCP loudspeakers boomed, "we will help get you home if you surrender to us.... Do not get close to Chiang."[66]

The Office of the Supreme Commander for the Allied Powers (SCAP) did not issue its first directive until September 2, just after the Japanese signed the official surrender treaty in Tokyo Bay. The order declared that "senior Japanese Commanders and all ground, sea, air and auxiliary forces within China (excluding Manchuria), Formosa and French Indo-China North of 16 degrees latitude, shall surrender to Generalissimo Chiang Kai Shek."[67] It is no wonder

that Japanese soldiers repatriating from Communist areas worried the occupation forces in charge. In fact, the entire issue of to whom and under what
circumstances the Japanese forces would surrender had significant impact on
the outcome of the Chinese civil war that followed Japan's withdrawal.[68]

KMT Propaganda Plans

Research on the growth of Chinese nationalism throughout the 1930s and
1940s highlights aspects of the symbiotic nature of Chinese propaganda during the war. Original Chinese interest in "awakening" *(juexing)* the Chinese
masses to their nationhood began with Sun Yat Sen, who followed the path
blazed by classical scholars and reformers Liang Qichao and Kang Youwei,
among others. This philosophy of the need to enlighten the masses spurred the
Communists' understanding of the importance of propaganda. (The CCP also
owed a debt to the Soviets for teaching them advanced propaganda methods).
Historians frequently note that a large portion of the Chinese who engaged in
KMT propaganda during the 1920s and 1930s were actually Communists. This
group included Mao Zedong who taught at the Peasant Movement Training
Institute in Guangzhou and Guo Moruo, noted writer and later Communist
leader, who for several years in the late 1930s headed the KMT Propaganda
Bureau.[69] Under Guo's direction the Propaganda Bureau arranged "comfort
visits" much like the United Service Organization (USO) performances the
United States military sponsored. The bureau also designed packages to send
to soldiers at the front, placing written materials and other goodies in the
parcels.[70]

Unfortunately the KMT continually monitored its ranks and to its detri-
ment tried to force the propagandists to join the Nationalist Party. Under the
relentless pressure, many eventually quit. Guo Moruo and many others left the
KMT's bureau and joined the swelling number of professional propagandists
who later shifted to the Communist side. After Guo left, the bureau floundered,
but by November 1940, in Chongqing, the KMT had created a cultural work
committee *(wenhua gongzuohui)* to research propaganda production techniques. This committee oversaw three departments: a cultural arts section, an
international issues research section, and an enemy analysis research section.
Once the Pacific War began in December 1941, two Japanese joined the enemy
analysis section, lecturing on how to spread pro-China propaganda among
the Japanese military. The two also headed up a Chinese and Japanese team
charged with collecting data at the front lines. The group disbanded at the end
of March 1945.

During the Chinese war of resistance against Japan, the KMT never relin-

This is an example of a Chinese poster used to rally the masses against the Japanese. The Manchukuo Daily Newspaper Company collected anti-Japanese and pro-Chinese nationalist posters and leaflets and published a collection of them in 1931. The slogan on the poster says, "Building Strong Soldiers' Bodies Can Save the Nation." Manshū Nippōsha, ed., *Jikyoku oyobi hainichi posutā shashinchō*, p. 85.

quished its goal to crush the nascent Communist movement, and this policy frequently thwarted its propaganda efforts against the Japanese. KMT censorship had squelched all non-KMT opinions even before the war. In 1941, once the KMT power center had relocated to Chongqing in Sichuan province, the party drafted a vague cultural policy propaganda plan that satisfied no one.[71] Unlike the CCP, even after the war against Japan ended in August 1945, the KMT still had no central policy concerning what type of literature or art it wished to produce. Throughout the war of resistance, from 1937–1945, and the subsequent civil war, from 1945–1949, the core of KMT cultural policy focused more on what it deemed unacceptable, rather than offering serious positive alternatives. KMT cultural policies centered on censorship laws and ordinances designed to obstruct, not create.

KMT propaganda plans against the Japanese started late in 1937 but were fairly disorganized and poorly maintained. In part, the plans were developed by paying close attention to what the Communists were doing, for the KMT worried not only about the Japanese but other Chinese. No regime on the Chinese mainland could afford to ignore the propaganda of the competing parties. It is clear that unlike the CCP propaganda forces, the KMT had difficulty in learning from its mistakes. For John Service, a US foreign service official in China during the war, lackluster KMT propaganda reflected its continued lack of central authority. Service's detailed memo to the American government made clear his position: KMT propaganda failed first and foremost, Service observed, because of the "Chinese tendency to multiply organizations without limiting their functions or unifying their control."[72]

Nonetheless, in terms of arousing international opinion against Japan, KMT propaganda generated significant international ire. Internationally educated Lin Yutang wrote numerous tracts in eloquent English lamenting the plight of his homeland, and public sympathy only increased as the public digested the works of Pearl Buck. Paul Robeson, noted American singer and performer, even recorded a melodious rendition of the Chinese national anthem, with perfect diction, in support of China against Japan.[73] The CCP was far less effective internationally with the west (except, of course, with the Soviet Union) since they had fewer conduits to the outside. Western journalists like Edgar Snow and Agnes Smedley were quite taken with CCP activities, but western governments stubbornly allied themselves with the Nationalists in the fight against fascism in Asia. The Japanese and the Japanese government knew they had a problem on their hands soon after October 4, 1937, for on that day *Life* magazine republished the photo made famous by the Hearst newspaper chain, of a young Chinese baby wailing amidst the ruins of a bombed

Shanghai city landscape.[74] American popular support for China only increased when *Time* magazine made Gen. Chiang Kai Shek and his wife Soong Mei Ling couple of the year in January 1938.

The KMT announced its own Japanese POW policy on October 15, 1937, with its *fulu chuli guize*, or "rules for dealing with POWs." Japanese POWs would be able to communicate with their families, the rules stated, and they would be free from threats, harassment, and coercion. Those who died would be properly buried and their families notified. The policy specifically forbade confiscation of personal items. The KMT document modeled itself on the Geneva Convention, and KMT officials hoped thereby to compete with the CCP treatment of POWs.[75] KMT authorities erected their first POW camp near Xian, the ancient capital of the Tang dynasty. Other camps followed later in Hunan, Guangxi, Guizhou, and Sichuan.[76] But a few years later KMT officials admitted that they still faced difficulties in educating the average KMT soldier about how to treat Japanese POWs. The greatest obstacle remained the lack of individuals at the front with specific responsibilities for taking care of Japanese POWs. Frequently, after having been taken prisoner, Japanese soldiers were stripped of their clothes and possessions, which were then given to soldiers in the KMT forces. The KMT could not admit defeat in regard to POW treatment, though, and the Nationalist report on the POW situation asserted that after the promulgation of the "treat POWs well" policy the number of these incidents supposedly shrank.[77]

In January 1939 the KMT Military Command in Guilin established a Japanese language training school and guerrilla warfare training school. At the Japanese language training school Kaji Wataru instructed would-be Chinese propagandists in the Japanese language. Kaji Wataru was a well-known Japanese author who had been arrested on charges of disturbing the peace in Japan. He fled to China in 1936 and later worked until the end of the war as a major organizer of KMT-sponsored anti-Japanese propaganda.

Kaji and his wife had escaped from escalating political violence in 1930s Japan and undertook the risky travel through Hong Kong and Shanghai in their opposition to Japan's war on the Chinese continent. It was an act that Japanese newspapers labeled "selling out the country." Kaji and his wife journeyed to Wuhan on March 18, 1938, a few months after China lost the city of Nanjing and on the cusp of the fierce fight over Xuzhou, where Japanese forces lost close to 30,000 troops. By the spring of 1938 severely wounded Japanese POWs started to trickle into KMT camps behind the battlefront. Even though the Japanese army said Japanese soldiers did not become POWs, no one could deny their existence. Many tried to commit suicide—cutting their tongues, crouching on a hand grenade—because their training had indoctrinated the soldiers to believe that the Chinese were barbaric and that their fate after surrender would be horrendous.

In a postwar article Kaji stated that it took him a while to convince the KMT of the possibility that Japanese soldiers would surrender. The KMT leadership finally acceded as they were pulling out of Wuhan in October 1938. Kaji paid his first visit to Japanese POWs at the KMT Number Three POW camp in Hunan province, in a camp called Pinghe (peace) village.[78] Kaji's group gathered about seventy Japanese POWs and began their reeducation. Success with these men and their efforts at the battlefront prompted the KMT to pay more attention to Kaji's activities.

After August 15, 1939, Kaji moved to Chongqing to escape the approaching Japanese army and engage in further propaganda work. The Nationalists had constructed a POW camp there, and Kaji assisted in establishing a Japanese antiwar alliance. Kaji and the KMT crew staffing the propaganda campaigns aimed at the Japanese faced a formidable foe. Along with general problems concerning the Japanese POWs, a major issue in reeducating POWs was their love of and attachment to Japan. Regardless of their status as lowly military men often fulfilling a mission they did not care for, Japanese soldiers still wanted to win the war.

KMT-sponsored Japanese POW propaganda troops traveled around China targeting Japanese forces. South of Guilin in Guangxi province, from December 29, 1939, to February 12, 1940, they patrolled the front with loudspeakers, appealing to Japanese soldiers.[79] In the afternoon these antiwar POW groups often taught Chinese soldiers simple Japanese, and in the evenings the POW groups returned to the front lines with loudspeakers.[80]

Unfortunately, efforts to employ Japanese POWs in the care of the KMT proved difficult and short-lived. Voices accusing Kaji of anti-KMT beliefs grew continually louder, proclaiming that he was trying to indoctrinate the POWs with Communist ideology. By August 1940 the order came from above to disband the antiwar POW group, and several months later Kaji returned to Chongqing where he helped organize study groups focused on analyzing conditions in Japan and studying the Japanese military.[81]

The KMT was not as adept as the CCP at using its Japanese POWs directly for assistance in developing Japanese-language propaganda, even though the suggestion continually arose. Guo Moruo argued that it was acceptable to use Chinese students returning from Japan as producers of Japanese-language propaganda, but the efforts still required help from native speakers. Guo used himself as an example. Born in 1892 in Sichuan, Guo had journeyed to Kyushu Imperial University in the south of Japan to study medicine. There he lived with a Japanese woman and fathered a family. With two other Chinese study-ing abroad at the time, Guo founded a magazine called *Creation Society,* but he later returned to China, where he joined the CCP. In 1928 he upset the KMT leadership so he fled to Japan to live in Chiba, a prefecture neighboring Tokyo. This second time Guo remained in Japan for about ten years. After the Marco Polo Bridge incident in July 1937, Guo once again returned to China and cooperated with the KMT, heading their anti-Japan propaganda programs. Even though Guo had lived in Japan for close to twenty years, he still felt that he had not completely mastered Japanese, or so he said. Guo recommended Kaji Wataru for the job of Japanese language instructor, which may be how Kaji found himself in the KMT offices in the first place.[82]

After the KMT dissolved Kaji's propaganda group, he returned to Chong-qing where he kept a small research office. He occupied his time writing and collecting documents pertaining to the war. Later, because Kaji's predictions about Japanese movements proved accurate, he became well known to the American propaganda agencies, the OWI and the OSS, predecessor of the Central Intelligence Agency (CIA). Two Japanese-Americans who worked on US propaganda against Japan, Koji Ariyoshi and Karl Yoneda, made trips to interview Kaji in Chongqing. The OWI invited Kaji several times to Kunming, where its office was headquartered, to create American anti-Japanese propa-ganda in China.

KMT failure at employing Japanese POWs for propaganda did not hinder attempts to utilize civilian Japanese for similar ends. Guo Moruo believed that Chinese propaganda campaigns against the Japanese were very important, and the KMT set about improving its product. The KMT had prepared poorly, but by the time Wuhan fell in December 1938 the pace picked up. The political bureau of the KMT, which was responsible for anti-Japanese propaganda, pub-lished two books, *Propaganda for Securing the Mind of the Enemy* and *A Col-lection of Anti-Japanese Wartime Propaganda Slogans.*[83] Agents distributed these books to every level of the political operations departments. The bureau also printed leaflets and a whole variety of safe-passage surrender passes for Japa-nese soldiers. However, obstacles continued to plague KMT propaganda efforts. It proved exceedingly difficult to get other KMT offices, both military and government agencies, to coordinate their efforts, especially to organize planes to drop the leaflets. Getting close to Japanese POWs and gaining their assistance posed even greater hurdles since POWs were placed under jurisdic-tion of the military, and the KMT military leadership appeared reluctant to provide access.[84]

Guo charged himself with the task of setting up various smaller divisions within the KMT propaganda section. These bureaus focused on developing propaganda from a variety of angles including mass mobilization, artistic propaganda, films, performance, and musical propaganda. A sudden order from above, ostensibly believed to be Chiang Kai Shek, created a bureau for counterpropaganda against the Japanese military. This bureau was further divided into several desks: the first desk focused on planning and translation; the second on collecting international information; the third concentrated on producing Japanese language materials.[85] At the outset, about three hundred people worked in all the propaganda-related sections. There were four platoons for anti-Japanese propaganda, one troupe of members who drew cartoons, and also related performing groups: a children's performance troupe and ten platoons of anti-Japanese performing propaganda troupes. The combined forces of these groups, plus various guards and associated workers came to about one thousand people.[86]

Not all members of the KMT propaganda bureau were Chinese. Another antiwar member of the inner KMT sanctum of propaganda activity was the Japanese proletarian writer Hasegawa Teru. Born in 1912 in Japan, Hasegawa had early on developed an interest in Esperanto, the artificial language created in Eastern Europe as a means to alleviate international miscommunication. Hasegawa published numerous articles and novels in Esperanto, but as she gained fame as a writer and involved herself more deeply in the Esperanto movement, the Japanese nation was withdrawing from international politics and slowly closing itself off to the outside world. In Japan, Hasegawa met her husband, Liu Ren, a Manchurian student studying in Japan on a scholarship from the newly created Japanese puppet state of Manchukuo. As Japan's adventures in China heated up, Liu returned to Shanghai and Hasegawa soon followed. By 1938 they were both in Guangzhou. At this point the KMT almost had Hasegawa classified as an enemy alien and deported, but fellow Chinese Esperantists and Guo Moruo intervened, and Liu and Hasegawa obtained permission to make their way to Hankou. Hasegawa toiled in the KMT propaganda bureau's international office as a member of the anti-Japan team for radio broadcasts to Japan. Japanese obviously heard Hasegawa's broadcasts because in Japan her family received bitter letters telling them to commit suicide to avoid the shame of having a daughter who performed propaganda for the enemy.[87] In a fashion similar to Kaji's efforts, Hasegawa's broadcasts seem to have produced a response. At a banquet for Guo Moruo that Hasegawa attended, Zhou Enlai turned to her at one point and called her a real patriot for her work. On November 1, 1938, in the Japanese newspaper, *Miyako shimbun*, Hasegawa's picture appeared under the headline "The real face of the coquettish traitor exposed here."[88]

Hasegawa was not the first Japanese female to star in KMT propaganda

子照川谷長・女る賣を國

The headline reads, "The real face of the coquettish traitor exposed here." The second line in from the right reads, "The eerie broadcast. Speaking fluent Japanese, she denigrates her homeland." *Miyako shimbun,* November 1, 1938.

radio. Previously, several Japanese women had broadcast for the party, but they were all wives of KMT officials. Hasegawa was not a party member. The general consensus, according to Kaji Wataru and others, was that these wives were often housemaids or hostesses who had fallen in love with overseas Chinese students studying in Japan. After marriage, they returned with their husbands to China and got swept up in the war. The problem with their broadcasts was that their heart was not truly in the project. Hasegawa's fervor for the Chinese struggle against Japan is probably one of the main reasons why the KMT hired her.[89]

In late October 1938 Hankou fell to the Japanese, but Hasegawa and her family had already moved with the KMT propaganda office to Hunan province, and later to the KMT capital in the interior, Chongqing. In Chongqing, Hasegawa worked directly for Guo Moruo in the political division of the KMT's central propaganda bureau. After the war the couple remained in China, but due to an infection from a miscarriage Hasegawa died in 1947 at the young age of thirty-five. A scant three months later her husband Liu also passed away.

In addition to leaflets, posters, and radio, cinema also played a role in KMT propaganda against Japan. American diplomatic cables from China to Washington DC explained that cinema was an important element for Chinese Nationalist military propaganda. Through US loans and materials obtained through other channels, several KMT troops in China obtained 35mm projectors. Charts indicate that these units projected films that were "patriotic productions of Chinese studios," "special compilations of the [Chinese] war of resistance," "collections designated as resistance songs," "a fair number of newsreels," and several educational and propaganda films.[90] American reports claim that cinemas frequently rejected showing propaganda films or educational shorts because they did not draw audiences. Chinese managers demanded feature films, for otherwise audiences stayed away from the cinemas.[91]

CCP success in drawing in sympathetic western journalists may also have stimulated similar KMT efforts. While the KMT did not monopolize domestic Chinese support, KMT ties to US government interests helped provide international backing for China's war of resistance. On the one hand the Chinese benefited freely from foreign-produced documentaries such as *The 400 Million*, filmed by Joris Ivens and shown to audiences around the world. Ivens's documentary, filmed in 1938, detailed the suffering of the Chinese in their war against Japanese aggression.[92] These images of suffering merely solidified what many Americans already believed when they read about beleaguered Chinese peasants in Pearl Buck's 1932 Pulitzer Prize-winning *The Good Earth*.

Guo Moruo's section in the KMT central propaganda headquarters also began promoting anti-Japanese feature films as a way of motivating the public. The KMT acquired the Wuhan Motion Picture Company in early 1938 and brought the studio to Chongqing. By 1940 the company produced numerous feature films for public consumption, including a movie cast with Japanese POWs. *Light of the East (Dongya zhi guang)* played in movie theaters in KMT-controlled areas in 1940. The film, partly shot on location in a KMT POW camp, and staffed with actual Japanese POWs, depicted Japanese soldiers recanting their former evil ways and blaming the Japanese military clique for their misfortune. "How glad we are to have run into our Chinese brothers in this land. It has made me reform myself and now I can see the true light of the east," exclaims one Japanese soldier in the production.[93]

Radio entertainment also played a feature role in propaganda on the mainland. The Japanese were already broadcasting several shows daily in a variety of dialects on the continent in an effort to win over the Chinese.[94] The KMT had used radio broadcasts beginning in the mid-1930s, in Nanjing, as part of its New Life Movement. Organizers quite often tried to incorporate *kaipian* (brief songs that introduced storytelling) into support for the movement's ideology.[95] The Nationalist New Life Movement was a short-lived effort that focused mainly on personal appearance, hygiene, and moral uprightness. Publishers frequently transcribed the broadcasts and sold them in magazine form.[96] Merchants appropriated many of these messages to use in advertising, thereby gaining new clients, but it seems that the KMT eschewed employing radio for the express intent of resisting the Japanese. In sum, the KMT did more to promote burgeoning markets than it did to disseminate anti-Japanese rhetoric. Chinese retailers used war slogans to "promote mass consumption" and advertisers followed a pattern similar to their counterparts in Japan by adopting the rhetoric of national revolution to ingratiate themselves with the authorities.[97]

In propaganda aimed abroad, not only did the Nationalists monopolize the ear of the American government, but they also took credit for most domestic propaganda success stories. KMT reports to foreign audiences tried to demonstrate the efficacy of Nationalist propaganda by detailing how captured Japanese soldiers' diaries obtained on the battlefields contained entries confessing low levels of morale and a desire to stop fighting with the Chinese. One of the KMT's main English propaganda organs, *China at War,* hammered home the issue that Chinese propaganda was effective. In one story six Japanese soldiers were said to have hanged themselves after Chinese propaganda troops blanketed their platoon with Japanese language antiwar handbills. KMT writers applauded their own efforts claiming, "most of the Japanese soldiers do not understand what they are fighting for."[98]

US Difficulties with Japanese Soldiers

As sketchy and unscientific as Chinese propaganda against the Japanese may have been, in several ways it was still progressive in comparison with Allied products. In contrast to the Chinese, who labored over how to get the Japanese to surrender, the United States faced a struggle in its propaganda efforts to convince US soldiers that the Japanese were even human beings. One marine who spent lengthy tours of duty on Peleliu island and experienced fighting on Okinawa recalled an incident that demonstrated the utter detestation some American troops felt for the Japanese. While on patrol his platoon leader took pains to shoot off the penis of a dead Japanese corpse. In addition, the platoon leader would not urinate normally while on reconnaissance missions, and whenever possible he "would locate a Japanese corpse, stand over it, and urinate in its mouth. It was the most repulsive thing I ever saw an American do in the war," stated the marine.[99] Even when authorities were convinced of the need to promote propaganda aimed at the Japanese, the attitude of the American troops on the group made it impossible. Moreover, one researcher studying the dismal impact of such US propaganda as there was noted that "[t]he reputed tenacious fighting abilities of the Japanese soldier and his penchant never to surrender were soon combined with a general lack of interest at all levels among the Allies with even bothering to try to take enemy soldiers captive."[100]

The dominant version of postwar American history often presents a picture of US propaganda and psychological policies that led to a victory for the hearts and minds of the Japanese, even though it faced an unfathomable enemy at the outset.[101] In contrast, a military historian of Japan, Edward Drea, places more emphasis on strategy, claiming that the war was won militarily and not psychologically:

> It does a disservice to the Allies, and gives far too much credit to the Japanese, to believe that the material power of the West simply overwhelmed the Japanese. ... Allied commanders out-thought and outmaneuvered their Japanese opponents, and Allied troops outfought them. They also show Japanese commanders did not think through the consequences of their actions.[102]

We should not completely discredit wartime US psychological operations crews and their strategic superiority in terms of overall efficiency, but the assessment that "[d]emoralization among Japanese combatants was directly related to their experiences on the battlefield" with Americans seems more sanguine.[103] For America this meant that until 1944, when the Japanese faced catastrophic losses in the Pacific Ocean, US propaganda was hardly effective. As the battle for Okinawa surged in April 1945, the OWI and the American armed forces began to assess their most comprehensive propaganda campaign launched to date. Out of a garrison of approximately 120,000 Japanese troops, 11,000 POWs were taken, but only 7,400 were Japanese soldiers. The others were Korean or Taiwanese laborers. While it was a partial success compared with efforts elsewhere, the approximately 50,000 German POWs per month who flooded into US camps from August 1944 until the spring of 1945 dwarfed Japanese surrender statistics.

Investigation of the Chinese and Japanese sides of the propaganda wars on the mainland reveals how differently the Chinese and Americans viewed anti-Japanese propaganda. The United States did not emphasize propaganda against the Japanese until the Americans were assured of military victory. As Brig. Gen. Bonner Fellers, the central figure in charge of US psychological warfare against Japan wrote, propaganda "can proceed no faster than winning armies."[104] American military and psychological warfare experts perceived propaganda to be meaningless, even if it could be developed against a foe they considered psychologically impervious, if the US military continued to lose on the battle-field. The US approach to propaganda was virtually the direct opposite of that pursued by the CCP and the KMT. As discussed above, even in 1939, when the CCP military power was far from threatening, the Japanese military under-stood the threat Chinese propaganda posed. If the Chinese propaganda pre-sented such a forceful psychological hazard to the Japanese at such an early stage, what stymied the Americans in the creation of a similar threat?

One major stumbling block stemmed from the US military's ignorance of both China and Japan, combined with an inadequate staff and poor analysis agencies that did not understand Japan or its program in Asia. In 1935 few Americans studied the language of Japan, and "no more than twenty people in all of the US were estimated to be concentrating on Japanese studies."[105] Moves to correct these deficiencies were slow in coming, but the situation changed once the United States declared war on Japan. Several military language schools were then established.

One reason behind the small numbers of Japanese soldiers captured by US forces may also have been the fact that US soldiers slaughtered wounded or surrendering Japanese soldiers. A historian of GI behavior toward the Japanese during the Pacific war notes, "Rampant rage failed to be extinguished even by orders from above. In a desperate effort to obtain prisoners for intelligence purposes, the American Division had to encourage its soldiers with the award of a case of beer or a bottle of whiskey for each Japanese captured alive."

In the Southwest Pacific, internal military memos reveal that the ante had to be upped to "three days leave and some ice cream" to coax soldiers to bring in live Japanese prisoners.[106]

By the beginning of 1944 the United States government recognized that it needed to take interest in what was happening in China, specifically regarding CCP propaganda programs concerning the Japanese and intelligence regarding Japan in general. John P. Davies, a foreign service officer assigned to Gen. Joseph Stilwell in China, had recommended a survey group be sent to Communist-held China because it had been over six years since firsthand, official American reports had been sent in from such locales. After months of haggling with the Chinese Nationalist authorities, in July 1944 a small US mission headed by Col. David Barrett was permitted to travel to Yenan, the Communist stronghold. The mission that Barrett headed was called the Dixie Mission. Barrett was an able leader; he had lived in China since 1924 as an officer with the US army and was fluent in Chinese.[107]

The Dixie Mission's primary goals were to gather intelligence about the Japanese and establish preliminary contacts with the Chinese Communists, who until then official US channels had ignored. Ironically, many of the men who participated in the Dixie mission and studied how to improve American wartime propaganda against Japan, later faced a battery of charges during the McCarthy hearings in the 1950s. The men were branded as Communist sympathizers who had displayed seditious behavior and should be held responsible for "losing China." In 1951 Koji Ariyoshi was arrested for being a member of the Communist Party and found guilty under the Smith Act in 1953. Five years later the Ninth Circuit Court reversed his conviction on appeal.

The fact that Japanese-American language interpreters accompanied the mission to Yenan suggests that the US government was keenly interested in interviewing Japanese POWs living in the Yenan camps and learning about CCP propaganda initiatives. The US mission opened an office in Yenan and staffed it with a variety of Americans until the end of the war; some military and intelligence men stayed for the duration, while others only spent a few weeks. John Emmerson, who was fluent in Japanese after years of political attaché work at the Tokyo embassy, had been specifically sent along with Koji Ariyoshi, a Nisei language officer working for the OWI, to talk with captured Japanese POWs.[108] Ariyoshi had grown up in Hawaii, but although his Japanese was excellent, he had never lived in prewar Japan. He had been given specific commands to utilize his time in Yenan investigating the Communists' anti-Japanese propaganda; however, his reports detailing CCP propaganda methodology and his analysis of their success angered his superior, Gen. Patrick Hurley.[109] In his memoirs Kagawa Takashi, a former Japanese POW, wrote about meeting Emmerson and Ariyoshi while in the Japanese school at Yenan.[110]

After meetings with Communist leaders and witnessing firsthand the propaganda work that the CCP had accomplished, Emmerson informed his superiors that he felt Japanese soldiers could, in fact, be convinced to surrender.[111] After returning to America in early 1945 Emmerson tried to promote the idea that Japanese POWs could be used further for propaganda activities and could serve as early liaisons for the ultimate occupation of Japan. On April 12, 1945, his efforts resulted in the establishment of an indoctrination school for Japanese POWs at Camp Huntsville in Texas. Since the war soon ended, however, the program never actually started.[112]

The Dixie Mission in Yenan reported its findings back to Washington DC, frequently to the surprise of its superiors. The American group discovered in Yenan an interesting melange of some two hundred Japanese POWs, trained and educated by Nosaka Sanzō. For the Americans, coming into contact with living, breathing Japanese soldiers was a rare opportunity. Prominent scholar of Chinese history John Fairbank, mobilized at that time as a US operative in China, remembered, "We knew that the only Japanese prisoners taken by American forces had usually been unconscious at the time."[113]

The real rationale behind the US mission to find out how the Communists could be so successful against the Japanese soldiers appears vividly in personal recollections from some of the other participants in America's anti-Japan propaganda activities. Karl Yoneda was one such actor. Yoneda was a second-generation Japanese-American and originally a member of the US Communist Party before he was forced to surrender his membership when the group excluded those of Japanese ancestry. After internment at a federal camp erected by the American government in the Midwest to detain Japanese-American citizens, he volunteered for military service and worked on Japanese-language propaganda campaigns in Burma and China. Yoneda's group produced reams of Japanese-language propaganda that he himself admitted did not convince a single Japanese soldier to surrender.[114] In June 1944 Emmerson told Yoneda about the Dixie Mission. Its goal, Emmerson said, was to investigate what the Chinese were doing concerning the reeducation of Japanese POWs, exchange propaganda techniques with the CCP's Eighth Route Army, and see firsthand the Japanese People's Liberation League.[115] Emmerson encouraged Yoneda to continue producing propaganda aimed at the Japanese in the China-Burma-India theater even though virtually everyone admitted that "[m]ost captured prisoners had read our leaflets, found them interesting, but denied that they had inspired a desire to surrender."[116]

The Dixie Mission appears to have had an impact on US production of anti-Japan propaganda. Yoneda recalled that his propaganda group in Burma put into action many of the suggestions detailed in the reports the mission had sent back. Yoneda even received a letter from his friend Ariyoshi, who had accompanied Emmerson to Yenan. Ariyoshi wrote, "[T]here is an excellent war school here which has amassed a wealth of experience in psychological war methodology. Compared to what they have here, our propaganda school is like an elementary school. Doesn't matter if it's Saturday or Sunday, every day here is study time." [117]

Emmerson and Ariyoshi arrived in Yenan on October 22, 1944, and immediately spent long hours with the Japanese POWs and Nosaka Sanzō, investigating how they crafted anti-Japan propaganda. Each day Emmerson and Ariyoshi went to talk to Japanese POWs and had them fill out questionnaires. The Japanese answered questions such as: "What kind of work did you do before the war?" "Do you think the China Incident was correct or not?" "If Japan wins do, you want to return?" "Is the emperor supporting the war?" "If Japan loses, do you think the emperor system should remain?" "If the United States invades Japan, to what extent do you think the Japanese people will resist?" "In order to speed the end of the war do you think you should support the Eighth Route Army? The American military?" [118]

American officers working on psychological warfare campaigns aimed at the Japanese did not merely want to observe Japanese POWs, they wanted their cooperation. The CCP's propaganda leaflets produced at Yenan impressed many members of the Dixie Mission, and Ariyoshi and others had brought with them a selection of leaflets produced in the United States for the POWs to analyze. Results of this study revealed chiefly that the US leaflets stressed American military strength too much and focused on the idea that Japan could not win the war. Japanese POWs felt that US leaflet propaganda missed the main point. They urged the Americans to stress that the US military desired only to remove the Japanese military clique from power and not to colonize Japan. [119] According to the POW criticism, America's insistence on Japan's inevitable loss actually brought about the opposite effect than the one desired, because American propaganda offered no way out for the Japanese. Focusing on the eventual loss aided Japan's own propaganda, the POWs said, because it made Japanese propaganda appear correct, that the Japanese military was saving Japan from the threatening American military. [120] The POWs offered numerous other suggestions. Many leaflets produced by the United States, they said, were too difficult both in Japanese language and style, and many remarked that the leaflets seemed to have been written first in English and then translated. (For many leaflets this was the case.) The POWs warned that while the United States had flooded various regions with leaflets, "quality is more important than quantity."[121]

While postwar American opinions about the value of the Dixie Mission range from derogatory to glowing, two things are clear.[122] First, the United States was puzzled as to why the Chinese Communist Party propaganda understood the psyche of the Japanese soldier where it befuddled the Allies. Second, with Asian-language experts at a premium, sending a few such treasured US officials to remote Yenan demonstrates how eager the US government and the US military were to gain intelligence that could help create effective psychological propaganda.

A military analysis report from the late summer of 1945 suggests the extent

An American propaganda leaflet dropped in China. The American military stated that their goal with this specific leaflet was "to impress the Chinese farmer and villager that by helping in a small way he can help defeat the Japanese." The US wartime translation was, "The Jap is strong, but our combined strength is even stronger." The image on the left shows an enormous but lone Japanese soldier held at bay by many soldiers and circling Allied and Chinese aircraft. Kenseishiryōshitsu, Anti-Japanese Propaganda Leaflets (no. 1) [shū 1233], National Diet Library, Tokyo.

to which the United States learned from CCP propaganda methods. The report noted that US-produced Japanese-language propaganda operations "were considerably enhanced by the addition of six [Japanese] prisoners of war to the staff. These prisoners were used in Burma for PW [psychological work] over a long period." Authors of the report concluded that using Japanese POWs to create and disseminate US-created anti-Japan propaganda had a "two fold effect in undermining Japanese morale in that it is convincing them they are losing the war and is destroying faith in their own news sources. Both the Chinese and the Japanese in Occupied China are starved for news and it is reported that news leaflets sell at a premium on the black market." While perhaps overstating actual numbers, the report also noted that

> Jap bodies have been found with morale leaflets on them, Chinese compete to pick up news leaflets despite drastic counter measures by the Japanese authorities, downed airmen attribute their rescues to leaflet instructions to the Chinese, Japanese work projects have been abandoned, communications clogged, active resistance encouraged and brought about, and interrogation of prisoners has revealed numerous instances of morale leaflets having a marked discouraging effect on the Jap soldiers who read them.[123]

By the end of the war it appears the United States had learned a lesson that the CCP had implemented early on—that the use of actual Japanese soldiers was indispensable to the creation of effective Japanese-language propaganda aimed at the enemy.

One final question remains that helps explain the divergence of opinion between the United States and China regarding propaganda. Why did the CCP, whom the Japanese often slaughtered and certainly wished to eradicate, reach out an olive branch to the Japanese military? This book asserts that they did so, in part, because early CCP leaders earnestly believed in their own social, political, and economic message and strove to convince the Japanese of its veracity. Many of the CCP and KMT leaders had also studied in Japan and still held Japan in high esteem, even if they despised the current political and military regime. These Chinese had developed personal relations with individual Japanese in the course of their studies and research abroad. In addition, since 1895 many Chinese had, for better or worse, regarded Japan as a model of modernity. The small country provided a glimpse of the power China might achieve if it could successfully modernize. Conversely, US higher officials, more often than not, felt little attachment to Japan; nor did they view the country as a model of modernity. For them Asia was an entirely foreign environment that offered little humanity or hope. Furthermore, the policy of treating Japanese POWs well made for effective CCP propaganda, for the Communists understood how to maintain meaningful propaganda. By putting into practice what they preached, they clearly demonstrated that their activities were the antithesis of the Japanese, and dissimilar to those of the KMT, and thus the CCP hoped to gain a mass following.

The propaganda policies conducted by the Chinese on the mainland forced the Japanese military to rethink its own initiatives on the continent. A paucity of military records do not allow us to make a complete assessment of the situation, but it is clear from extant sources that the Japanese worried about the impact of Communist propaganda on the imperial forces. This may not have translated into a change in Japanese military policy, but it does illuminate the fact that the Japanese were not ignorant of the Chinese threat; nor were they completely indifferent about it. However, even an understanding of the threat posed by CCP propaganda appeared to have no effect on the Japanese military's ability to use Chinese POWs for propaganda. In fact, military records concerning Chinese taken alive as POWs and used for propaganda purposes are conspicuous in their absence. The Japanese did use white Allied POWs for radio and movie propaganda, both inside the empire and abroad, but either racial protocol or hubris prevented a similar policy with regard to the Chinese.[124] The very failure of the Japanese to recognize this incongruity only adds to the tragedy when we consider the sheer numbers of Chinese, military and civilian, who never even made it to a Japanese POW camp. The appearance of the United States on the scene, as student of CCP propaganda, only adds to the evidence that leads us to understand that the propaganda struggle on the mainland was not a forgone conclusion for any party. The Chinese and Japanese struggled for each supporter, regardless of nationality. America's entry into the fray, after 1941, merely added another voice to an already complex cacophony of competitive propaganda.

CHAPTER SIX

Preparing for Defeat

If initiating a war requires complex strategies, concluding a war involves similar schemes. Previous chapters have illuminated the massive superstructure of competing agencies underlying the Japanese wartime propaganda campaigns. The Special Higher Police constantly surveyed the population to analyze statistically the level of its acquiescence to government pronouncements concerning the war. At the same time the military used a heavy hand to censor news that it felt could shake this fragile public opinion. In light of the extreme complexity and nature of these efforts we are left with a puzzling question: if the Japanese implemented propaganda to such a level, how were the Americans able to occupy the country so quickly and with a minimum amount of civic disturbance?[1]

The one major work in English on wartime Japanese propaganda, by the eminent historian of Japan John Dower, asks just this question. Following in the research footsteps of Christopher Thorne and Akira Iriye, Dower dubbed Japan's war with the west a race war, and one without mercy. During the four years the United States fought Japan, racial stereotypes permeated the propaganda on all sides, but in Dower's estimation these labels proved "remarkably flexible and malleable" immediately following the war. In the final analysis, "the same stereotypes that fed superpatriotism and outright race hate were adaptable to cooperation."[2] While that assessment may stand as an accurate assessment for the elite of Japanese society, the thesis obfuscates the actual effects of wartime Japanese propaganda. Perhaps more importantly, it clouds a realistic assessment of how the occupation of Japan unfolded. The Japanese did not freely and easily shrug off the decade and a half of constant propagandistic influence. Dower does not exactly imply that they did, but the process still remains mysterious. The war changed Japanese society in profound ways and to accept the American occupation, a whole new strata of propaganda became necessary to dissolve the social attitudes that the wars against China and the west had created.[3]

These social attitudes, which the Japanese controlled even after surrender, rested on a description of the Japanese situation after the war, when the nation "embraced defeat." To understand the circumstances leading up to the American occupation, it would not be incorrect to say that, in fact, the Japanese actually *prepared* for defeat. Scholarship on the occupation often leads readers to believe that the detente of the occupation sprang from American ingenuity or at least good-heartedness. American films, such as *Teahouse of the August Moon*, occasionally reflect the ambiguity as to just which power ruled during the early years of the Cold War. In the movie version, Marlon Brando plays an Okinawan, Sakini, caught between townspeople who want to rebuild their local teahouse and stock it with geisha and the bumbling occupation officers who want to rebuild educational institutions. As this postwar American comedy perhaps unwittingly demonstrated, there were many factors that explain the ease of the occupation. American planning did play a role. However, it was Japanese planning in advance that appears to have exerted the primary influence in the occupation's smooth evolution. After all, it was the Japanese who spoke the language, knew the region, and had experience in governing the country. The US overseers just sat on top. The same Japanese agencies that only weeks earlier had touted their spiritual fortitude to repel the barbarians quickly switched over to mandating new public behavior and ordering Japanese imperial subjects to accept the occupation so that Japan could rise again. How the Japanese managed suddenly to convince a population mobilized to fight America to now embrace the west is the focus of this chapter.

The ultimate goal of Japanese wartime propaganda was to connect the home front to the battlefront and structure a stable Japanese society that could help Japan win the war. The relationship between "defeat propaganda" and wartime propaganda becomes clearer if we recognize that Japan faced a new and greater problem following the war. With the imminent arrival of Americans, propaganda had to once again orient Japanese society in a certain direction. The Japanese authorities were interested in both maintaining the fiction of their success in the war and protecting their *kokutai,* or national polity. The very language used in the emperor's famous surrender broadcast of August 15, 1945, and the language Japanese officials employed domestically with the population, reflected this attitude. Books have been devoted to this slippery Japanese term, *kokutai,* and not every Japanese even understood what it meant. Following the surrender, however, Japanese politicians continually employed the term in speeches and secret government documents as a synonym for national integrity, or even nationalism. Since they lacked a new postwar term to express the idea, Japanese officials employed terms from before 1945 with which the Japanese public were quite familiar.

The end of Japan's war carried with it obstacles that only linguistic acrobatics could surmount. In Japanese, the terms to describe Japan's situation at the end of the war oscillate between two poles, between *haisen,* "defeat" and *shūsen,* "end of the war." Japanese authorities assiduously avoided using the concise word for defeat, *haisen.* In contrast, *shūsen,* a word that merely described the war as having come to a close, ignored the notion of defeat or even victory. As a result of such careful linguistic monitoring on the part of Japanese officials, the entire postwar vocabulary helped diffuse responsibility for the war, obscure its goals, and evade the reasons why Japan lost. The lesson of Japan's defeat became "to never lose again," and this new strategy did not allow for personal reflection on the root causes of the war or investigation into where responsibility lay. Japanese government records demonstrate the degree to which the postwar Japanese government was quite concerned with saving the *kokutai,* or national polity, and preserving intact as much of prewar ideology as it could. This act of salvation was important for at least two reasons. First, Japanese leaders were eager to continue their own hold on power after the surrender. And second, Japanese wartime leaders felt that Japan faced a crisis, this time not a threat from an unstable China but from a foreign occupying army. Under such circumstances, stability was seen as a way of keeping occupation interference to a minimum.[4]

Propaganda programs, police bureaus, and military and civilian agencies employed to keep the population in line before defeat mirrored the policies that survived into postwar Japan. The Japanese may have taken the defeat in stride, or "embraced it," but the maintenance of social order demonstrates something else. For wartime Japanese leaders and early postwar Japan, maintaining social order in the face of crushing defeat was of paramount importance. The ravages of the Fifteen-Year War on Japan have been ably described elsewhere, but it is important to remember that economic woes were not the only travails that the newly conquered Japanese faced. "At war's end, millions of demobilized soldiers, war widows, and other displaced persons began to make their way back into the cities and, as virtually all moral and government restraints subsequently collapsed, the [Japanese] mob strengthened its grip on the municipal economy."[5] Once the occupation forces arrived, Tokyo became a hotbed of intrigue and debauchery, to the extent that the "moat around the Imperial Palace was so clogged with used condoms it had to be cleaned out once a week with a big wire scoop."[6]

The Japanese defeat was orchestrated and the population that met the occupying Allied forces had been trained for the task. Random acts of kindness toward US soldiers may have been just that, but it is important to remember that often these actions had been taught. Early postwar Japanese reactions to the occupation were not always completely spontaneous.

In any case the occupying Allied forces deemed spontaneity counter to their occupation plans. The first contingency of US soldiers did not actually arrive on Japanese shores until August 28, 1945. General MacArthur arrived on August 30—a full two weeks after the Japanese acquiescence to surrender on August 15. Four years of heavy island fighting in the Pacific and dogmatic Japanese propaganda had burned into the minds of many American leaders the image of an imperial fighting force that would never surrender no matter what the costs. US military leaders were not eager to leap into what they feared would be a maelstrom on the Japanese home islands. Domestic Japanese leaders also coveted those weeks to rally the population behind new postwar goals of accepting defeat in order to protect Japan. Gaining support for the occupation was not going to be easy. Only a week before Emperor Hirohito's imperial announcement to surrender, a crowd of civilian Japanese, including young and old women, took turns beating to death a US airman whose B-29 bomber had the misfortune to crash near Tokyo.[7]

Even after the imperial government announced the decision to surrender, US uncertainty as to how the Japanese archipelago would react to actual American military landings paled in comparison to general anxiety concerning the behavior of the several million Japanese troops still stationed in China. In a June 1944 report to Washington DC regarding the situation in China, John Service provided a harsh estimate of China's military capabilities against Japan. "China is dying a lingering death by slow strangulation. China *does not* now constitute any threat to Japan. And China cannot, if the present situation continues, successfully resist a determined Japanese drive to seize our defensive bases in East China."[8] The Japanese also displayed distress regarding order in their ranks in China. In contrast to the military situation throughout the Pacific and Southeast Asia, Japan's military on the Chinese mainland, while bogged down and constantly harassed by Chinese guerrilla forces, never faced clear military defeat. In late 1944 the Kwantung Army launched its Operation Ichigo and managed to penetrate deep into southwestern China. The offensive mobilized one of the largest forces the Japanese had mustered since the start of the war with China in 1937, including approximately 500,000 Japanese soldiers, 100,000 horses, and 10,555 vehicles. This massive show of might carved its way over 1,500 kilometers of harsh territory to attack Nationalist strongholds in southwest China.[9] By the time of Japan's surrender in the late summer of 1945, many judged that a full and immediate Japanese demobilization on the mainland was, in light of recent Japanese efforts against China, not a simple task.

The occupation of Japan slowly forced the United States into the role of authority partly due to fears over potential violence regarding the transition. The actual surrender signed on the battleship USS *Missouri* took place on September 2, 1945, in Tokyo Bay. In the two-week interval between surrender and signature, the Home Ministry and Cabinet Board of Information, along with the police, worked furiously on a variety of new propaganda programs to help the population accept an occupation presence. The brief respite before the Allied forces arrived did not allow for internal dissent to the surrender. In contrast to their role only weeks before, after August 15 police agencies carefully quelled any lack of support for the surrender, coming from either the left or the right. It is difficult to ascertain whether these propaganda plans, that predated the American arrival, prevented widespread rebellion. However, one thing is certain. The Japanese authorities did not want to wait and find out for themselves. The appearance of these new police policies, antirumor campaigns, and the supervision of Korean activities demonstrate the uncertainty of the initial occupation. No one was sure what was going to happen, and no agency could predict with assurance the reaction of the Japanese public at large, so the Japanese tried to plan ahead.

Kessen or Final Battle Mentality

From 1943 onward the Japanese Special Higher Police focused intensely on what they termed *minshin dōkō*, or the "trends of the hearts and minds of the people." The Special Higher Police were specifically interested in popular attitudes toward official proclamations and announcements. Nor did they always keep their findings secret. The Home Ministry often published its data in inhouse magazines like *The Voice of the Street* and *Weekly Report of Public Opinion*, both of which the Japanese higher authorities used as reference journals.[10] The Special Higher Police was a key agency that the government employed to prepare the groundwork for social stability. In the face of a collapsing social structure, as the war sputtered toward defeat, keeping Japanese society in line and acquiescent were deemed absolute necessities.

The Special Higher Police particularly kept tabs on the public as the Japanese military faced a precarious situation in the late summer of 1944, when it could no longer hide the obvious fact that the war was taking a turn for the worse. The Imperial General Headquarters admitted to its domestic audience, employing vague terminology, that Saipan had been lost to the Americans. When that news hit the streets, the Special Higher Police scrambled around the country to chart the people's reaction. In a top-secret memo to the Home Ministry from August 1944, police officials admitted that the news had been a shock to the whole country. Many people attributed the loss to a tactical military failure and inadequate government planning. Even so, most police recognized that the population had also been psychologically prepared for this eventuality.[11] In light of the fact that the police assumed most Japanese had mentally prepared for such a catastrophe, the Special Higher Police reported that most Japanese were responding positively to the announcement. Japanese were quoted as saying that the country must continue its efforts to unite and to vanquish the enemy.[12]

The police gathered rumors that ranged from the plausible to the incredible. On April 20, 1944, the police magazine *Shisō junpō* published a section labeled "trends within recent rumors." This section noted that the number of comments against the authorities had increased since the previous summer, when food shortage problems had grown urgent. The report mentioned that the two most prevalent rumors were that Japanese forces on various islands throughout the Pacific had all committed suicide and that the war was "virtually over." Laborers were overheard rejoicing, poorly disguising their fatigue with the war. "If the war is lost, then only those at the top will be killed, we poor workers and villagers at the bottom don't have to worry. Whether we win or lose, we won't be killed," the report quoted workers as saying.[13]

Irrational and strange rumors intrigued the police enough for them to write detailed accounts in their reports during 1944. In one small town, a report documented, a rumor developed that someone had been born who looked like a four-legged cow. Villagers stated that the war would end sometime that year, and when it ended, a pestilence would spread around the country. The rumor urged people to eat *umeboshi* (dried salted plums) and scallions so that they would not get sick.[14] Another rumor spoke of a white-haired old man or woman—it was not clear which—who carried around a bottomless *tokkuri* (vessel for pouring sake). If one poured sake into the vessel, the rumor advised, the war would end in the near future. Peasants believed in this rumor to the point that one peasant was said to have followed this old person out of the village but the person supposedly disappeared along the path.[15] Yet another rumor spoke of a rare mushroom that grew inside a local shrine. It was said that this mushroom had grown at the same shrine during the Russo-Japanese war and that it was an omen that the war would end soon.[16]

Special Higher Police files and reports, analyzing as they did the mood and trends within wartime Japanese society, demonstrate the attention the agencies concerned with propaganda paid to the hopes and fears of the domestic audience. This calculus of public opinion was key in the construction of effective propaganda and counterpropaganda. The police kept tab of rumors circulating in factories, public toilets, even under bridges, and in conversations overheard in public bars, cafeterias, or on the street.

However, as much as the Japanese population throughout the empire groaned with discomfort, the war did not completely erase political activity during the war, as was the case in Germany. Japanese political cabinets rose and fell, reflecting the weight domestic opinion carried and how results from the battlefield influenced the political landscape.[17] Even as the war reached its apex, the military situation and popular opinion still had an impact on political fortunes. The loss of Saipan in the summer of 1944 deprived the Tōjō Cabinet of crucial support, which led to its replacement by the Koiso Cabinet on July 22. Regardless of military control, public opinion still remained crucial to social stability during the war.

According to the 1944 summary of Special Higher Police reports, people mostly complained that the military was riding in first- and second-class trains while civilians had difficulty procuring any tickets at all. The Japanese grumbled that if the war effort failed, everyone's lifestyle would suffer. Less commonly, some griped that the war was unjust or detrimental to Asia, which was stifling under the Japanese yoke.[18] The police outlined what they deemed the cause of social unrest in an April 1944 memo. In clear and precise language —rare for a document of this nature—the police revealed that "the people's greatest interest at the moment is not the war but the problems they encounter trying to live."[19] This lesson was not lost on the police. They were mindful of the fact that one of Japan's greatest riots, the 1918 rice riots, exploded due to a scarcity and overpricing of rice. The riots shut down the capital, spread throughout the nation, and virtually reformed the government. The fact that the Special Higher Police mentioned such historical precedents in their records suggests they were mindful of the chaos food shortages could cause. A similar study noted that of approximately 10,000 students surveyed in Kōchi city, more than half reported that they did not have enough to eat. Out of that majority, about 1,290 students ate so little nourishing food that they could not bring a *bentō* (boxed lunch) to school.[20]

The Special Higher Police worried not just about the failure of the country's youth to maintain a proper diet, but they also continued to fret over people's personal habits. In April 1944 the authorities worried about women staying at home after their husbands had been drafted. Sexual affairs and sleeping around, it seemed, were directly related to the war effort.[21]

Frequently reports dealing with the military loss of critical islands or battles did not explicitly employ the words "loss" or "failure." Instead, authorities used language that informed the population when the next decisive step would be taken, usually in the form of preparing for *kessen*, the final battle. The imperial military's inability to admit defeat mirrors the ambiguous terminology the postwar Japanese government used concerning Japan's surrender in August 1945.

Last Months before Surrender

By the late summer of 1945 Allied troops had essentially wiped out Japanese forces fighting in the Pacific, on the Marshall islands, Guadalcanal, Luzon, and elsewhere. The fierce confrontation for the control of the islands of Okinawa escalated to a frenzy in the hot summer of 1945. Losses on both sides, especially the Japanese, staggered even the most battle-scarred officers. Okinawa, the last major battle of the Pacific War, lasted from April 1 to June 22, 1945. The conflict involved mass numbers of troops from both sides, and the fighting included an enormous deployment of aircraft, including Japanese kamikaze efforts. Japanese deaths, including civilians, totaled over 150,000. US troops suffered 12,281 combat deaths, 50,000 troops wounded, and 14,000 combat fatigue casualties. Japan would be defeated, but it was going to cost both sides dearly. While Japanese troops in China, Manchuria, and Southeast Asia were not surrendering in massive numbers, many were choosing escape through suicide.

Amidst this tragic development of seemingly inevitable defeat for the Japanese navy, Japanese army forces on the Chinese mainland still constituted a formidable force, and conditions on the Japanese home islands seemed to portend major bloodshed. Initial American military estimates placed Japanese troops deployed in the south of the Japanese archipelago at around 230,000, a figure later radically adjusted upward to 680,000 by late July 1945.[22] Japanese propaganda and the military's prior performance on the battlefield convinced the United States that Japan would fight to the last woman and child to defend the motherland. A full discussion of America's rationale for dropping the atomic bombs is outside the scope of this book, but Japanese propaganda, supported by the frequent failure of Japanese soldiers to surrender, deeply affected American attitudes. It is safe to say that such attitudes at least influenced the decision to use the atom bomb against Japan.

Numerous English- and Japanese-language studies have portrayed Japan as exhausted and on the verge of collapse as the war drew to a close. However, the situation varied greatly by locale. Even though the Americans had bombed Tokyo to rubble, it remained the seat of national authority and thus conflicted over the fate of Japan. On July 12, 1945, in the burned-out embers of Nakano, a section of western Tokyo, the police reminded inhabitants about the pressing contingency of the "final battle" to defend Japan. In a message that was passed from household to household, members of each *tonarigumi* (neighborhood association),[23] were required to show up at the police station two days later for military practice from five to six in the morning.[24] The early hour was specifically chosen so that those who worked could not use their jobs as an excuse not to participate.

The Japanese parliament made its attitude to take a final battle stance quite clear in a message to the people in late January 1945, when the war was obviously getting worse. The Diet decided, after the United States had reclaimed the island of Luzon in the Philippines, that Japan's wartime goals must be explicit.

The parliament's directive read that the enemy's goal was "to subjugate Japan and hegemonize the world." The Japanese government claimed that the United States was waging war to "liberate" countries that "we have already liberated." The parliament called such ideas a "sham," asserting that the west merely wished to recolonize territories Japan helped to become independent.[25]

Mirroring the fact that wartime propaganda really had permeated national attitudes, individual Japanese exhorted the government how to act in the last few months of the war. Japanese did not just listen to the government, they directed it. A few months prior to the January 1945 parliamentary declaration, a reader named Ōta Masataka from the Kōjimachi section of Tokyo wrote to the government's Cabinet Board of Information weekly magazine, *Weekly Report*, to request that newspapers not print any depressing news about potential capitulation to the Allies or cessation of fighting. Ōta claimed that articles along those lines only caused people to become depressed and led the Japanese to "begin to harbor fears of losing the war." A similarly excited reader wrote in complaining that the radio should be used only to mobilize people for the war effort. This unidentified writer felt that the government should limit music on the airwaves: "Now is the crossroads of our fate and we should not be distracted with music....We should be focusing all our effort into the war."[26]

Not everyone seemed as melancholy as the writer to the *Weekly Report*. In information gleaned from censored domestic mail, the Special Higher Police learned that not everyone was apathetic; some were downright hawks. In March 1945 a war supporter from Hokkaido, Japan's northernmost island, declared, "We will fight until the last of the last of the Yamato race is slain, and I have made up my mind, even alone, to die killing many of the American devils."

Warlike talk was not limited to Japanese men. A woman, also from Hokkaido, exclaimed in her letter that "if I could trade places with the kamikaze pilots, I would. I am so ready, I would even use my own body as a weapon against a battleship."[27] Other Japanese were probably not as happy with the situation but that was not necessarily because they did not support the war, but because they felt their leaders were mishandling the situation. One man's comments about such ineptitude captured that feeling. "More than planes and bombs, what Japan really needs now is a great statesmen," he lamented.[28]

As the war raged, reports from the Home Ministry describing conditions from June through August 1945, painted a picture of a people concerned more with escaping the daily bombings and managing life in the face of a thriving black market, empty store shelves, and worsening health. Most urban inhabitants, the reports emphasized, sought merely to survive rather than actually wage war.[29]

In this chaotic, desperate situation the authorities responsible for public security were keenly interested in maintaining as much of a facade of social tranquility as possible to keep the factories functioning and war materials in production. To facilitate such production meant keeping a watchful eye on the tens of thousands of Koreans and Chinese whom the Japanese had dragooned to Japan and forced to work under grotesque conditions. The police, no friend of the Koreans, noted that rumors concerning Koreans and their supposed suspicious activities increased during the spring and summer of 1945. Koreans were rumored to kill Japanese women and eat or sell their flesh on the black market. Others claimed that Koreans rejoiced when they saw an Allied plane and were unhappy upon sighting a Japanese plane. One prevalent rumor stated that Koreans were busy preparing their best western suits to welcome the Americans when they landed on Japanese shores. The police also investigated the fears that circulated among the Koreans themselves. Most anguished that as the "air raids worsen, the Japanese are probably going to kill us anyway." Koreans fears were not completely unfounded, since hundreds had been massacred following the great 1923 Kantō earthquake. When the frequency of Allied air raids over the main islands diminished in mid-1945, the rumor about Koreans dressing in a western suit to welcome the landing Allied forces mutated to "one had to wear a suit to welcome the Allied forces," or that if a Korean greeted US soldiers wearing Korean costume, it would assure that individual's safety.[30]

Perhaps in response to its determined efforts to track every rumor and piece of graffiti, or more importantly, to turn such slander into its own weapon, the Special Higher Police devised a plan in late June 1945 to mount its own rumor campaign. To take advantage of what seemed to be a natural tendency among Japanese at this late stage of the war, this word-of-mouth propaganda campaign was supposed to augment and supplement the propaganda already circulating in newspapers and on radio. The campaign instructed unnamed private and government media agencies to follow orders directed by the Cabinet Board of Information, Plans called for dispatch of rumor platoons across the country to coordinate maneuvers. Rumor platoons were to be staffed with journalists, writers, and whomever else seemed suited for the job. The staff was to be organized into groups and sent out across the country in order to rally the spirit of the people.[31] It is difficult to ascertain whether the plan was implemented or not, but efforts to coordinate it certainly were serious.

On July 31, 1945, two weeks before Japan unconditionally surrendered to the Allies, the chief of the Metropolitan Police Headquarters Intelligence Bureau posted letters to the heads of the national newspapers concerning the verbal propaganda platoons and asked for their support and active participation.[32] The Japanese military may have been losing ground in the Pacific, but the Special Higher Police continued to establish propaganda policies that encouraged the domestic population to continue supporting the war effort.

July 1945 was a busy month for the police in general. They fielded and uncovered numerous complaints about the lack of food, the military's hoarding of precious resources, and a general malaise concerning the war. Excerpts from *The Voice of the Street* detail specific charges of incompetence leveled against the government. One irate Japanese complained that while the government was trying to promote bank savings, banks consistently closed at noontime. The post office did not have enough savings passbooks, the writer observed, so they turn people away from the bank window. Nonetheless, the government had no immediate plan; nor was it demonstrating a plethora of solutions. Thus, as the people saw it, the writer decided, "the government is incompetent."[33] As the many rumor lists compiled by the police noted, people were angry at the way in which the government mishandled the war, not necessarily toward the war itself.

On one of the last days of July, the police department of the Home Ministry published in *Shisō junpō* interviews collected from various Japanese leaders and important opinion makers concerning the Potsdam declaration. Several Japanese politicians replied that the Japanese government's *mokusatsu* or silent-treatment response was appropriate. Another added that whatever the west and China spouted was entirely propaganda. Demonstrating the extent to which Japanese authorities wished to shield their public from the actual situation of the war, one member of the House of Peers stated that the cabinet even debated whether to release the content of the Allied conditions for peace to the public.[34]

The Special Higher Police were not immune to the social conditions surrounding the impending defeat—they could see the writing on the wall. Ironically, they would be among the first to start plying the population with new rules in order to welcome the incoming occupation forces.

A *Shisō junpō* report from July 21, 1945, focusing on public opinion about the air raids, openly observed that Japan was being bombed almost daily, but that it was important to keep the following points in mind concerning the people's state of mind and body under this situation. The problem of people losing their taste for the war is tied into their feeling of safety, the report enunciated. More people were pushing for peace and fewer believed in the military. Those who have not been bombed are loathed by those who have, the report concluded. In short, the war is dividing the population between the haves and the have nots.[35]

The Special Higher Police issued a directive, "Understanding the Hearts and Minds of the People," on August 1, 1945, only two weeks before the surrender. The police seemed to have grasped the situation and described what they felt directly influenced people's decreasing faith in the war: escalation of the air attacks, worsening food supply, inflation, enemy propaganda actions, and fear concerning the final battle for the main island.[36]

Nearing Defeat

Upon surrender, Japan did not simply subordinate itself to the Allied occupation forces. The Japanese met the Allies at the doorstep and in true Japanese style made US soldiers take off their shoes before entering. In order to operate effectively in the Japanese environment, the Americans needed to conduct their policy through Japanese interlocutors. To be sure, every day did not proceed smoothly—rape, pillage, petty theft, and prostitution developed into serious problems. But to think for a moment that a docile Japanese population merely traded one overlord for another, that they simply allowed the chrysanthemum throne to be shrouded in US military olive drab, is to miss the point of what went on before the Allied forces arrived.

On August 10, 1945, four days after the atomic bombing of Hiroshima and one day after the atomic bombing of Nagasaki, the director of the Metropolitan Police Peace and Public Security Bureau at the Home Ministry, Okazaki Eijō, sent a directive discussing the end of the war to the national police headquarters Special Higher Police chief, Osaka city's public security chief, and the police chief of each prefectural police force. The director stated that since the Soviet Union had entered the fray, extra precautions needed to be put into place to maintain the public peace. The USSR's declaration of war against Japan on August 8, 1945, had galvanized the Japanese authorities into action. Japanese bureaucrats were already jittery about the influence they believed that the Communists had wielded in the prewar era. Now they faced the prospect of having the dreaded Soviets actually occupy Japanese imperial land as part of the Allied occupation forces. Okazaki's letter outlined several areas where the police and Special Higher Police should be especially vigilant. Police were told to be aware of left-wing activities, to take notice of accidental or frivolous acts of violence by youth group members, and to strive to the best of their ability to keep the right wing from disrupting the capital. If that was not possible, official measures required the police at least to notify the authorities in Tokyo in advance. The Japanese authorities expected criticism and popular debate concerning responsibility for the war—whether it was the government or army's fault—so the police forces were ordered to stifle or at least limit this type of discussion because it could potentially harm imperial prestige and lead to a chaotic state of postwar affairs.[37]

Near the end of the war the police were poised to keep an eye on Koreans and others who were felt to be less than sympathetic toward Japan's fate. This supervision might have been one reason why the head of the Osaka police force received a specific directive from the Home Ministry. By 1945 tens of thousands of Korean nationals resided in Osaka. Koreans were not the only source of worry for the Japanese authorities. An August 1945 police report specified that the authorities had to be aware of "those Christians" in Hiroshima as well. Those Christians referred to "hidden Christians" in the south of Japan. Southern Japan had been a hotbed of Christianity in the early 1600s when Portuguese and Christian missionaries first visited Japan. From 1633 to 1638, the Tokugawa rulers crushed a Christian uprising, called the Shimabara rebellion, slaughtering an estimated 30,000 adherents to the western religion. For over two hundred years the shoguns believed that they had eradicated the heretics from the islands, only to discover after the opening of Japan in 1868 that pockets of believers had merely gone underground. Christianity maintained a stronghold in some parts of southern Japan.

From July to August, bridging the gap between the end of war and the beginning of the occupation, the same organizations that were responsible for social order, primarily the police and military, employed familiar old methods for keeping society calm. The content of the propaganda changed dramatically, but those in charge and those executing the propaganda activities remained in power as Japan jerkily shifted from war to peace.

After the Surrender

The Fifteen Year War (1931–1945) devastated Japan. A decade and a half of military madness had squandered Japan's limited natural resources. Postwar estimates place the number of Japanese military deaths at 1.74 million soldiers, but the numbers almost double if civilian deaths are included. When the first foreign journalists entered Japan's flattened cities, they discovered that the war had pulverized over one quarter of the country's entire wealth.[38] Almost immediately after the surrender, an estimated 7 million Japanese stranded abroad, out of a total population of 74 million people, began trickling back to the motherland, straining an already desperate situation.[39] The fact that Japan's empire spread across the Asian continent and over the Pacific Ocean meant that getting mobilized Japanese soldiers to surrender was going to be a formidable task.[40] Even assuming they surrendered, the sheer complexity of repatriating 7 million Japanese military and civilians from the former empire would be among the largest forced movements of people in history. Europeans repatriating after the war moved in greater numbers, but their return did not always necessitate third-party transport; nor did they have to move over a body of water. For the most part, returnees in Europe could travel under their own steam and on their own timetable. In the Japanese case, repatriation followed a policy the Allies dictated.

On August 15, 1945, in a radio broadcast largely unintelligible to the common listener, the Shōwa emperor called on the Japanese nation to protect the *kokutai,* the national polity, and "bear the unbearable." Not everyone rose to their feet. Several groups of soldiers commandeered airplanes and flew over Tokyo and the surrounding areas. Soldiers who could not accept defeat printed up thousands of leaflets and distributed them. The leaflets sprouted up around the capital and metropolitan areas. In an ironic twist of fate, the Special Higher Police now collected these leaflets opposed to surrender and classified them as "seditious." Only days before, the same police had been canvassing the population, weeding out any who desired surrender. Leaflets were discovered at the train station in Tachikawa city, west of Tokyo, on August 16, 1945, and in the fashionable district of Shibuya on August 17. In Shinagawa, in southern Tokyo, many saw leaflets against the surrender fall from the sky and land as far away as Shibuya and Kanda. All the leaflets exhorted Japan to continue the war. The messages against surrender reminded the Japanese that it was better to die an honorable death fighting to the end than to submit to the enemy.

The more politically oriented leaflets actually labeled the surrender a "Badoglio-like" action, referring to Pietro Badoglio, the key figure who helped initiate Italy's surrender to the Allies and who took charge of Italy after Mussolini fell. One prowar leaflet managed to play on themes similar to those the Communists used to portray the war as a battle between economic classes. "A message to the people of the country. The Badoglio-like leaders of the country are deceiving you. They are only securing an idle life for themselves and enslaving you." Other leaflets cried out for more soldiers to join the kamikaze forces or admonished the people that surrender was absolutely not the way of real peace.[41]

Before the Americans arrived the domestic situation was not the picture of serenity that the Japanese authorities desired. On August 24 in Shimane prefecture, on Japan's southwest coast, fifty-three people set fire to the prefecture government building in opposition to the surrender. Most participants were youths in their twenties, including about twenty women. The courts sentenced the leader, Okazaki Tsutomu, to life in prison, but he was released in 1952.[42]

The day after the emperor's August 15 surrender broadcast, the Special Higher Police concentrated on the Korean issue. On August 16, authorities sent a directive to the police in Chiba prefecture concerning Koreans residing there.

Japanese authorities deeply worried about how Koreans would react to Japan's defeat. The fact that the Special Higher Police drafted this directive the day after the surrender, a day when most Japanese would still have been in a state of shock over the swiftness of the surrender, demonstrates the high degree of their anxiety. The police felt that they could lose control of the domestic situation at any time, and the Japanese authorities did not wish to have the Allied occupation forces deal with the Korean issue. Japanese officials strove to prepare a stable domestic front for the arrival of the Americans and to stifle, in advance, potential Korean unrest. Preparing for defeat meant taking control of minority affairs before the Americans arrived. The instructions stated that the police were anxious about Koreans behaving rashly, so action should be taken quickly to promote the smooth, quick transport back to Korea for those who wished to return. However, since the labor shortage in Japan was acute—the tens of thousands of Koreans had originally been forced to Japan to work for this reason—the commands stipulated that those working in factories should remain at their work until further notice. Authorities also instructed Japanese living in areas surrounding Koreans not to engage in behavior or activities that could potentially arouse Korean ire.[43]

On September 1, in an obvious bid to preserve its energy sources and prepare to survive a winter under strict occupation guidelines, the Ministry of Health and Welfare and the Home Ministry both sent directives to the heads of local agencies concerning the movements of Koreans. Authorities exhorted local leaders to retain Korean workers with mining skills and put those who possessed no real labor skills on boats back to Korea first.[44] Repatriating the Koreans was important to the Japanese to preserve social stability following defeat, but they also did not want the process to upset Japan's already extremely precarious economic situation.

The clampdown on Korean dissatisfaction paralleled general anxiety concerning Japanese public reaction to the surrender. Notices to the police chief of Iwai city in Tottori prefecture on Japan's west coast, several days after the surrender, underscored how the authorities saw the need to keep a tight clamp on Japanese society. The memos noted that Japan was now at a crossroads where its survival or demise was to be decided. The report stressed, among other issues, the necessity for the authorities to maintain the support and understanding of the masses in order to direct Japan toward salvation.[45]

Takami Jun, a noted prewar Japanese writer and essayist, wrote in his diary about the efforts of the Japanese to keep things quiet after the surrender.[46] In some ways while Takami foresaw the end of the war, it was not clear to him until the emperor's announcement which way it would finish. Nonetheless, Takami did not blame defeat on the government. He lamented that during the war everyone dissimulated. "Everyone deceived one another. The government deceived the populace and the populace in turn deceived the government. The military deceived the government and the government deceived the military and so on."[47]

Takami, an intellectual, had the capacity to be critical of Japan, but his diary demonstrates that perhaps not everything was a deception. He wanted to share in the glory that he felt Japan had almost attained. On August 16, the day after Japan's surrender, Takami mourned in his diary, "Japan's defeat is not something I wished for. Japan's defeat is not something over which we should be joyous. I wanted Japan, somehow or another, to win. As such, I exhausted all efforts to help achieve that goal. My heart is now filled with pain and my love goes out to Japan and all Japanese."[48]

Preparation for defeat meant more than stifling dissent and a heart filled with pain, as Takami wrote. Postwar propaganda needed to educate the Japanese that the Allies were good. The most fascinating preparations for defeat were those in which the police taught the Japanese that the advancing Allied forces would not engage in wholesale slaughter and that the populace should remain in place. In what must remain to date the fastest turnaround from an anti-American to a pro-American stance for any government agency, an August 27 notification to the police chief of Chiba prefecture detailed the drastic changes that had taken place. This was *less than two full weeks* after the announced decision to surrender, but still days before an official surrender was signed on the USS *Missouri* on September 2. The police notice explained how to treat the Allied forces that would soon be arriving. It said that the police were to make it known to the local populations that in the event of an Allied plane accident, the people were now ordered to help the pilots or passengers, as opposed to what they did during the war. But local residents were also told that they should, of course, notify the police if they or any others were subjected to violent behavior by any members of the Allied occupying army.[49]

Preparations for defeat did not end with the arrival of US occupation forces. In order to deal effectively with the occupying forces, which would have soon spread into even the most remote corners of the country, the Special Higher Police prepared an unusual document on October 2, only two days before they had been ordered by SCAP authorities to disband. The Special Higher Police dispatched their suggestions to police forces around the country, obviously hoping that the document, "Various Aspects of American Personality Characteristics," would serve as a guidebook so that those dealing with the enemy for the first time would be able to do so in a friendly manner. In contrast to the barbaric image attributed to the average American only a few weeks before in Japanese wartime propaganda, the new descriptions portrayed Americans as "tidy, clear, happy, precise (especially in keeping time)." The report advised Japanese not to be overly polite, *enryō,* in the presence of Americans. Unlike in Japan, where a high value was placed on such behavior, the report stated, overly polite behavior merely annoyed Americans. Locals were educated not to point, to make sure to shave and keep their hair managed, not to expose their bodies (especially women), to be sure to give women priority seating on transportation, to take their hats off in elevators, not to urinate in public, not to pick flowers from the public garden, not to spit on the street, not to talk too openly about their mistresses or behave immorally in front of others, and not to smoke in front of women, etc. People were also encouraged to sit next to Allied forces on public transport but were told not to salute if they saw soldiers in uniform.

The same report, in somewhat delicately expressed language, remarked that while the United States was white and racist, the war had helped transform American attitudes, and their Christian way of thinking had aided them to see the error of their stereotypes. The conclusion is a symphony of ideas, allowing a brief glimpse into how the Japanese authorities at the time interpreted Japan's war and the defeat.

> In summation . . . the people should continue to have the same national ideas they held during the war. Today, even though the war has ended, they should not consider themselves servile as they were prewar toward England and America. The Japanese should hold the belief that they are equal [to the west] and that in the future their mutual cooperation will lead to world peace. Before the start of the war Americans praised the Japanese . . . now we must not lose pride in our race and nobly make efforts to rebuild in the postwar.[50]

Early postwar Japanese propaganda played on positive prewar Japanese attitudes toward America and the west. All the same, many Japanese remained convinced of western sloth and laziness, and defeat did not damage wartime ideals regarding the Japanese belief in their own superiority. In the immediate postwar period, the speed and zest with which defeated Japan took to western ways convinced many foreign participants of the occupation that the domestic wartime population had never taken Japanese propaganda seriously. Their lack of understanding for the reasons behind this conversion shows they did not comprehend how Japanese propaganda worked. Japanese wartime propaganda effectively controlled a wartime population, but it never managed—because it was not necessary to do so—to eradicate pro-western attitudes completely, and these resurfaced after defeat. As this chapter demonstrates, postwar Japanese reappraisal of western democracy was not spontaneous but emanated from an official policy to reorient society so that the occupation would proceed smoothly and Japan could rebuild. The Japanese police, government officials, and the educated elite quickly comprehended that accepting defeat would be in their own best interest.

The rumors that the police had always monitored so carefully continued to worry officials even after the surrender. Both during the war and after, the Japanese authorities prized social stability as the necessary fulcrum to wage a victorious war. During the postwar era, Japan defined the war as one of national salvation and of not becoming a flunky to the west. Postwar goals defined the new battle as the need to rebuild.

A report on August 18, 1945, discusses a false notice in Kyushu which claimed that "the enemy is landing at Nagasaki, Fukuoka, Monji, and Shimonoseki and that women and children are starting to evacuate." The report carefully makes clear that police will inform the locals that the enemy will land according to procedures decided on in the surrender accord and that it will be implemented in an orderly fashion. In any event it was not scheduled until some days in the future. As further assurance, the notification added, "When the enemy lands, if circumstances arise and it becomes necessary to evacuate, we will notify you ahead of time."[51] Although defeated, it took several weeks for official reports to change their terminology. In numerous reports Japanese continued to refer to the Allies as "the enemy."

Numerous scholars assert that the precarious nature of the period surrounding Japan's surrender rested uneasily on the shoulders of a population in a state of shock. However, I propose that a less universal description approaches the actual situation. Some Japanese were relieved, others depressed—responses varied. Postwar Japanese scholarship's overarching historical depiction of the nation as exhausted from fifteen years of war has painted a monochromatic picture of a defeated Japan. The United States entered a Japan that had been militarily defeated, but socially and politically the country remained extremely viable.

While the average Japanese may have been *kyodatsu,* exhausted, the country's leaders were not. Japanese officials worked frantically on a multitude of plans to lessen the need for—and deplete the effectiveness of and deflect the brunt of—large portions of US occupation policy. At the outset, most Japanese were negatively disposed toward the surrender decision, but as the occupation got under way, this negativity turned into positive support rather quickly. However, this change in attitude cannot be attributed solely to the benevolence of the US occupation. Both the Japanese and Americans spent time and money on complex postwar propaganda efforts to help the average Japanese feel affinity toward America and denigrate Japan's own military for the war's mistakes.

Soon after the surrender, the imprint of Japanese propaganda was still apparent. At the time of the surrender then Prime Minister Suzuki Kantarō delivered a radio broadcast concerning the "termination of the Greater East Asia War." In his final broadcast before leaving office Suzuki attempted to clarify to the people that Japan's biggest failure in the war was the backwardness of its scientific endeavors—the war was lost because Japan did not have the same engineering prowess as the United States. In the future, Suzuki urged, the people must dedicate their efforts, using their local governments, creativity, and labor, to rebuild a Japan that would make a contribution to world civilization. "This is the only way they can reciprocate the emperor's great and unbounded benevolence."[52] A few days later Japanese newspapers highlighted the former prime minister's broadcast.[53]

The actual surrender did little to alleviate all the problems Japan had created in Asia, but it did allow Japan to concentrate on domestic issues to the exclusion of the imperial concerns that had obsessed the nation for over fifteen years.

The Allies' first major concern was to demobilize the millions of Japanese, both military and civilian, who lived in the disparate regions of the former empire. At the same time all of the Allied powers had to deal with Koreans, Allied POWs, and other nationalities stranded in Japan. The Allied agencies recognized that the process of repatriation was going to take years. Due to the complex organization needed to implement such mass repatriation and the torpid pace of the process, the Allies commenced various propaganda campaigns within POW camps housing demobilized Japanese soldiers around Asia. The Allies wanted to prepare Japanese soldiers about what to expect from the new Japan. In this regard SCAP policy mirrored Japanese desires for the postwar era; the highest priority was to contain anti-American rhetoric and maintain stability. SCAP was not the only authority interested in investigating the emotional health of repatriates. Following the surrender to the Allies, the Japanese police and other Japanese authorities also felt it necessary to restrain anti-American activities. The Special Higher Police (who continued to wield power until the end of 1945) wished to know whether deep-seated wartime attitudes continued to threaten the postwar social order. Officials also wanted to detect whether the quick change from labeling Americans "barbarian devils" to suddenly embracing them had weakened the social fabric.

The end of the war brought demands for a different kind of propaganda and thus the need to gauge public opinion with a renewed vigor. Japanese government teams interviewed recently demobilized soldiers around the country and sent back their findings to their own police headquarters. These interviews demonstrated what authorities feared most. The population was confused during this period of sudden change, and the society showed signs of losing its bearings. Post-surrender propaganda became imperative to reorient the shaky society. One soldier interviewed during this time, a thirty-year-old army sergeant from Shibuya, Tokyo, stationed in neighboring Chiba prefecture, stated that he had been prepared to fight to the death for the homeland when he heard that the war had ended. "Suddenly the war ceased and when I heard of the surrender, I thought surely that's complete nonsense. Japan can still fight on. This was obviously the treacherous work of spies who had sold out the country." [54] A twenty-four-year-old university student who had enlisted in the kamikaze corps and trained in Ibaraki prefecture was awaiting orders to crash his plane headlong into enemy ships. When he heard the rumor of surrender, he thought it was merely enemy propaganda. [55]

In an effort to make sure that the masses understood the situation of the surrender clearly, the Japanese armed forces took out advertisements in the major newspapers notifying the population of how troops would be moved and how the locals should behave. One such advertisement, in the August 22 Tokyo metropolitan *Asahi* newspaper, alerted the people that the Japanese military was pulling out of Kanagawa prefecture for the arrival of the occupation forces. However, even after the "enemy arrives," as the paper stated, "the military police will be there protecting public security so there is no cause for worry." [56]

Along with interviews and reeducation campaigns for Japanese POWs, Japanese authorities targeted specific areas that were slated to have foreign troops in their midst. The police sent out orders to detail how the occupation would proceed. Proclamations urged Japanese locals not to make contact with the occupation soldiers on a one-to-one basis. It was assumed that communication would probably be tough at times, so the police encouraged local groups to find men who could speak some English. Women and children were told to take special precautions. "Women and girls should not wear any suggestive clothing, and do not expose your breasts in public under any circumstances," orders stipulated. An addendum at the end of the ordinance suggested that women abstain from showing their bare feet to any Chinese occupying forces. The ordinance also suggested women refrain from responding to calls of "Hello" or "Hi" from foreign military men. [57]

Japan's plans to rebuild the nation called for heeding the voice of the people, though as previous chapters have articulated, this function had not been absent during the war. As the following example makes clear, however, officials were also at times unclear about their new roles and how to execute the government's new orders. Post-surrender Japan was chaotic. No one was quite sure what was happening; nor was anyone sure of what was going to happen. All the hopes and dreams of imperial empire had evaporated in a quick moment following the emperor's recorded broadcast. Nowhere was this more apparent than in political actions following the surrender.

After the surrender, the new Prime Minister Higashikuni Naruhiko suggested that the government wanted to hear the voice of the people and listen to their grievances and concerns. Those interested should write to the prime minister, they were told, and the government would examine the matter. Isaji Yoshijirō, from Gifu prefecture, obviously took this proposal to heart. Basically illiterate, Isaji made what must have been a fairly arduous journey to Tokyo in order to voice his opinion directly to the prime minister concerning food shortages and other issues. On September 24 the police apprehended and arrested him because Isaji supposedly looked suspicious, loitering around the capital. Through his interrogation the police came to understand why he had come to Tokyo. The entire episode was written up and forwarded to Yamazaki Iwao, the minister for Home Affairs, and Okino Satoru, the governor of Gifu prefecture.[58]

Arrival of the Americans

Japanese feared, vilified, abhorred, liked, disliked, and loved Americans; they made them the object of a very ambiguous affection. Americans supposedly epitomized all that Japan had been fighting against, and yet the occupation proceeded fairly smoothly, at least according to many firsthand reports.[59] American motives were not merely altruistic regarding Japan. The US occupation was not vindictive because the US authorities believed that would be counterproductive. That Japan became an ally in the early Cold War hostilities between the United States and the Soviet Union and the United States and Communist China also ensured a relatively benign occupation.

The massive project of repatriation and reorientation of a wartime society left little to chance and thus required new organizations to keep track of where Japanese society was heading. A US military intelligence secret report for the period August 10–20, 1945, entitled "Japanese Propaganda Lines and Morale Tendencies," provides clear insight into how the Japanese and Americans planned for the occupation. The report began by pointing out that after the emperor's announcement to surrender the Japanese news agency, Dōmei,

> . . . lost no time in proclaiming to the world Japanese plans for post-war political stability and reconstruction. These plans and pronouncements were apparently designed to convince the world of Japan's ability to maintain order and live up to the surrender agreement. There was also talk of democratic reforms. It seems to us Japan seeks to avoid the impression that she is a defeated and prostrate nation, but rather to show that she is ready and able to take care of her own future.[60]

US military intelligence was aware that Tokyo had avoided the word "surrender." American intelligence groups analyzed why Japanese news emphasized that Japan "endured the unendurable," that "Japan fought a just war," and that "Japan's national polity remains intact" because "to save the nation the people must remain united and obey the emperor." The Japanese conducted these postwar rhetorical ploys to execute a form of postwar propaganda and assist the country in avoiding a total psychological breakdown in the face of utter defeat.[61]

General Headquarters and Japanese Propaganda

Just as the Japanese sought to calculate public opinion about the surrender and occupation, US occupying forces zeroed in on intelligence concerning how the Japanese public accepted its role as an occupied, defeated country. US military authorities wanted to make it clear that their goal was to "democratize, or rather teach democracy" to the Japanese, not to enslave them. To this end the Civil Information and Education (CIE) department was established. The United States had not prepared for the fact that the Japanese media would still be so healthy once the occupation began, so it needed to adapt quickly and absorb the domestic Japanese media under occupation guidelines to wrench it away from the continued influence of the Japanese government.[62] Japan was exhausted after the war but many of its domestic industries remained viable, virtually springing up from the ashes of defeat.

Although American occupation planners had several uses for the CIE, the division often acted as a postwar domestic propaganda unit within Japan. The CIE had actually begun as the US military's psychological warfare section, which then reformed itself to work with the civilian government in Japan. On September 22, along with a few other changes and addition of personnel, the military psychological operations reorganized and called itself the CIE department. It was later placed directly under SCAP authority in Japan. The CIE, which was composed of sections for research, operations, press and publications, radio, motion pictures, as well as schools and organizations, quickly appealed to Japanese media outlets and created its own media to implement a plan for postwar enlightenment propaganda activities within Japan.[63]

CIE's stated ideals were to educate Japanese so that the country could achieve the goals the occupation set out for it. To cover such broad ground CIE grew rapidly as an organization. Intelligence officers employed a variety of media strategies to show the Japanese public how the military had failed them and the Greater East Asian Co-prosperity Sphere had been misguided. The research and planning section of the CIE busied itself trying to figure out how best to promote this message to the Japanese. The CIE's policy was "defined so that the occupation forces do not take responsibility, but create a situation in which the Japanese can themselves undertake responsibility" for changing Japan.[64] The department felt it should remove the social and political barriers that had stymied the Japanese from enacting change and create conditions conducive for such behavior. CIE staff wished to encourage, but it would not explicitly replace, Japanese actions.

The CIE department aimed to spread information and education throughout Japan concerning democracy and how it functioned. The department also wished to establish groundwork for creating a free and viable publishing and newspaper industry in Japan—ostensibly so that the occupation General Headquarters (GHQ) could easily transmit its own messages to the Japanese public via a conduit other than the Japanese government. The CIE relegated to secondary importance the tasks of informing the Japanese about the causes of the war, their responsibility for it, and war crimes. CIE deemed social stability as a primary target and postmortems concerning the war did not appear to be a productive way to move forward.

The American occupiers realized they could not accomplish their goals unilaterally. They understood, for linguistic and sociological reasons, that they were impotent unless they gained Japanese assistance. For their part, the Japanese recognized the same held true for them. To become the dominant voice in the court of public opinion, the Japanese and Americans competed for statistical advantage. For the CIE, data about public opinion was crucial for postwar manipulation of the public, and to such an end they established a research and information division, later renamed the Public Opinion and Sociological Research Division. Both SCAP headquarters and the Japanese authorities continued to keep a check on the pulse of the people. Both sought to manipulate social attitudes through careful observation of popular trends, and this required sophisticated new public-opinion measuring devices.

The Japanese government did not want SCAP authorities to be the sole arbiter of public opinion, so they made efforts of their own to establish agencies to court the postwar Japanese population. Promulgation of Imperial Decree #503 created the Naikaku Chōsakyoku, or Cabinet Survey Bureau.[65] The newly created bureau hired 77 surveyors, for a total staff of 159. It soon dissolved, but the same day, December 24, 1945, a new public opinion survey agency opened, called the Naikaku Shingishitsu or Cabinet Investigation Office. This agency housed a public opinion survey section manned by a staff of eight. Tsukahara Matsurō headed the unit, with prewar propaganda theorist Koyama Eizō as an advisor. Two-thirds of the staff transferred directly from the Cabinet Board of Information, a pivotal Japanese agency among the wartime government's agencies for civilian propaganda. The public opinion section accepted its first mission between December 1945 and January 1946, when it analyzed 337 letters that Japanese citizens had sent to the authorities. From 1946 onward, the Cabinet Investigation Office planned to work with the Ministry for Demobilization (Fukuinshō) to conduct surveys of returning soldiers, but GHQ did not provide authorization.[66]

The various Japanese government agencies that analyzed letters to Japanese and GHQ officials began almost immediately after the surrender. A mere two weeks after defeat, on August 31, Prime Minister Higashikuni had called on the people of Japan to send letters to newspapers in order to voice their concerns. The Tokyo *Asahi* newspaper headline that day read, "It is permitted to write letters to the Prime Minister. The office wishes to hear directly the voice of the people."[67] At first letters only trickled in, but the numbers soon surged upwards of eight to nine hundred a day. However, the Japanese government was not unanimous in its approval of the prime minister's decision to loosen the reins on speech; many felt that such an outpouring of potential discontent could disrupt social stability.[68]

To establish the United States as the powerbroker who controlled the keys to Japan's future, American occupiers realized they had to compete with the Japanese and its new polling operations. SCAP's concern with public opinion seems logical, but the American decision to employ Japanese wartime propagandists, or to allow them to avoid being purged from government work, appears incongruous unless we understand the predicament Americans faced. What prompted the United States to hire the very individuals who only a few months before had produced invective against it?

It may have been the case that SCAP believed it had no choice in the matter but to hire wartime propagandists for American postwar occupation propaganda activities. On the eve of the surrender no element of Japan had been left untouched by the military, and when the Japanese surrendered they left a massive military presence in the lurch. Even at the end of the war the combined forces of the army and navy ran upwards of 7 million soldiers.[69] Of course military supplies, equipment, and rations were in tremendously short supply, and much of this materiel existed on paper only. By the summer of 1945, even though it still theoretically maintained large reserves, the Japanese military was essentially finished. To be sure, a lack of supplies, equipment, and rations rendered their ability to wage war virtually nil. But no one could estimate definitely what the psychological response was going to be. More serious, though, was the breakdown of internal military order. Japanese leaders, as well as the United States, worried whether the Japanese military could actually surrender and disarm. To avoid conflict before the US arrival, the Japanese authorities dispatched orders to begin disarming the troops on the home islands. Demobilizing soldiers abroad proved to be an even more enormous undertaking.[70]

It is important to remember that at the end of 1945 the number of Americans soldiers who could ably use the Japanese language was minuscule. The United States obviously needed to use the Japanese to occupy Japan. Even as the United States was demobilizing the country, GHQ sections were hunting for former Japanese military and police to assist them with the occupation and to assert Japan's role in the Cold War.

To maintain an efficient demobilization project the Allies placed many of the higher officers who had worked for the General Staff Headquarters in charge of the Japanese government departments that were responsible for military repatriation and demobilization. Gen. Charles Willoughby, the American in charge of G-2 (America's military intelligence bureau within the occupation government), hired former Japanese military men from the army to work on a Japanese military history project for the occupation. The project began in 1947 and continued until 1951 under the sponsorship of Captain Hattori Takushirō, the former chief of the anti-American wartime strategy section of the General Staff Headquarters. The Americans also employed numerous Japanese officers who had worked in Japanese intelligence against the Russians. (They operated similar efforts in Germany, gathering Nazis who could break and analyze Soviet codes.)[71] The Japanese anti-Russian group assisted the United States in its bid to deal with the Japanese Communist Party and its activities in what was considered the fragile state of postwar Japanese politics.[72]

The Allied authorities and occupied Japanese government competed for the attention and support of the Japanese public. SCAP may even have allowed the CIE department to persist as a department specifically as a buffer against Japanese obstruction of GHQ plans, or at least as an agency that could evaluate Japanese public opinion on its own. The Americans did not want to rely solely on the Japanese for statistics concerning the hearts and minds of the people.[73]

In a sense the occupation faced an enormous dilemma. To be effective the United States could implement only a fraction of its original plans. To operate efficiently in a totally foreign environment required unforeseen adjustments. GHQ and the Japanese government's reliance on wartime propagandists, such as public opinion surveyor Koyama Eizō and Yoneyama Keizō, emphasizes this dilemma. Postwar authorities often employed the same men who worked against the enemy prior to the surrender.

The appearance of professional propagandists like Koyama Eizō as central characters in postwar Japanese propaganda demonstrates that many of the social and political ideologies and agencies that led Japan to war also helped revive Japan after 1945. Both before and after the war Koyama was a prolific writer. During the war Koyama penned three important works on Japanese propaganda: *Theories on the Craft of Propaganda* (1937), *A Theory of Wartime*

Propaganda (1942), and *Propaganda War* (1943). Koyama also feverishly promoted wartime tourism. In 1938 he wrote "War and International Tourism Propaganda." Koyama claimed that tourists, unlike reporters and sketch artists for the newspapers, returned home to their own countries after their trips and transmit news about their destinations.[74] Koyama's intense interest regarding the influence of public opinion held true after the war as well. During the occupation he worked in the Public Opinion Department in the Cabinet Board of Information. In 1949 he became head of the National Public Opinion Investigation Institute, and in 1953 he returned to Rikkyō University as a professor.[75]

The fact that SCAP employed Koyama and did not purge him clearly underscores the fact that to fight the Cold War against the Soviet Union and build a Japan that would ally itself with America, occupation forces chose the path of least resistance. SCAP preferred professionals to thugs, and thus employed Japanese propagandists who months earlier had been writing tracts vilifying the west.

The Allied authorities who managed the occupation employed known wartime propagandists because these professionals were the only ones who had experience in polling Japanese public opinion. SCAP probably had ulterior motives in using Japanese wartime propagandists for occupation propaganda also because US occupation authorities believed these Japanese former propagandists could be counted on to take a paternal view of manipulating society for the common good. Occupation-era Japanese media research paralleled prewar Japanese government paternalism toward the general public, and "Koyama's role in developing opinion research in the Occupation period continued to be based on a strong sense of the relationship between public opinion and propaganda—now defined as 'opinion leadership.'"[76] In postwar Japan, both the American and Japanese authorities deemed "opinion leadership" to be of paramount importance, especially in light of the extreme economic dislocation most Japanese faced in the early years of the occupation.[77]

Koyama's role in developing supportive media that aided the government and the war, and his subsequent impact on postwar Japanese media studies, cannot be overstated. At one point a Japanese study group convened to publish his papers and a book on his work and life, but it failed to coalesce. One professor of Japanese history privately lamented that for a Japanese scholar to attempt a complete examination of Koyama would essentially be career suicide. His students and disciples hold powerful posts at top universities. To delve into the questions concerning the link between prewar media studies, wartime propaganda, and postwar media studies would be uncomfortable and unwelcomed by many.

American occupation officials hired another well-known, influential wartime professional propagandist, Yoneyama Keizō. Before the war Yoneyama had been a professor at Keiō University and during the war he authored many articles dealing with wartime propaganda.[78] After the war Yoneyama Keizō remained a professor at Keiō in the Newspaper Research Institute.[79] Extant records of his employment and salary history reveal that Yoneyama started work on January 4, 1949, as advisor to the public opinion and sociological research division of SCAP's CIE. Originally employed for a salary of approximately 9,000 yen a month, within a year requests placed to superiors augmented his salary to over 11,000 yen per month.[80]

This trend to allow and even recruit former Japanese propagandists into academia and government positions of authority may explain why, until recently, Japanese archives and research collections concerning the war were notoriously difficult to use. Yokomizo Mitsuteru, who had served as the first head of the Cabinet Information Bureau in 1940, as governor of Okayama prefecture, and later as the chief of the Health and Welfare Ministry's Social Bureau, actually worked as an advisor to the National Cabinet archives after the war.[81] The Japanese government was not interested in public declarations of investigating wartime responsibility or in divulging that the same bureaucrats who brought Japan to the edge of disaster continued in similar functionary roles after the surrender. Postwar Japan's immediate concern focused on reconstruction, and to do that both Japanese and Americans felt they needed expertise on social management, regardless of its origins.

Before, during, and after World War Two, groups that molded and shaped Japanese public opinion remained in positions of power. Prior to the surrender, the Special Higher Police and the military worked together to guarantee that Japan operated smoothly to avoid conflict with the occupiers. Immediately before and after the surrender, the Japanese authorities used the massive domestic police network to continue to manipulate the population, only this time the propaganda nudged the Japanese to embrace the Allies, not fight them. The same agencies involved—the Special Higher Police, and the Japanese military men who worked for the GHQ—were all part of the propaganda apparatus before the war.[82]

This continuity should come as no surprise. In order to manage society the Japanese government needed to employ the same men who worked on campaigns that had incited popular ire toward the west. The Allies were also complicit in the persistent use of wartime propagandists and their agencies to mold postwar Japanese public opinion. SCAP realized it had neither the manpower nor skills necessary to realign the Japanese population toward American goals. A successful occupation, SCAP believed, mandated the use of domestic Japanese propaganda professionals.

However, questions remain unanswered concerning the long-term impact of continuity, prewar to postwar. Only recently has contemporary Japanese scholarship on media studies begun to question its wartime roots, and slowly analyze the connections among the many stalwarts who led the field immediately after the war. As outlined through select examples in this chapter, the number of elite Japanese who remained in positions of influence in the media and tangential industries is thought-provoking. In some ways this continuity of leadership might help us understand the general reluctance of postwar Japanese authorities to come to terms with issues of wartime responsibility and the lack of desire to probe further into historical issues concerning the war.

Conclusion

We will fight until there is a lone leaf on a single tree standing on the burnt ground of Okinawa!
　　—Rear Admiral Ota Minoru

apanese wartime propaganda persisted because it evolved from multiple centers of production. The Cabinet Board of Information, the Ministry of Foreign Affairs, military propaganda platoons sent to the Chinese mainland, the Special Higher Police, private individuals, advertisers, comedians, publishers, and writers all worked to urge the nation to support the war. The aim of the propaganda was also multivocal. It championed a variety of messages to a diverse nation and empire, not simply blind devotion to the emperor. Japanese propaganda attempted to convince the Japanese that fighting for Japan meant fighting for modernity. Even when the heady Japanese propaganda abroad ultimately failed in its purpose, the message of Japan as organized, clean, and in pursuit of modernity struck a chord.

In the early years of the Japanese occupation of the Philippines, in 1942, one well-respected Japanese propagandist working for the military took to traveling around the countryside delivering fiery orations filled with allegory about Japan's mission in Asia. Another Japanese listening to both the speech and the translation burst out laughing and had to explain himself. It turned out the lofty presentation had not only gone over the translator's head, it had totally surpassed his ability in Japanese as well, so he had simply told another story in Tagalog about "when I went to Japan as a study-abroad student, this is what I saw."[1]

In Japan and often elsewhere, the vision that wartime propaganda frequently offered seemed appealing because it showed a modern Japan that symbolized healthy people, fast and timely trains, fine consumer products, extensive urban centers, and efficient government. This image of modernity was precisely what the Filipino translator had retained from his stay in Japan. These representations of modernity also made the propaganda resilient, and that is why wartime propaganda survived into the postwar era. In the same manner, postwar Japan remained a projection of what wartime propaganda had initially espoused—a modern, economically viable Asian nation offering itself as the model for the rest of the region. This idea of transwar continuity in politics, government, and economy is not new, but the assertion that the same propaganda agencies carried Japan through the war and the occupation is.[2]

In ways very different from the Nazi experience, Japanese wartime propaganda survived the war precisely because a small coterie of bureaucratic cronies did not dominate. Instead, a large and diffuse body of individuals created both the wartime and the postwar propaganda. Moreover, the process reinforced itself. Japanese propaganda convinced the authorities and the Japanese people that social stability necessitated good propaganda. Few Japanese viewed propaganda as a necessary evil, but rather defined it as a desirable tool for keeping society unified and on the track toward modernization. Even though Japan "swallowed defeat," voices in Japan's public sphere did not thereupon clamor for reduced propaganda efforts. Quite the contrary, bureaucrats and the population at large called for redoubled efforts since the war had dissolved so much of what, paradoxically, wartime propaganda had envisioned.

For men and for women as well, the war offered a place in the new society. Wartime Japanese society vigorously promoted the institution of marriage and clear identities for women in a mobilized society. Wartime women's magazines established roles for women that included producing future soldiers, providing additional labor in the war effort, and acting as cheerleaders to spur the society on from the home front.[3] This wartime society also considered "loose" women—those who engaged in illicit love affairs—not only as antiwar, but as threatening the fabric of Japanese society and thus disrupting the sensitive relationship between battlefront and home front.

Japanese wartime propaganda also endured during the occupation because of the broad social consensus surrounding its implementation. Obviously, the goals of the Japanese state changed after the war, but the mechanisms for influencing such decisions remained constant. Even the individuals who espoused these goals remained the same. Comedians who had performed during the war often later headed various performers' associations. Both the Japanese and the Americans considered it imperative for the police to maintain social order, but they differed on which path to follow. In the end, "the confusion characterizing the relationship between SCAP and Japanese government officials was complemented by an ambivalent reform program that demanded radical change on one hand and a stable sociopolitical environment on the other."[4] Immediately after the war no one knew what was going to occur. SCAP felt that the police would be absolutely necessary in maintaining public order.

Advertising and media professionals, whose images of Japan postwar domestic audiences avidly consumed, were the same media technicians who had created wartime visions of Japanese modernity and leadership for Asia. These were not a band of misfits or outcasts. Quite the contrary, these professional propagandists often represented the best and brightest Japan had to offer.

Notwithstanding this continued propaganda and its impact, attitudes concerning Japanese wartime propaganda are colored by Japan's defeat. For many years the defeat itself impeded the inclusion of Japanese wartime propaganda as a topic worthy of academic inquiry. The Tokyo War Crimes Trial made the Japanese military, not Japanese civil society, appear responsible for the war, and because of this, discussions concerning Japanese wartime propaganda failed to develop in the early years of the occupation. No broad social movement developed to probe the painful issues relating to the near-universal social responsibility for Japanese expansion and the war. In fact, as Norma Field and Ian Buruma have demonstrated, national discussions concerning popular support for the war remain deeply contested in postwar Japanese society even to this day.[5]

This practiced historical amnesia concerning the roots of Japan's Fifteen-Year War, apparent within days of the surrender, helped Japanese society in its postwar efforts to rebuild quickly and retain the notion that the national polity had not been compromised. However, rebuilding quickly and under the American defense umbrella required utilizing the same propaganda methods and agencies that had led the country to ruin in the first place. If responsibility for the destructive war were laid on the propagandists' shoulders, however, it would be nearly impossible to mobilize the country for redevelopment. Japanese society did not have the time, inclination, or liberty to pursue a penetrating inquiry into the structural collusion that had supported Japan's wartime activities, with its extensive cast of advertisers, media professors, entertainers, Special Higher Police officers, and others who had aided in its construction.

Postwar Japanese opinion as to why Japan was defeated often masks this transwar continuity and thus the success of the wartime propaganda machine. Wartime patriot and political powerbroker Ishihara Hiroichirō offered such an opinion. In Ishihara's eyes, technology did not fail Japan. Ishihara believed Japan's spirit failed Japan. Japan's propaganda failed to mobilize society adequately, Ishihara pronounced, because the propaganda never struck a deep enough chord with the Japanese public. During the Russo-Japanese war, Ishihara wrote, Japan had outlined clear goals for itself, while the stated goals of the Greater East Asia War never managed to align themselves directly with the lives of Japanese individuals. Ishihara concluded that Japan's wartime propaganda did not imbue the population with the spirit needed to fight to the death.

To rally the fighting spirit of the nation the government had its National Spiritual Mobilization Campaign, its slogans, leaflets, whistles and drums, all making a commotion. But the people never developed an enthusiasm, and within a short time these movements all vanished from the stage. After that, followed national reorganization and the situation shifted to the Imperial Rule Assistance Association, organizations for village associations, ordering the people to wear patriotic dress, telling women to wear cotton trousers, focusing on style only but never putting real spirit into the propaganda. This was the method the government and military used, they became obsessed with theory and form . . . but society is an organic structure and does not follow logic, it reflects nature. This is why the population failed to put its backbone into the war. The nation was dragged along by the military and government and merely went through the motions to make the best of the situation.[6]

Ishihara himself helped initiate the trend of blaming the failure of the war, not on the misguided goals of the war, but on the military and government propaganda that, he claimed, failed to ignite Japanese support. Ishihara's own personal failure to come to terms with defeat perhaps forced him to take such a stand.

Prime Minister Suzuki Kantarō clearly disagreed with Ishihara's assessment of Japan's defeat. In his August 1945 broadcast when he stepped down as prime minister after Japan's defeat, Suzuki declared that Japan lost the war because the west was scientifically more advanced. Suzuki held obvious motives in asserting this view. While his logic differed from Ishihara's, Suzuki wanted the Japanese public to remain hopeful. Both Suzuki and Ishihara assiduously avoided talking about direct causes of the war, or its aims.

The two men's discussions of the war distort the actual picture of wartime propaganda because both fall into the same trap. They judged wartime propaganda solely on the basis of its failing to produce military success. This one-sided approach ignores the entire social side of the mobilization. Militaries demobilize, but societies do not. Societies retain an elastic memory that lingers long after the barracks have been torn down. Japanese wartime propaganda crossed many boundaries into a variety of social spheres. Wartime Japanese propaganda permitted a very small nation, situated on the periphery of the Pacific Ocean, to threaten a western hegemony, disrupt Asia, dislocate millions, and destroy millions more. These are not facts that can be ignored, and neither can the propaganda that inspired a society to bring them about. Consequently, an examination of wartime propaganda must go beyond the military and analyze its relation to the society as a whole. Examined in this manner, Japanese wartime propaganda does not appear to merit the judgment of "failure" it originally received. In contrast, were we to judge America on the basis of its propaganda aimed at the Japanese soldiers and not for its military victories, it would appear to have been a total failure since the propaganda rarely persuaded Japanese soldiers to surrender.

As other historians have demonstrated, racism played a key role in the friction between Japan and the rest of the world, including China, but racism was not the main thrust of wartime Japanese propaganda. Had it been, how could the Japanese have switched so quickly to embracing America? Racism may have been a factor, but the pursuit of modernity and empire was the greater inspiration. During the war this desire to be modern aided in Japan's quest to build an empire in opposition to the west. In the postwar era, Japan embraced the United States not because America had suddenly shed its racist attitudes (or the Japanese shed theirs), but because the United States now offered Japan the best opportunity to recreate its modern world. Suzuki Kantarō said as much in his first postwar speech, and Japan's preparation for defeat and propaganda agencies pushed this new objective. Accepting American culture became an element of postwar Japanese propaganda, as can be seen in the guide to US characteristics mentioned in Chapter Six, but the greater goal was still to rebuild Japan, using America merely was the method.

As much as attitudes toward America changed due to postwar necessity and the surrender, even after the war Japanese society continued strong-arm tactics with Asian victims of its wartime policies, perhaps reflecting that many elements of wartime propaganda had never been eliminated. A most egregious example of this concerned Liu Lianren, a Chinese dragooned as a laborer in the Shandong province of China and brought to Japan in 1944. Liu fled cruel and dangerous conditions working in a Japanese mine, escaped to a remote area of Japan's northernmost island of Hokkaido, and hid, never knowing that the war had ended. Villagers finally discovered him in February 1958. By that time not only was the war over, but Kishi Nobusuke had also become prime minister. During the war Kishi had served in a number of high-level positions dealing with industrializing Manchukuo and maintaining Japan's armaments. The occupation government initially charged Kishi as a war criminal but eventually dropped the charges. Not one to be sentimental about Japan's wartime excesses, and obviously feeling no remorse over Japan's atrocities during the war, Kishi summarily had Liu deported as an alien illegally residing in the country. The Japanese government offered no apology or restitution.[7]

Postwar Japan also mirrored wartime Japan in the government's appeal to social management. As the occupation progressed, the Japanese government continued, as it had in the prewar era, to guide public opinion. It is interesting to note that just as before the war only the Communists continued to voice opposition toward these efforts at social mobilization. Nosaka Sanzō, eager to realign Japan after his reelection to the Diet in 1949, plagued the government with his concerns over such guidance. On November 7, 1949, in an open Diet session, Nosaka pointedly asked the prime minister's office what the Ministry of Foreign Affairs was doing sending people from its offices around the country delivering lectures on "international affairs." Nosaka implied that this action resembled prewar policies where the ministry played a role in propaganda campaigns. Nosaka wanted to know who was paying, how much the overall budget was, when and where the talks were held, and who was directly responsible for the program. The prime minister's office responded in a manner that reflected its prewar and wartime attitude toward social management, saying that the talks themselves had not been planned by the Ministry of Foreign Affairs but were, in fact, provided in response to local requests. The prime minister's office elaborated this point, stating, "the dissemination of knowledge concerning international affairs . . . should be one of the major duties of the Ministry of Foreign Affairs." Over a ten-month period the ministry had sponsored 1,248 lectures in 1,215 different locales around the country.[8] Nosaka never received a direct answer to his queries, but his questions demonstrate the extent to which the postwar Japanese government continued actively to guide public opinion, just as it had in the prewar and wartime eras.

Japan's dependence on professional social management policies to guide society is indicative of a larger process at work before and after the war. The wartime elite who worked on Japan's propaganda programs were hired because they were skilled professionals and defeat did not lessen Japan's dependence on their abilities. Former military officials, many of whom also worked directly for the agencies involved in wartime propaganda, remained in positions of executive power in postwar Japan. Fujiwara Iwaichi, head of the Fujiwara propaganda platoon that had helped wartime and postwar activities in Indonesia leading to independence from Holland, later became director of a branch of the Self Defense Forces School. Kawabe Torashirō and Omae Toshikazu played key roles in assisting US occupation forces manage Japan. Kawabe was a lieutenant general in the imperial army and a deputy chief on the general staff by the end of the war. Omae was a captain in the imperial navy and also worked closely with occupation leadership. In the days soon after Japan's defeat, Kawabe and Omae had traveled to Manila to iron out details concerning the Americans' arrival and how the occupation would proceed. Arisue Seizō, a former general and onetime chief of the General Staff Headquarter's overseas propaganda section—he was also responsible for creating Bunka Camp, the POW unit charged with broadcasting Japanese radio propaganda—became a key interlocutor between Japanese authorities and American occupiers. At one point during the war, Arisue had also headed the Nakano school, the institute at which Onoda Hirō and Yokoi Shōichi trained before tramping off to the jungles of Southeast Asia to fight for thirty years.[9] At the end of August 1945, the general had been part of the first Japanese military contingent that met US forces at Atsugi Airfield when American troops landed in the first days of the occupation. It is no coincidence that such men as Arisue, Fujiwara, Kawabe, and Omae were continually active in areas where social management and propaganda guided wartime and postwar Japanese society. Japanese society valued these men's skills during the war, and after the war the need for their professional expertise did not diminish.[10]

Perhaps it was historically naïve to pretend that Japan had changed overnight. After all, Japan had a long history of social mobilization. In a collection of postwar reminiscences about the history of the Home Ministry, one elderly bureaucrat recalled that during the prewar era, often before roads were paved, the ministry made sure police telephone lines had been strung. Even in remote areas, where transportation might be backward, the police kept track of the pulse of the nation.[11] Propaganda helped unite Japan in its bid to modernize in the prewar era, and the importance of such activity did not fade after the surrender. Japan lost the war, but through determination and careful application of propaganda it did not lose the nation.

Notes

Propaganda for Everyone

1. For all of the lyrics, see Komota et al., eds., *Shinpan nihon ryūkōkashi (chūkan)*, p. 113. "Shanhai dayori" is a 1938 song with a catchy tune harking back, Yazawa Kan says, to the trumpet melodies used in songs from the Russo-Japanese war. This similarity made it popular within Japan and throughout the rest of the empire; Yazawa, *Sensō to ryūkōka*, pp. 75–76.

2. Komota et al., *Shinpan nihon ryūkōkashi (chūkan)*, p. 146.

3. The lyrics can be read and the song can be heard online at http://www.d1.dion .ne.jp/~j_kihira/band/midi/daitoa_ke.html.

4. I have personally heard Senryū's routine live several times, and it is also available in recorded form on the CD *Kokon tōzai hanashika shinshiroku*, produced by the APP company. I am indebted to Okamoto Kōichi for providing me with a recording. In Japanese this rarely recorded routine is called *Gākon*. Senryū performs the routine tongue in cheek. His ability to recall the myriad songs from this era and joke about them makes the routine amusing. He is by no means a right-wing comedian.

5. Kobayashi Yoshinori, *Discourse on the War* (Shin gomanizumu sengen Special sensōron), *Discourse on the War II* (Shin gomanizumu sengen Special sensōron 2), *Discourse on the War III* (Shin gomanizumu sengen Special sensōron 3), *Discourse on Taiwan* (Shin gomanizumu sengen Special Taiwanron). For some of the debate he has stimulated, see Kobayashi and King, *Nyūkoku kyohi [Taiwanron] wa naze yakareta ka*.

6. Welch, *The Third Reich*, p. 2. Welch states that he examines the propaganda of the Nazis to "explain the popular base of National Socialism and its ability to sustain a consensus (of sorts) over a twelve-year period."

7. Cunningham, *The Idea of Propaganda*, p. 4

8. Jowett and O'Donnell, *Propaganda and Persuasion*, p. 16

9. Minami, *Shakai ishiki to rekishi ishiki*, p. 385.

10. Ibid., p. 398.

11. Kashiwagi Hiroshi, "Senji senden no modanizumu," *Geijutsuronchō* (December 1989): 38.

12. In his book *The Pacific War*, p. 208, historian Ienaga Saburō notes that "there was almost no organized illegal resistance in Japan" during the war. Japan did face extensive racism abroad, however, as the various US exclusion acts demonstrate. Many Japanese may have chosen to stay at home, rather than try to assimilate in a hostile foreign environment.

13. Welch, *Propaganda and the German Cinema*, pp. 34–35.

14. Nicholas Cull discusses the American view of propaganda in the introduction to *Selling War*. Gerd Horton, in *Radio Goes to War*, p. 16, points out that Americans were reluctant to accept propaganda because they felt it had dragged them into World War One. Brett Gary, *Nervous Liberals*, p. 9, states that in the United States, "propaganda came to be understood exclusively as a technique for the dissemination of anti-democratic ideas." See also two books by Doob, *Propaganda* and *Public Opinion and Propaganda*. Rossingnol, *Histoire de la propagande en France de 1940 a 1944*.

15. There are some notable exceptions. See Dower, *War Without Mercy* and *Japan in War and Peace*; Havens, *Valley of Darkness*; Young, *Japan's Total Empire*; Garon, *Molding Japanese Minds*; Shillony, *Politics and Culture in Wartime Japan*. Except for Dower, few of these studies focus specifically on Japanese propaganda. See also Rei Okamoto, "Pictorial propaganda in Japanese comic art, 1941–1945."

16. The Chinese and Japanese sources are too numerous to list here but representative of the Japanese interest in domestic wartime propaganda studies is Akazawa, Awaya, et al., eds., *Sensōka no senden to bunka*.

17. So diverse and demanding was wartime Japanese propaganda that it forced the Japanese to think about themselves in ways they never had; this included the Japanese language. Within the empire it began to be necessary for Japan to have a coherent, across-the-board policy regarding the teaching of Japanese to nonnatives. This debate caused an even greater flurry within intellectual circles regarding what type of Japanese to teach, and what constituted proper Japanese. For more on these debates that touched on the core of how Japan wished to present its civilization abroad, see Shi, *Shokuminchi shihai to nihongo (zōhoban)* and Kawamura, *Umi o watatta nihongo*.

18. This racial hierarchy was spelled out most clearly in the Ministry of Health and Welfare's population policy program, originally published in 1942. Kōseishō kenkyūbu jinkō minzokubu, ed., *Minzoku jinkō seisaku kenkyū shiryō*.

19. Kanda Kōichi, *Shisōsen to senden;* Koyama, *Senden gijutsuron,* and *Senji sendenron;* Muneo, *Shisōsen;* Yoneyama, *Shisō tōsō to senden.*

20. Extended explanations of slogans can be found in Ozarasha Publishing Company, ed., *Senjika hyōgoshū;* Mikuni, *Senchū yōgoshū;* and *Daitōa kyōdō sengen.* See also Lone, *Japan's First Modern War;* Ōtani, "'Shinbun sōjū' kara 'taigai senden' e."

21. Cook and Cook, *Japan at War*, p. 16. See also Ohnuki-Thierney, *Kamikaze, Cherry Blossoms and Nationalisms,* for a discussion of the diverse reasons kamikaze pilots joined the war effort; and Aramata, *Kessenka no yūtopia.* For details on the emperor's wartime life, see Bix, *Hirohito and the Making of Modern Japan;* Fujiwara Akira and Awaya, eds. *Tettei kenshō shōwa tennō (dokuhakuroku);* and Large, *Emperor Hirohito and Showa Japan.*

22. Paxton is a historian who can be credited with almost single-handedly urging the French to reexamine their own attitudes and concepts of national history through their recollection of the war; see his *Vichy France.*

23. Both Edward Drea, *In the Service of the Emperor,* and Michael Barnhart, *Japan Prepares for Total War,* detail the lacunae in histories of Japanese military and intelligence policies. Hori Eizō also outlines military failings in his book on the same topic,

Daihonei sanbō no jōhōsenki pp. 273–274. Hori believed that the US military accurately reported on the main reasons why Japanese intelligence lost the war for Japan: the Japanese underestimated the national strength of opposing forces, lost air power superiority, failed to organize properly, disregarded the importance of informed intelligence data, and placed exaggerated emphasis on the Japanese spirit.

24. See Lebra, *Jungle Alliance and Japanese-trained Armies in Southeast Asia;* also see Ba Maw, *Breakthrough in Burma* and Fujiwara Iwaichi, *F. kikan.*

25. This notion is somewhat accurate but fails to take into account the degree of support for Japan among Black Americans, at least until the start of the Pacific War. See Satō and Kushner, "'Negro Propaganda Operations,'" pp. 5–26. Also see Allen, "Waiting for Tojo."

26. Don Brown Collection, B-17–12–62, "Shinri bira." Located in the Yokohama Kaikō Shiryōkan, Yokohama, Japan. The leaflet was directed toward Allied soldiers in Southeast Asia and Australia.

27. As quoted in Argall, *My Life with the Enemy,* pp. 164–165.

28. Kaplan and Dubro's *Yakuza* supports this stereotype. There may be more truth in Kaplan's other assertion that the CIA used film in postwar Japan to orient Japan toward America's Cold War policy. See also Kaplan, "U.S. Propaganda Efforts in Postwar Japan," on the website http://www.jpri.org/publications/critiques/critique_IV_1 .html; and Richard Storry, *The Double Patriots.*

29. Jansen uncovers this relation in *The Japanese and Sun Yat-Sen.*

30. Awaya and Yoshida, eds., *Kokusai kensatsu kyoku (IPS) jinmon chōsho,* vol. 8, pp. 397–497. Doihara, a leading military member of the Special Forces in China, operated many campaigns to bring the Chinese to the Japanese side. However, to extrapolate that he was therefore central to the Black Dragon Society seems unreasonable.

31. Okamoto, *Impressions of the Front.* Recent scholarship suggests that Japanese government propaganda efforts may have begun even earlier, with Japan's punitive expedition to Taiwan in 1874. See Eskildsen, "Of Civilization and Savages."

32. Swinton, *In Battle's Light.*

33. Keene, *Emperor of Japan,* p. 493.

34. Yui Masanomi, "Joron: Sōdōin taisei no kakuritsu to hōkai," in Kano and Yui, eds., *Kindai nihon no tōgō to teikō,* vol. 4, p. 12.

35. Akira Iriye details the boundaries of this clash of cultures in *Power and Culture* and *The Origins of the Second World War in Asia and the Pacific.* See also Iriye and Cohen, eds., *American, Chinese, and Japanese Perspectives on Wartime Asia.*

36. Muneo, *Shisōsen,* pp. 10–11. Satō Takumi, "The System of Total War."

Chapter 1: Master Propagandists and Their Craft

1. "Kokumin wa kō omou," *Bungei shunjū* (January 1940): 151–161. For more polls of the public, see Yoshida and Yoshimi, eds. *Shiryō nihon gendaishi 10, Nicchū sensōki no kokumin sōdō 1.*

2. A full discussion of the intersection between propaganda and product promotion can be seen in Gao Yuan's work on Japanese tourism in Manchukuo. Gao Yuan,

"[Futatsu no kindai] no konseki" and "[Rakudo] o hashiru kankō basu." For resources on Dōmei, see Purdy, "The Ears and Voice of the Nation."

3. Some of the numerous reports include: Allied Translator and Interpreter Section South West Pacific Area, "Control by Rumor in the Japanese Armed Forces," April 20, 1945. Ibid., "Prominent Factors in Japanese Military Psychology," Feb. 7, 1945. Ibid., "Defects Arising from the Doctrine of 'Spiritual Superiority' as Factors in Japanese Military Psychology," Oct. 10, 1945. Ibid., "Hokō: The Spy-Hostage System of Group Control—the Clue to Japanese Psychology," April 26, 1945. Ibid., "Japanese Reactions to Allied Leaflets," Dec. 1, 1945. All these documents are in the Kensei shiryō room of the National Diet Library, Tokyo, Japan. Although many studies missed the mark, the tremendous breadth of US analyses of Japanese propaganda was stupendous, all the more so in the face of the extreme lack of qualified linguists at the outset of the war. One difficulty with wartime US sources is their tendency to judge US propaganda as being more effective than it was against the Japanese. Even though scant evidence attests to the effectiveness of US propaganda against the Japanese military, a belief still persists that US propaganda helped "turn" Japanese soldiers.

4. Shimada and Tsuganesawa, eds., *Puresuaruto*. This collection is a complete reprint of the original run of the magazine.

5. Yoshimi Yoshiaki, *Kusa no ne no fashizumu*.

6. Garon, *Molding Japanese Minds*, p. 6. In "Abortion Before Birth Control," Christine Norgren follows a similar debate in Japan that examines how social groups mediate state policy.

7. Garon, *Molding Japanese Minds*, p. 7

8. Yui Masanomi, "Joron," pp. 11–12.

9. Nagahama, *Kokumin seishin sōdōin no shisō to kōzō*, pp. 18–20.

10. This is clearly stated in Messinger, *British Propaganda*, and Taylor, *British Propaganda*.

11. Early Japanese efforts in propaganda are keenly described in Ōtani, *Kindai nihon no taigai senden*; Ōtani's volume edited with Hara, *Nisshin sensō no shakaishi: [bunmei sensō] to minshū*; and Valliant, "The Selling of Japan."

12. Hasegawa, "Senden no nihonteki seikaku." Yoshida Saburō voiced a similar critique of Japanese propaganda methods in "Bunkasen no kiso."

13. Shibuya, *Showa kōkoku shōgenshi*, p. 181.

14. Newman, *Goodbye Japan*, p. 120.

15. Iritani, *Nihonjin no shūdan shinri*. The quote is taken from the English version, *Group Psychology of the Japanese People in Wartime*, p. 26.

16. Iritani, *Group Psychology of the Japanese People in Wartime*, p. 60.

17. Kato, *The Lost War*.

18. Ariyama, "Senji taisei to kokuminka," pp. 1–36.

19. Ellul, *Propaganda*, p. 25.

20. Naikaku, ed., *Shisōsen tenrankai kiroku zukan*, p. 1. This quote is taken from the Home Ministry's published version of Yokomizo's talk, which was broadcast originally from Tokyo on February 8, 1938. Naiseishi, ed., *Yokomizo Mitsuteru shi danwa sokkiroku (ge)*.

21. Naiseishi, ed., *Arai Zentarōshi danwa sokkiroku,* Interview number 14, p. 152.

22. Tsuganesawa and Satō, eds., *Naikaku jōhōbu jōhōsenden kenkyū shiryō,* vol. 8, p. 384. *Nanjing* was the second part of a popular documentary-style trilogy produced between movies on Shanghai and Beijing. As Mark Nornes notes in *Japanese Documentary Film,* p. 151, the movie *Nanjing* showed the city falling into Japanese hands, but the "camera remains far away from the actual fighting, and many of the scenes appear to have been staged." On p. 112, Nornes also notes that cameramen recorded in their diaries that they heard and saw the Japanese military looting and pillaging but did not include such footage in the final, distributed version of the film. Most Japanese enjoyed the film, as did important members of the intelligentsia like film critic Tsumura Hideo. In *Teikoku no ginmaku,* p. 92, Peter High states that Tsumura, a well-known film critic, praised the film and felt that it represented Japan's true aims in Asia, for it contained, among other things, scenes of Japanese military doctors treating wounded Chinese. See also Nornes and Fukushima, eds. *Media Wars Then and Now.*

23. Tsuganesawa and Satō, eds., *Naikaku jōhōbu jōhōsenden kenkyū shiryō,* vol. 8, p. 385.

24. Ibid., p. 401.

25. Kido Nikki Kenkyūkai, ed., *Kido Kōichi kankei monjo,* p. 186. Cited from the reproduced document January 10, 1935, "Tainai kokusaku yōkōan ni kansuru kenkyūan (chōsahan)."

26. *Senzen no jōhō kikō yōran,* p. 73.

27. Ibid., p. 317.

28. Nanba, *Uchiteshi yamamu taiheiyō sensō to kōkoku no gijutsushatachi,* p. 55.

29. Nagahama, *Kokumin seishin sōdōin no shisō to kōzō,* p. 64.

30. Akazawa, Kitagawa, and Yui, eds., *Shiryō nihon gendaishi,* vol. 12, *Taiseiyokusankai.* See the documents numbered 130 and 131, pp. 406–409.

31. Ibid. See document number 136, "Daisanjūyongō." The letters were received after a January 18th lecture called "Taigai mondai kōenkai no hankyō," p. 420.

32. Ibid. See document number 138, "Sankō jōhō dai yonjūyon."

33. Taiseiyokusankai, *Yokusan seijikai shiryō, kokumin seikatsu kankei.* See "Chōnaikai, tonarigumi no seibi kyōka ni kansuru chōsa," a document from 1943 that provides details on the inner workings of these groups.

34. Ibid. See the document (marked secret) from January 1943, "Shunpō seikatsu no tettei to sono gutaiteki hōsaku ni kansuru chōsa hōkoku fushoku sankōsho," p. 50.

35. *Senzen no jōhō kikō yōran,* p. 147

36. *Kokumin engeki* (June 1941): first page.

37. Matsuhara, "Nōmin to kokumin engeki," p. 130.

38. Ibid, p. 137.

39. Awaya and Kawashima, eds., *Haisenji zenkoku chian jōhō,* p. 10. The Japanese expression is *"kuchi de yokusan, kokoro wa yokusan,"* which loosely translates as "supporting with your mouth, but plotting with your heart." In Japanese the IRAA is pronounced "taiseiyokusankai." The play on words is with "yokusan," which, depending on the characters used, can mean support or plotting.

40. Research on Koyama is fragmentary; no thorough biography exists. Two arti-

cles that cover the long span of his life and work are Miura, "Koyama Eizō no kōhō ikōru PR seisaku ni tsuite" and Iwai, "Koyama Eizō no yoron kenkyūshi ni tsuite."

41. Satō, "Senjika nihon no senden kenkyū."

42. Morris-Suzuki, "Ethnic Engineering." See chapter 10 in Dower, *War without Mercy,* for a detailed discussion behind the discovery of these documents and the impact.

43. Koyama, *Senden gijutsuron,* p. 132.

44. Ibid., pp. 132–133.

45. Koyama, *Senji sendenron,* pp. 4–5.

46. Ibid., p. 2, in the English article at the back of the book.

47. One wonders if Koyama was trying to respond to Lasker and Roman, *Propaganda from China and Japan.*

48. *Kokusai kankō* (October 1938): opening leaf.

49. Koyama, "Kankō seisaku to minzoku ninshiki."

50. *Kokusai kankō* (April 1939): 96.

51. Koyama, "Shōseiken no bunka senden seisaku."

52. Koyama, *Daitōa sensō to chūgoku minshū no dōkō,* p. 133.

53. Tsurumi, "Dainihon no kōryū ni tsuite kokumin ni utau," p. 207. For more on the complex relations between intellectuals and the war, see Barshay, *State and Intellectual in Imperial Japan* and Fletcher, *The Search for a New Order.*

54. Kitaoka, ed., *Yūjō no hito Tsurumi Yūsuke sensei,* p. 201.

55. Fogel, *The Literature of Travel,* p. 170.

56. "Taibei kankō senden dashin," *Kokusai kankō* (October 1, 1939): 21. Issues of the wartime tourist magazines and papers can be found in the Tokyo Shisei Chōsakai Shisei Senmon Toshokan, Tokyo, Japan (Tokyo Institute for Municipal Research Special Library).

57. Kitaoka, ed., *Yūjō no hito Tsurumi Yūsuke sensei,* p. 202.

58. Dower, *Empire and Aftermath.*

59. As quoted in Kitaoka, ed., *Yūjō no hito Tsurumi Yūsuke sensei,* p. 205.

60. There were numerous firsthand reports and diaries published during the war that spoke about these activities and informed the public. See Koba, *Rikusentai senbuki;* Shimazaki, *Senbuhan;* Kagawa, *Hokushi senbukō;* Nakano, "Senbuhan Kara." See also Kawayase Fuhō, *Senbukō.*

61. *Kokusai kankō* (January 1938): 62. These same pamphlets were translated into other languages like Arabic and Malay to be used as propaganda in Southeast Asia. For images, see Osaka Mainichi Company, *Japan Today and Tomorrow.*

62. For an excerpt of the declaration and an article on it published in English, see Nagasaka, "New Information Chief Amau." This is reprinted in Amō Eiji's diaries, see Amō Eiji nikki shiryōshū kankōkai ed., *Amō Eiji nikki shiryōshū dai yonkan,* pp. 692–698.

63. The Chinese remembered Amō's declaration concerning Japan's Monroe Doctrine in the Far East. In 1940 the calls for improved Chinese propaganda and social mobilization still dredged up his name and his proclamations as despised examples of

Japanese imperial designs on the Chinese nation. See Wenhua gongyingshe, ed., *Kangzhan jianguo shouce*, p. 657.

64. K.2.1.0(6) *Naigai ryokō annai zakken*, document number 63, November 20, 1934, letter from JTB jimuriji Takahisa Jinnosuke to Amō Eiji. Located in the Gaikōshiryōkan, Tokyo.

65. K.2.1.0(6) *Naigai ryokō annai zakken*, unnumbered and undated document by Amō Eiji "Kokusai kankō kokuei goshūnen ni tsuite." Located in the Gaikōshiryōkan, Tokyo.

66. K.2.1.0(5–2) *Gaikokujin torai kankei zakken, gaikokujin yūin oyobi dōyō kikan kankei*, "Kokusai daigorakujo kensetsu shuisho." Located in the Gaikōshiryōkan, Tokyo.

67. *Asahi shimbun* (Tokyo edition), April 4, 1935 (S. 5.4.10), located in file, *Gaikokujin torai kankei zakken, gaikokujin yūin oyobi dōyō kikan kankei*, Shōwa, 3.7–5.12, vol, K.2.1.0 (5–2). Located in the Gaikōshiryōkan, Tokyo.

68. A.1.1.0(30–2) *Shina jihen ikken, yoron narabi shinbun ronchō*, September 1938 document, "Shina jihen ni okeru jōhō senden kōsaku gaiyō, p. 104. Located in the Gaikōshiryōkan, Tokyo.

69. A.1.1.0(30–2) *Shina jihen ikken, yoron narabi shinbun ronchō*, "Shina jihen ni okeru jōhō senden kōsaku gaiyō," pp. 116–120. Located in the Gaikōshiryōkan, Tokyo.

70. A.1.1.0(30–2) *Shina jihen ikken, yoron narabi shinbun ronchō*, "Shina jihen ni okeru jōhō senden kōsaku gaiyō," p. 9. Located in the Gaikōshiryōkan, Tokyo.

71. Kajimoto, "Online Documentary."

72. Williams, *Behind the News in China*, forward.

73. Kajimoto, "Online Documentary," p. 63.

74. Ibid., p. 66.

75. A.3.5.0(2–1) *Gaikoku shinbun kisha tsūshinin kankei zakken, beikokujin no bu, daiyonkan*, S-W, "Uinsento," folder, memo from December 12, 1932, Portland Consulate Nakamura Toyoichi. Located in the Gaikōshiryōkan, Tokyo.

76. A.3.5.0(2–1) *Gaikoku shinbun kisha tsūshinin kankei zakken, beikokujin no bu, daiyonkan*, S-W, "Uinsento," folder, memo from January 19, 1933, Arita to Kubota. Located in the Gaikōshiryōkan, Tokyo.

77. A.3.5.0(2–1) *Gaikoku shinbun kisha tsūshinin kankei zakken, beikokujin no bu, daiyonkan*, S-W, "Furederikku Uiriamu," folder, May 9, 1938 telegram from Ambassador Ueda in Xinjing, Manchukuo, to Minister of Foreign Affairs Hirota. Located in the Gaikōshiryōkan, Tokyo.

78. A.3.5.0(2–1) *Gaikoku shinbun kisha tsūshinin kankei zakken, beikokujin no bu, daiyonkan*, S-W, "Furederikku Uiriamu," folder, top-secret cable from Consul Satō in San Francisco to Foreign Affairs Minister Matsuoka on September 12, 1940. Located in the Gaikōshiryōkan, Tokyo.

79. Kajimoto, "Online Documentary," p. 66.

80. M.2.3.0(1) *Ryōjikaigi kankei zakken, January 1936–1937*. Located in the Gaikōshiryōkan, Tokyo.

81. "Jihenka no kokusai kankō jigyō o kataru zadankai," *Kokusai kankō* (October

1938): 36–52. Suzuki later became chief editor of the Japanese version of *Reader's Digest* during the US occupation.

82. For more on Takarazuka, leisure, and the war, see Jennifer Robertson's chapter on wartime leisure in Linhart and Fruhstuck, eds., *The Culture of Japan*. Also see Robertson, *Takarazuka*.

83. "Bunka to shite no kankō senden o kataru zadankai," *Kokusai kankō* (July 1939): 42–55.

84. Kawamura, *Manshūtetsudō maboroshi ryokō;* Ishizuka and Narita, *Tokyoto no hyakunen.*

85. For more on Manchukuo and urban planning, see Koshizawa, *Manshūkoku no shuto keikaku.*

86. *Kigen nisen roppyaku nen*, p. 850. Reference number [2a 37–4 ki1]. Located in the Kokuritsu Kobunshokan, Tokyo.

87. The early architect of imperial policy on Taiwan and Manchuria, Gotō Shimpei, promoted the railroads in such a manner. See Yoshihisa, "The Making of Japanese Manchuria," pp. 181–185. Yamagata Aritomo, founder of the modern armed forces in Japan, also developed a keen interest in linking all of Asia through rail travel as part of Japan's imperial project. Yamagata did not, of course, envision an underground tunnel to do so. See Duus, *The Abacus and the Sword*, p. 119.

88. Young, *Japan's Total Empire*, pp. 260–266.

89. Senji kōtsūhen ed., *Nihon kokuyū tetsudōhan nihon rikuun shiryō*, Vol. 3, *Nihon rikuun jūnenshi*, p. 99. While the statistics are unclear, from other sources one can surmise that these foreign visitors were primarily from western countries.

90. Daniels, "Japanese Sport," p. 182.

91. Maema, *Dangan ressha*, p. 345. The author included a page from a March 1942 issue of *Kagakushugi kōgyō*. This article displayed a map showing projected rail lines winding through the Asian continent all the way to Singapore and down to Batavia. Also see Gakushūkenkyūsha, ed., *[Zusetsu] Shinkansen zenshi*, pp. 30–36.

92. One author claimed that people at the time referred to the train plans as an "Olympic Era Special Express." See Yanagita, "Berurin Tōkyō orinpikku mahi," p. 71.

93. Maema, *Dangan ressha*, p. 335.

94. Harada, ed., *Daitōa jūkan tetsudō kankeishorui*. The documents in this collection deal with the plans for a transportation network throughout Asia. The South Manchurian Railway Company had planned an enormous train and transport system, at least on paper, for the entire Asian continent, linking Singapore, Australia, and connecting routes to Europe. These documents are mostly from 1942, but plans actually started much earlier, in the mid 1930s. After the war the Japanese adopted a different term to describe the high-speed train, labeling it the *shinkansen* (new trunk line). However, the English term remains "bullet train." Also see Yamamoto Hirofumi, ed., *Technological Innovation*, p. 170.

95. Maema, *Dangan ressha*, p. 330.

96. Ibid., p. 175.

97. "Roku dai toshi oyobi shuto ni okeru chōhei kensa kekka no hikaku," *Toshi mondai* (January 1937): 123–126.

98. Taikaikai naimushōshi henshū iinkai, ed., *Naimushōshi,* vol. 4, p. 592.

99. Shimizu Katsuyoshi, ed., *Shōwa senzenki nihon no kōshū eiseishi,* pp. 20–21.

100. Ibid., p. 658.

101. The quote is from *Asahi shimbun* (Tokyo edition) August 1, 1936. A slightly different English version was quoted in an article in *The New York Times,* August 2, 1936.

102. *Asahi shimbun* (Tokyo edition), August 2, 1936.

103. Ibid. , August 14, 1936.

104. Ibid., August 6, 1936.

105. Ibid., August 5, 1936.

106. Ibid., August 2, 1936.

107. Minami, ed., *Kindai shomin seikatsushi,* vol. 8, p. 225.

Chapter 2: Defining the Limits of Society

1. Katō, *Rikugun nakano gakkō no zenbō,* p. 209. In 1984 news of a boy who murdered his parents with a metal bat shocked Onoda. In response to what he felt was a crisis among Japanese youth, Onoda established the Onoda Nature School, located in Fukushima prefecture, with additional offices in Tokyo. Onoda felt that he could take what he learned during thirty years in the jungles to better educate young Japanese by teaching them these skills. See also Onoda Hiroo, *No Surrender;* and Asahi Shimbun Tokuha Kishadan, *28 Years in the Guam Jungle.*

2. United States Strategic Bombing Survey, ed., *The Effects of Strategic Bombing.*

3. Ogino, ed., *Tokkō keisatsu kankei shiryō kaisetsu,* p. 13.

4. Ibid., p. 318.

5. Ibid., p. 324. See also Mitchell, *Janus-faced Justice;* and *Thought Control in Prewar Japan.*

6. Ogino, ed., *Tokkō keisatsu kankei shiryō shūsei,* vol. 20, p. 552. From the 1945 police manual titled, *Tokkō keisatsu jimu hikkei.*

7. Dunnigan and Nofi, eds., *The Pacific War Encyclopedia,* vol. 2, M-Z, p. 513. The documentary, *Japanese Devils* (2001 Riben Guizi Production Committee), produced by Matsui Minoru, provides testimony from numerous Japanese soldiers about the atrocities they committed against Chinese military and civilian POWs.

8. Yui and Kosuge, *Rengōkoku horyo gyakutai to sensō sekinin,* p. 38. Hirakushi, *Daihonei hōdōbu,* p. 27, recounts a slightly different version of events. Hirakushi says Akiyama had been drinking late one night with a journalist friend who recounted the story. He claims that Akiyama then appropriated the story as his own for his broadcast.

9. *Asahi shimbun* (Tokyo edition), December 5, 1942.

10. *Kagayaku butai* (August 17, 1939), reprinted in the Fuji Shuppan reproduction of the same name.

11. Record Group 331, (SCAP files), Box 1425, *Bunka POW Camp Folder, File #1.* Ikeda Norizane filed an affidavit for the International Military Tribunal for the Far East, November 1946. Located in US National Archives II, College Park, Maryland. See Ikeda's own version of the story, where he makes himself out to be much more of a humanitarian; Ikeda, *Puropaganda senshi.* For more on Ikeda's role, see Satō and Kushner, "'Negro Propaganda Operations.'"

12. Record Group 331, (SCAP files), Box 1425, *Bunka POW Camp Folder, File #2.* Located in US National Archives II, College Park, Maryland.

13. Tsuneishi, *Shinri sakusen no kaisō.* As a Japanese-American imprisoned by the Japanese and a POW in the Bunka Camp, Frank Fujita's experience differed from that of the white POWs. Due to the fact that he was an Asian-American and had no broadcasting experience, but was an artist, his recollections of Bunka Camp detail a magnitude of suffering Ikeda failed to describe; see Fujita, *Foo.*

14. See the document *Taigai senden no tame kikan yokuryū tekikokujin riyō jōkyō,* in Ariyama and Nishiyama, eds., *Jōhōkyoku kankei shiryō dai yonkan, [Jōhōkyoku senden tōsei kankei shiryō],* vol. 4, pp. 9–34. In *Quiet Passages,* P. Scott Corbett discusses the details of the plans to repatriate the Japanese and Americans in the early years of the war, the problems encountered, and how the transfer almost did not take place.

15. Johnson, *An Instance of Treason.*

16. It is estimated that soon after the earthquake, vicious Japanese mobs killed several hundred, if not thousands, of Koreans.

17. Ogino, ed., *Tokkō keisatsu kankei shiryō shūsei,* vol. 30, p. 31. See the Home Ministry police document, "Hokushi jihen ni kansuru jōhō naimushō keisatsuhokyoku," August 1937–March 1938.

18. Ibid., p. 77, same document.

19. Ibid., p. 56. Document "Hokushi jihen ni kansuru jōhō (sono yon)," August 26, 1937, Naimushō keihokyoku hoanbu, marked secret.

20. (Kei9, 4 E: 15–2, No. 223) *Keihokyokuchō kessai shorui,* 1937 (shimo), document 20, "Shusseiguntai kangei sōgei ni kansuru ken," November 20, 1937. Located in the Kokuritsu Kobunshokan, Tokyo.

21. *Kagayaku butai* (October 17, 1937), special issue on imperial entertainment forces.

22. Ogino, ed., *Tokkō keisatsu kankei shiryō shūsei,* vol. 20, p. 578.

23. Uchikawa, ed., *Gendaishi shiryō,* vol. 41, *Masu media tōsei,* 2, p. 146. See the August 1938 document concerning publishing regulations, "Shuppan torishimari sono hoka ni taisuru iken chōsa ni kansuru ken."

24. Ibid., p. 150.

25. The Supreme Command for the Allied Powers (SCAP) purged Kan after the war. Following the end of the occupation, however, he was elected several times to the lower house of Parliament.

26. Naimushōshi kenkyūkai, ed., *Naimushō to kokumin,* p. 243. Elise Tipton talks about this in *The Japanese Police State.*

27. Keishichōshi hensaniinkai, *Keishichōshi shōwazenhen,* pp. 1073–1074. These

derogatory attitudes toward Koreans, Chinese, and Taiwanese still exist today in Japan. See the comments of Ishihara Shintarō, the mayor of Tokyo, for similar remarks in the October 29, 2003, *Mainichi shimbun* (Tokyo edition).

28. Keishichōshi hensaniinkai, *Keishichōshi shōwazenhen*, p. 1075. Italics mine.

29. Jay Rubin devotes a whole chapter to censorship, literature, and the war in *Injurious to Public Morals*. Media historian Matsuura Sōzō spends almost twenty pages on the litany of laws and ordinances relating to censorship and media regulations that expanded as the Japanese military's aggression in China augmented; see his *Senchū senryōka no masukomi*, pp. 229–245; also his *Tennō to masukomi*.

30. Takagi and Fukuda, "Nihon fashizumu keiseiki no masu media tōsei (2)," p. 80. Takasaki, *Pen to sensō* and *Senjika no jānārizumu*.

31. Takagi and Fukuda, "Nihon fashizumu keiseiki no masu media tōsei (2)," p. 83.

32. Uchikawa, ed., *Gendaishi shiryō*, vol. 41, p. 137. See the document "Fujin zasshi ni taisuru torishimari hōshin," May 1938.

33. Fujime, *Sei no rekishigaku*, pp. 288–309.

34. Suzuki Yūko, *Feminizumu to sensō*, p. 67.

35. The best collection in color reproduction of these propaganda leaflets is Heiwa Hakubutsukan o Tsukuru Kai, ed., *Kami no sensō dendan*.

36. Shimokawa, *Shōwa seisōshi*, pp. 236–237.

37. The scholarship on the *ianfu*, or "comfort women," has grown over the last few years. See Hicks, *The Comfort Women*, and Yoshimi Yoshiaki, *Comfort Women*.

38. Uchikawa, ed., *Gendaishi shiryō*, vol. 41, p. 141. Previously, the ministry had already called in publishers of women's magazines to talk to them about cleaning up ads in women's magazines. Ibid., p. 154. See the September 1938 regulations on journal and serial advertising.

39. Ibid., p. 158.

40. Ariyama, "Sōryokusen to gunbu media seisaku," pp. 114–116.

41. Ibid., p. 128.

42. Kitayama, *Rajio Tōkyō*. Kitayama deals more with broadcasts aimed abroad, while Takeyama's book concerns domestic radio. Takeyama, *Sensō to hōsō*; Fukuda, *Sugata naki senpei*; Kaigai Hōsō Kenkyū Gurūpu, ed., *NHK senji kaigai hōsō*.

43. See Sakuramoto, *Bunkajintachi no daitōa sensō*. For a firsthand, slightly biased account, see Machida, *Aru gunjin no shihi*.

44. Katō Yūzaburō, "Shin naikaku no shisei taikō to keisatsu no ninmu," p. 12.

45. *Gaiji geppō* (June 1943): 109–110.

46. Ibid. (March 1943): 21–22.

47. Ibid. (February 1944): 9.

Chapter 3: Advertising as Propaganda

1. "Hōdō gijutsu kenkyūkai kaisoku," envelope 23.2, Papers of the Imaizumi Takeji collection, Ritsumeikan University, Kyoto, Japan.

2. Imaizumi, "Jiyū no atarashisa," p. 48.

3. Tsuganesawa, "[Puresuaruto] ni miru senjiki dezainā no kenkyū (jō)."

4. Komota et al., eds., *Shinpan nihon ryūkōkashi*, p. 114.

5. Yamana, Imaizumi, and Arai, eds., *Sensō to senden gijutsusha*, p. 36.

6. Arai, "Senden ippeisotsu no shuki."

7. "Jihenka kōkoku zadankaiki," *Waseda kōkokugaku kenkyū* (June 1940): 132–133.

8. Imaizumi, "Kokka to hōdō gijutsu," (Shōwa 15nen), envelope 23.2. Papers of the Imaizumi Takeji collection.

9. As quoted in Inoue, "Hōdō gijutsu kenkyūkai no [gijutsu] to sakuhin-senjika no aru kōkokujin gurūpu," p. 85.

10. Ibid., p. 86.

11. Ibid., p. 93.

12. Nanba, *Uchiteshi yamamu taiheiyō sensō to kōkoku no gijutsushatachi*, pp. 130–134. Personal recollections of the various advertising clerks who worked on this type of propaganda can be found in Dezain shōshi henshūkai, ed., *Nihon dezain shōshi*.

13. Hōdō Gijutsu Kenkyūkai, ed., *Senden gijutsu*.

14. Tagawa, "Taigai sendeshi [Front] no kiroku," p. 29.

15. Mikami, "Nandaka omoshiroin desu yo, kaisha no naka ga," p. 14.

16. Kashiwagi, *Shōzō no naka no kenryoku*, pp. 54–55.

17. Tagawa, *Sensō no gurafizumu kaisō no [FRONT]*, p. 228. It is unclear whether SCAP actually released such a statement. Nonetheless, the Tōhō staff believed that it had and quickly came out of hiding.

18. Weisenfeld, "Touring Japan-as-Museum"; Weisenfeld asserts that Natori is the father of Japanese photojournalism.

19. Nanba, *Uchiteshi yamamu taiheiyō sensō to kōkoku no gijutsushatachi*, p. 40.

20. Ibid., p. 38.

21. Ibid., p. 50.

22. Yamana, Imaizumi, and Arai, eds., *Sensō to senden gijutsusha*. For more complete personal recollections, see Yamana, *Taikenteki na dezainshi*; and Arai, *Aru kōkokujin no kiroku*.

23. Nanba, *Uchiteshi yamamu taiheiyō sensō to kōkoku no gijutsushatachi*, p. 53.

24. Ibid., p. 212.

25. Yamamoto Akira, "Senji senden bira no ideorogī (1)." See reprints of the leaflets in Heiwa Hakubutsukan wo Tsukuru Kai, ed., *Kami no sensō dendan*.

26. Nishioka, *Hōdōsensen kara mita "Nicchū sensō,"* p. 7.

27. Hino's famous book of his first time on the front with soldiers in China, *Wheat and Soldiers,* was actually a quasi record of his journey with the military on its 1938 battle in Joshū, (Xuzhou in Chinese) in Jiangsu province. The expedition evolved into an enormous loss for Japan and marked a decisive turn that changed Japan's military aims toward China. The battle began at the end of 1937, moved slowly south, and by April 1938 Japanese forces found themselves surrounded by the Chinese, suffering heavy losses. At the end of the battle Chiang Kai Shek's forces headed southwest, breaking the dykes of the Yellow River so that the Japanese army could not follow in pursuit. It is estimated that millions of Chinese peasants perished in the aftermath.

28. For a detailed view of wartime literature see Donald Keene's three articles: "Japanese Writers and the Greater East Asia War," "Japanese Literature and Politics in the 1930s," and "The Barren Years." Also see Rubin, *Injurious to Public Morals,* pp. 272–278. For a slightly different take on wartime literature, see Kawamura, *Manshū hōkai-daitōa bungaku to sakkatachi,* and his *Sakubun no naka no dainihon teikoku.*

29. Rosenfeld, *Unhappy Soldier,* p. 13.

30. Ibid., p. 24.

31. Nishioka, *Hōdōsensen kara mita "Nicchū sensō,"* p. 133.

32. Ibid., p. 294.

33. Takasaki, *Zasshi media no sensō sekinin,* p. 78.

34. For a personal perspective on the work of these writers, see Machida, *Aru gunjin no shihi.*

35. Nishioka, *Hōdōsensen kara mita "Nicchū sensō,"* p. 181.

36. Sakuramoto, *Bunkatachi no daitōa sensō PK butai ga yuku,* pp. 29–37, lists the authors and numerous articles they wrote around the time of the battle for Hankou in China.

37. Nishioka, *Hōdōsensen kara mita "Nicchū sensō,"* p. 182.

38. Mabuchi Itsuo, *Hōdō sensō.*

39. Ozaki, "Nihon no PK Butai (1)."

40. Sakuramoto, *Bunkatachi no daitōa sensō PK butai ga yuku,* p. 9.

41. Ibid., pp. 68, 70–72. For a sample of the personal memoirs and similar writings on embedded reporter experiences, PK *butai* memoirs, and pen platoon writings that the Japanese public would have consumed at that time, see Ozaki, *Bungaku butai;* Kageyama, *Marē kessen kamera senki;* Koyanagi and Ishikawa, *Jūgun kameraman no sensō.*

42. Machida, *Tatakau bunka butai,* forward.

43. Takenouchi, ed., *Dai niki gendai manga,* vol. 11, pp. 305–308. After the war Mizuki became known for his comics about monsters and Japanese trolls in *Kappa no sanpei: Yōkai daisakusen,* and *Gegege no kitarō,* as well as the popular TV series *Akumu-kun.* See also Akiyama, ed. *Maboroshi no sensō manga no sekai.*

44. Matsumoto, *Daihonei haken no kishatachi.*

45. One such account by a pacification platoon member was published in the *Bungei shunjū* magazine in January 1938. See Nakano, "Senbuhan kara."

46. A complete synopsis of primary documents concerning the function and breadth of the Imperial General Headquarters can be found in Inaba, *Gendaishi shiryō,* vol. 37, *Daihonei,* see p. lxxiii and p. 353.

47. Uchikawa, ed., *Gendaishi shiryō,* vol. 40, Masu media tōsei (1), p. 654. See the military document, "Rikugunshō shinbunhan ni tsuite (Matsumura Hideitsu sensei kōjutsusho)."

48. A sample of such writing can be seen in Takada, *Biruma minzoku kaihōroku* (Takada was a military reporter for the army); Sakai, *Marē senki* (Sakai was an *Asahi* reporter but followed the army in the invasion of Malaysia); Daihonei kaigun hōdōbu, ed., *Sangokai kaisen* (a volume completed by the Imperial General Headquarters Navy Media Division about the Coral Sea Battle).

49. Shina Hakengun Hōdōbu, ed., *Shidan*.

50. Iwasaki's chapter in the book was entitled "Return from the North China Battle" ("Sen no hokushi yori kaerite").

Chapter 4: A Funny Thing Happened to Me on the Way to the Front

1. Kiyosawa, *A Diary of Darkness*. Japanese are not the only ones who label their war in this manner. The French consider their occupation by Nazi Germany to have been *"les années noires."*

2. Allied Translators and Interpreters Section, "Prominent Factors in Japanese Military Psychology," WTS 1 Series 10-RR-76.2 (microfiche), p. 2.

3. The most popular study during the war was Ruth Benedict, *The Chrysanthemum and the Sword: Patterns of Japanese Culture.*

4. Allied Translators and Interpreters Section, "Prominent Factors in Japanese Military Psychology," WTS 1 Series 10-RR-76.2 (microfiche), p. 3. Located in the National Diet Library, Kensei shiryō room, Tokyo, Japan.

5. A notable exception would be the famous Japanese/Chinese film actress Ri Kō Ran.

6. There is a growing consensus that many Japanese on the home islands supported the war and even thrived during the war years. See Yoshimi, *Kusa no ne no fashizumu.* Research focused on social mobilization demonstrates that Japanese efforts at mobilizing the population began sporadically after World War One and increased after the great 1923 Kantō earthquake. See Nagahama, *Kokumin seishin sōdōin no shisō to kōzō*, pp. 16–19. Akazawa Shirō's research points out that Japanese government policies concerning leisure and entertainment emerged more forcefully when the Hamaguchi administration initiated its Kyōka Sōdōin (Education Mobilization) in 1929. For more, see Akazawa Shirō, *Kindai nihon no shisō dōin to shūkyō tōsei.* Also see Akazawa, *Nihon fashizumu to taishū bunka*, pp. 32–44. Takeyama Akiko explains how the visual media worked itself into the process of creating a culture that supported military aims abroad. The cinema, in most circumstances, allowed people to enjoy the fruits of the battle and bathe in its glory without the horror of actual combat; see Takeyama, "Media ibento toshiteno nyūsu eiga." For work on film propaganda, see Baskett, "The Attractive Empire"; and High, *Teikoku no ginmaku.* Also see Nornes and Yukio, eds., *Media Wars Then and Now.* Popular culture was significant in providing outlets for wartime propaganda; even music became a vehicle. See Kitagawa Kenzō's article, "Sensōka no sesō fūzoku to bunka" and Tonoshita, "Ongaku ni yoru kokumin kyōka dōin."

7. Bytwerk, "The Dolt Laughs."

8. Rentscheler, *The Ministry of Illusion*, p. 112.

9. Stites, *Russian Popular Culture*, p. 108. For a fuller description, see Horton, ed., *Inside Soviet Film Satire;* and the translated comedy routines in Yershov, *Comedy in the Soviet Theater.*

10. Stites, *Russian Popular Culture*, p. 118.

11. According to a Tokyo city investigation committee, from 1937 to 1939 annual cinema attendance rose from 4,900,000 to 9,800,000. These statistics translate to at

least 7.8 movie visits per person in 1937, and this increases to over 14.5 times a year only two years later; as quoted in Minami, ed., *Shōwa bunka*, p. 77.

12. Ishikawa, *Goraku no senzenshi*, pp. 134–135. The police were not prudish; legal prostitution abounded. But the authorities wanted to control where sexual entertainment occurred.

13. An excellent source in English on the history of *rakugo* is Morioka and Sasaki, *Rakugo*.

14. For a discussion of the various types of *manzai*, see Sawada Takaharu, *Warai o tsukuru*; Kurata, *Meiji taishō no minshū goraku*; Kurata and Fujinami, eds. *Nihon geinō jinmei jiten*.

15. This difference in comedic tastes makes the translation of wartime routines all the more difficult. Much of the humor is lost when the routine is put into written form (let alone translated) because it deprives the performance of the voice, tone, and cadence of the original performer.

16. The title and content of each production changes slightly but generally follows "Rakugoka no heitai," transcribed from the CD encyclopedia of *rakugo* humor, *Kokon tōzai hanashika shinshiroku*, produced by Maruzen, 1999.

17. Transcribed from the film *Up in Arms* (1944, Goldwyn).

18. Kojima, ed., *Taishū geinō shiryō shūsei*, vol. 7, *Manzai*, pp. 210–214.

19. For more on Akita, see Tomioka, *Manzai sakusha Akita Minoru*.

20. NHK, ed., *Rekishi e no shōtai, shōwahen*, vol. 22, p. 87.

21. The event where the Japanese army claimed that they were attacked by Chinese forces and thereupon launched a counteroffensive is known as the Manchurian Incident of September 18, 1931.

22. Readers should not confuse *imon butai* with *ianfu* (comfort women). Following the 1937 Nanjing massacre, with the army's increased use of forced prostitution, there might have been a connection. I have only found one account that spoke clearly of the amusement area that a soldier visited which diagramed a temporary cinema and temporary brothels around the corner. It is entirely possible that entertainment performances were held in this area, but until further proof is found, it is wise to assume that these two activities were apparently separated.

23. Yoshimoto, *Yoshimoto hachijūnen no ayumi*, p. 48.

24. Ibid., p. 49.

25. Ibid., p. 52.

26. Ibid., p. 86

27. Ibid., p. 87.

28. Ishikawa, ed., *Yoka goraku kenkyū kiso bunkenshū, kaisetsu*; quoted on p. 6.

29. Shigeta, *Fūzoku keisatsu no riron to jissai*, p. 201.

30. Yamashita Keitarō, *Nakiwarai gojūnen*, p. 68.

31. Ibid., p. 107.

32. Koronbia Gojūnenshi Henshū Iinkai, ed., *Nihon koronbia*, no page numbers in this book.

33. Kurata, *Nihon rekōdo bunkashi*, p. 348.

34. Ibid., p. 362.

35. Naimushō, *Shuppan keisatsu gaikan*, p. 596.

36. (Kei9, 4 E: 15–2, No. 219) *Keihokyokuchō kessai shorui*, document "Shōwa kyūnen, chikuonki rekōdo ni kansuru ken tsūchō, March 14, 1934." Located in the Kokuritsu Kobunshokan, Tokyo, Japan.

37. Kojima, *Rakugo sanbyakunen*, p. 44.

38. The name of *Eloquence* in Japanese is *Yūben*.

39. (Kei9, 4 E: 15–3, No. 284) *Naimushō daijin Kessai shorui*, Shōwa jūninen (shimo) shorui #23, "Kōgyō torishimari ni kansuru ken, November 13, 1937." Located in the Kokuritsu Kobunshokan, Tokyo, Japan.

40. Gonda, "Shintaisei ni okeru iangoraku mondai."

41. Gonda, "Senjika ni okeru shimin goraku mondai."

42. Kurata, *Nihon rekōdo bunkashi*, pp. 437–438.

43. Ogawa, *Ryūkōka to sesō*, prologue.

44. "Warawashitai" is a play on the causitive form of the verb "to laugh" and the word for "platoon." Washi also means "eagle," so Warawashitai has another potential meaning suggesting, "our eagle platoons."

45. Yamashita, *Nakiwarai gojūnen*, p. 151.

46. Yoshimoto, *Yoshimoto hachijūnen no ayumi*, p. 67.

47. Kurata, *Nihon rekōdo bunkashi*, p. 435.

48. Ishida and Kyōyama, *Warawashitai hōkokuki kōgun imon no tabi*, p. 6. Located in the special collections room, National Diet Library, Tokyo.

49. Ibid., p. 18.

50. Sanyūteikinba, "Hokushi kenbutsu," p. 540.

51. Misu Wakana's ability to mimic both domestic and other Asian accents can be verified by listening to the routine "Zenkoku fujin taikai," released on CD in the comedy compilation *Owarai hyakkajiten: Shōwa 12nen–20nen senran no naka no warai.*

52. Azabu, "Sensen imon yori kaerite."

53. "Warawashitai gaisen omiyage banashi," *Shūkan asahi* (May 1939): 21–24.

54. Tamamatsu, *Wakana Ichirō kessaku manzaishū*, p. 59.

55. Ibid., p. 44. This is a fairly free translation to capture some of the original song's mood and parodic qualities.

56. Ibid., pp. 44–45.

57. See the April 5, 1939, report and others on Communist propaganda directed at the Japanese military, "Kyosantō no wagaguntai ni taisuru shisōteki gakai kōsaku no shinsō to kore ga bōatsu hōsaku," Kita shina hōmen gunshireibu, Shōwa jūyonnen shigatsu itsuka, pp. 327–381, marked top secret, in Awaya and Chatani, eds., *Nicchū sensō taichūgoku jōhōsen shiryō, dai sankan (shōwa 14nen).*

58. Kojima, ed., *Taishū geinō shiryō shūsei*, vol. 7, *Manzai*, p. 230. One can identify parallels in the structure of the gags to Abbott and Costello routines, but neither group was aware of the other.

59. Transcribed from the film *Buck Privates* (1941, Universal).

60. Teruoka, "Jikyoku to yūmoa."

61. Kojima, *Manzai sesōshi*, p. 148. I checked with the authorities at the Yasukuni shrine to verify this fact, but they were unable to determine conclusively whether a ceremony had actually taken place and, if it had, what form it took.

62. Kojima, ed., *Taishū geinō shiryō shūsei*, vol. 7, *Manzai*, pp. 345–346.

63. Yamachi, *Kokumin goraku engei dokuhon*, p. 168.

64. Ibid., p. 169.

65. Hagi, *Kasen no haha*, p. 35.

66. Ibid., pp. 50–51.

67. Ibid., p. 69.

68. Kojima, *Rakugo sanbyakunen*, p. 23. The same *rakugo* association unearthed and rehabilitated these routines after the war in a similar ceremony on September 3, 1946.

69. This was a special issue of the magazine *Itaria* devoted to "various problems concerning national entertainment."

70. Nakajima, "Kokumin goraku no shiten," p. 194.

71. NHK, *Rekishi e no shōtai, shōwahen*, vol. 22, p. 101.

72. "Charging into the Jungle" is the name of this routine, performed by Misu Wakana and Tamamatsu Ichirō and released on record in 1942. The script can be found in the pamphlet that comes with the contemporary CD entitled *Sensō no omote to ura* (Teichiku Company, 1995).

73. Yokozuna is the highest ranking sumo wrestler.

74. Kojima, *Manzai sesōshi*, pp. 165–167. This section is a "sumo match" between the United States and Japan a hundred years into the future. To make it more comprehensible, I have changed it into a boxing-match announcing style.

75. A *benshi* was a professional who sat to the side of a movie screen during a silent film and narrated the action.

76. Kurata, *Nihon rekōdo bunkashi*, p. 474.

77. Kōriyama, *Kessen manzai sakura hinode kessakushū*, pp. 24–37.

78. Tozaki et al., "Sensō to rekōdo," p. 11.

79. Shibusawa, *Kōgun imon*.

80. Ibid., p. 56.

81. Ibid., p. 86.

82. Ibid., pp. 146–147.

83. Ibid., pp. 164–165.

84. Kokonteishinshō, *Binbō jiman*, p. 204.

85. Ibid., p. 225.

86. Kojima, *Rakugo sanbyakunen*, p. 7.

87. Akazawa, "Kyōka dōin seisaku no tenkai," p. 39.

88. As quoted in Takaoka, "Haisenchokugo no bunka jōkyō to bunka undō," p. 176.

89. Shulte-Sasse, *Entertaining the Third Reich*, p. 4.

90. E. Taylor Atkins discusses similar issues concerning wartime jazz in Japan in his book *Blue Nippon*. See the chapter "'Jazz for the Country's Sake': Toward a New Cultural Order in Wartime Japan," pp. 127–164.

91. Douglas, *War, Memory, and the Politics of Humor,* p. 4. Douglas poses this question with regard to humor in France during World War One, and it seems applicable to the Japanese case.

Chapter 5: The Japanese Propaganda Struggle on the Chinese Mainland

1. Hoshi, "Wasureenu shichisanichi butai no kyōki," p. 50. Shinotsuka was one of the few surviving members of Unit 731 courageous enough to provide courtroom testimony for the many legal suits still active in Japanese courts dealing with issues related to these atrocities.

2. Junshi weiyuanhui zhengzhibu translation, *Shibing bixu zhi,* (translated into Chinese from Japanese), 501–519, located in the KMT Central Party Headquarters Archives, Taipei, Taiwan.

3. The literature on Japanese atrocities committed during the war is vast and growing. Honda Katsuichi, a journalist, launched the first salvo when he went to China and conducted personal interviews. See his *Chūgoku no tabi,* and the work edited by Frank Gibney and translated into English by Karne Sandness as *The Nanjing Massacre.* See also Toshiyuki Tanaka, *Hidden Horrors,* for a more comprehensive account of atrocities all around the Japanese empire.

4. Karnow, *In Our Image,* esp. pp. 190–195, concerning Gen. Jacob Smith's brutal campaigns in the Philippines.

5. Odoric Wu calls for such cross-border analysis of Japan's war in China. He says scholars have ignored the "incessant interaction" among the Japanese, the Communists, and the Nationalists. See his "Communist Sources for Localizing the Study of the Sino-Japanese War," pp. 226–235. See also Eastman, *The Abortive Revolution* and his *Seeds of Destruction,* as well as the volume he edited with Jerome Ch'en, *The Nationalist Era in China;* and Ryū, *Kankan saiban.*

6. Coble, *Facing Japan,* p. 284. Hata, *Gun fashizumu undō shi; Nihonjin horyo (Jō); Nicchū sensō shi; Nihon rikukaigun sōgōjiten;* and *Senzenki nihon kanryōsei no seido soshiki jinji.*

7. Japanese propaganda flyer from June 11, 1939, *Senden bira sappu keikaku sōfu no ken (sono go) Roshūdan sanbōchō Numata Takezō.* Report addressed to Rikugun jikan Yamawaki Masataka, in Awaya and Chatani, eds., *Nicchū sensō taichūgoku jōhōsen shiryō, dai sankan (shōwa 14nen),* p. 27. Many of these archives have still not been catalogued and can be found in the Bōeichō Archives, Tokyo, Japan (Ministry of Defense Archives).

8. Japanese propaganda flyer from July 12, 1939, ibid., p. 54.

9. Japanese propaganda leaflets from September 13, 1939, ibid., pp. 90–94.

10. Japanese propaganda leaflet reports from October 19, 1939, ibid., pp. 110–111.

11. Murakami, "Posutā haifu ni kansuru chōsa," pp. 67–72.

12. Tanimoto, "Posutā no kōkateki sakusei to sono riyō," p. 42.

13. *Nihongun Sanpu Bira*, call # Shū 1236, located in the National Diet Library, Kensei Shiryō Room, Tokyo, Japan.

14. For a detailed description of Japanese military propaganda orders relating to propaganda in North China, see Chapter 5, "Ideological Control," in Li, *The Japanese Army in North China*. See also Furuya, ed. *Nicchū sensōshi kenkyū*.

15. April 5, 1939, report on Communist propaganda directed at the Japanese military, *Kyōsantō no wagaguntai ni taisuru shisōteki gakai kōsaku no shinsō to korega bōatsu hōsaku*, Kitashina hōmengun shireibu, marked top secret, in Awaya and Chatani, eds., *Nicchū sensō taichūgoku jōhōsen shiryō, dai sankan (shōwa 14nen)*, p. 330. (Hereafter, this item is called April 5, 1939, report on Communist propaganda).

16. April 5, 1939, report on Communist propaganda, pp. 338–339.

17. Liao, "Duidi xuanchuan gongzuo zhi jianshi," pp. 16–21.

18. Takahashi, "Kōtō senden o jūshi seyo," pp. 2–7.

19. April 5, 1939, report on Communist propaganda, p. 340.

20. These scare tactics and campaigns of brutality were mocked in postwar Japanese film comedies, but they remain as visual evidence of the manner in which officers would slap, denigrate, and generally mistreat enlisted soldiers. See Baskett, "Dying for a Laugh."

21. April 5, 1939, report on Communist propaganda, p. 344.

22. One example, originally written in Japanese and translated into Chinese, is Hu Lei, *Fulu riji*. Located in the KMT Central Party Headquarters Archives, Taipei, Taiwan. For a contemporary account of POW life written by a Japanese soldier after the war, see Kobayashi, *Zai zhongguo de tudi shang*. For a comparison of how Japanese POWs felt under American authority, see Ōoka, *Taken Captive*. Ōoka was an educated, thirty-five-year-old Japanese intellectual, a translator of French literature, whom the Americans captured in January 1945 in the Philippines.

23. April 5, 1939, report on Communist propaganda, p. 356.

24. Ibid., p. 357.

25. Ibid., pp. 366–367.

26. Ouchi, "Kanminzoku to senden," as quoted on p. 12. On the Manchurian Film Company, see Yamaguchi Takeshi, *Aishū no manshū eiga*.

27. In Japanese the article was entitled "Kōsen shindankai to nihon shinsaku," pp. 113–118. Zhou gave the speech on March 7, 1938.

28. Imai, "1940 nen zengo no nihon no kōsen chūgoku ninshiki."

29. April 5, 1939, report on Communist propaganda, p. 371.

30. Ibid., p. 372.

31. Kawano, "Gyokusai no shisō to hakuhei shōtotsu," p. 156.

32. Ibid., p. 159.

33. Satō Tadao, "Kusa no ne no gunkokushugi," p. 9.

34. Kuwajima, *Kahoku senki*, p. 38. See also Fogel, ed. *The Nanjing Massacre in History and Historiography*.

35. Kuwajima, *Kahoku senki*, p. 136.

36. Ibid., p. 137. Mussolini's career as dictator ceased in the summer of 1943, and the Americans hit the shores of Tarawa in late November 1943.

37. Ibid., p. 140.

38. Ibid., p. 141.

39. Himeta, "Sōron, nicchū sensō to kōnichi sensō no hazama," p. 11. Shakai mondai shiryō kenkyūkai, ed., *Shina jihen ni okeru shinagun no bōryaku senden bunsho*. Smedley, *China Fights Back*; Snow, *Red Star over China*.

40. Peter Sano describes the very harsh conditions most Japanese soldiers were eager to avoid in his memoir, *One Thousand Days in Siberia*.

41. Himeta, "Sōron, nicchū sensō to kōnichi sensō no hazama," p. 34.

42. Holm, *Art and Ideology in Revolutionary China*, pp. 24–25. Holm remarks on p. 47 that since many of the songs and plays produced as CCP propaganda were "too Europeanized" due to their Soviet roots, "in most cases contact between intellectuals and the masses was superficial."

43. Kagawa and Maeda, *Hachirogun no nihonheitachi*, pp. 17–18.

44. This phenomenon of being "reborn" was also spoken about by those working with Japanese POWs in America. See Gilmore, "'We have been reborn.'"

45. As quoted in Hata, *Nihonjin horyo (Jō)*, p. 102.

46. Kagawa and Maeda, *Hachirogun no nihonheitachi*, p. 22.

47. "Enan no bunka undō gensei," *Senden geppō* (May 1941): 81–85.

48. Kagawa and Maeda, *Hachirogun no nihonheitachi*, p. 38.

49. Nosaka employed a multitude of aliases including Lin Zhe, Hayashi Tetsu in Japanese, and Okano Susumu. Following Japan's surrender, after sixteen years away, Nosaka returned to Japan in January 1946 and entered the first elections in March of that year. He won a seat in the lower house from a Tokyo district and stayed in office until June 6, 1950, when he was forcibly removed from government service on MacArthur's order. In July 1956 Nosaka returned to elected office in the upper house as a representative from a Tokyo district.

50. Kagawa and Maeda, *Hachirogun no nihonheitachi*, p. 58.

51. Hata, *Nihonjin horyo (Jō)*, p. 123.

52. Ibid., p. 183.

53. Yasui, "Kōnichi sensō jiki kaihōku ni okeru nihonjin no hansen undō," p. 43.

54. Nosaka, *Nosaka Sanzō senshū (senjihen)*, p. 307.

55. Ibid., p. 312.

56. Ibid., pp. 314–315.

57. Ibid., p. 318.

58. Ibid., p. 320.

59. Ibid., p. 321.

60. Ibid., p. 323.

61. Ibid., p. 324.

62. Ibid., p. 342.

63. Ibid., p. 345.

64. Barrett, *Dixie Mission*, p. 35; Selden, *China in Revolution*.

65. Beechert and Beechert, eds., *From Kona to Yenan*, p. 124.

66. Kuwajima, *Kahoku senki*, p. 237.

67. Japanese Ministry of Foreign Affairs, Division of Special Records, *Documents concerning the Allied Occupation of Japan*, vol. 1, *Basic Documents*, p. 35.

68. Levine and Hsiung, eds., *China's Bitter Victory*; also see Levine, *Anvil of Victory*. For research that discusses the close ties between surrendering Japanese forces and Nationalist Chinese forces, see Gillin and Etter, "Staying On."

69. Fitzgerald, *Awakening China*.

70. Xiao and Zhong, eds., *Kangri zhanzheng wenhuashi*, p. 234.

71. Zhang Qiang, "Guomindang kangzhan shiqi de wenyi zhengce."

72. Esherick, ed., *Lost Chance in China*, p. 65. This comment was part of Service's analysis in his July 10, 1942, report "Memorandum on Propaganda, Psychological Warfare and Morale Agencies in Free China."

73. I thank Andrew Jones for pointing this out. *Chee Lai: Songs of New China, Paul Robeson with Chinese Chorus*, conducted by Liu Liang-mo, Keynote Recordings, Album No. 109 (pressed in 1942).

74. Henry Luce, the owner of *Life* magazine, had grown up with missionary parents in China and felt an affinity for the country. For similar accounts that moved some to the plight of the Chinese, see Snow, *Red Star over China*, and Smedley, *China Fights Back*. The magazine's reprint of the photograph announced that through quick distribution by the International News Service, other newspapers, Movietone News, and other newsreel companies, within a few weeks "the Chinese baby's potential audience [had reached] 136,000,000."

75. Uchida and Mizutani, "Jūkei kokumin seifu to nihonjin horyo seisaku," pp. 47–48.

76. Ibid., p. 50.

77. Wenhua Jiaoyu Yanjiuhui ed., *Diwo zai xuanchuan zhanxianshang*, pp. 252–253. Located in the KMT Ministry of Justice, Bureau of Investigation Archives, Taipei, Taiwan.

78. Kaji, *Kotoba to dangan*, pp. 4–5; Fujiwara Akira, "Nihon no chūgoku shinryaku to hansen dōmei," in Fujiwara et al., eds., *Nihonjinmin hansen dōmei shiryō (bekkan)*.

79. Uchida and Mizutani, "Jūkei kokumin seifu to nihonjin horyo seisaku," p. 54.

80. Ibid., p. 55. See also Guo, *Zhangshi xuanchuan gongzuo*; and Tan Luo Fei. *Kangzhan shiqi de Guo Moruo*.

81. Fujiwara Akira, "Nihon no chūgoku shinryaku to hansen dōmei," in Fujiwara et al., eds., *Nihonjinmin hansen dōmei shiryō (bekkan)*, p. 8. For a discussion regarding the shifts in KMT policy toward Japanese POWs, see Uchida, "Jūkei kokumin seifu no kōnichi seiji senden seisaku to nihonjin hansen undō."

82. Guo, *Kōnichisen kaisōroku*, p. 45.

83. The Chinese titles were *Duidi xuanchuan xinde* and *Duidi xuanchuan biaoyu heyanyiji*.

84. Guo, *Kōnichisen kaisōroku*, p. 110.

85. Ibid., p. 41.

86. Ibid., p. 42.

87. Hasegawa, *Arashi no naka no sasayaki*, p. 190. This book originally appeared in its entirety in China in 1945. Hasegawa published in Esperanto under the name of Verda Majo or "Green May."

88. Iwao, "Hasegawa Teru kenkyū," p. 110. Also see *Miyako shimbun*, November 1, 1938.

89. Iwao, "Hasegawa Teru kenkyū," p. 109.

90. United States State Department. Confidential US State Department Central Files (microfilm), *China: Internal Affairs, 1940–44,* Reel 30, "Letter from US Embassy to Sec. State, January 29, 1943."

91. Ibid., "Dept. of State, Division of Far Eastern Affairs, memo, March 18, 1943" and "US Embassy Chungking China Report, April 7, 1943." See also Xiao and Zhong, eds., *Kangri zhanzheng wenhuashi*, p. 275. The editors of this Chinese volume accept that wartime Chongqing produced an enormous number of plays. However, they do not identify film as a cultural activity that attracted large audiences in the Nationalist-controlled regions.

92. Ivens, *The Camera and I*. Ivens describes the entrenched reluctance that the KMT manifested toward his self-financed project because the government could not fathom why he would want to help the Chinese cause with no seeming gain for himself.

93. Cheng, ed., *Zhongguo dianying fazhanshi*, p. 44.

94. See Fukuda, *Sugata naki senpei*.

95. Benson, "From Teahouse to Radio," p. 143. See also Walter and Ruth Meserve, "From Teahouse to Loudspeaker."

96. Benson, "From Teahouse to Radio," p. 149.

97. Ibid., p. 341.

98. *China at War*, September 1939. An article on January 1940, p. 8, exclaimed that the "poor fighting morale" of Japanese soldiers was credited to the Chinese "spiritual mobilization" of troops and civilians. *China at War* was an English-language magazine published by the Nationalists for western wartime audiences.

99. Sledge, *With the Old Breed*, pp. 198–199.

100. Laurie, "The Ultimate Dilemma of Psychological Warfare in the Pacific," pp. 110–111.

101. American historians are not the only ones to support this thesis; others also overestimate US propaganda. To be sure, as Yamamoto Taketoshi states in his book on US propaganda, *Nihonhei horyo wa nani o shabetta ka*, p. 47, American efforts were often more systemic and organized compared with what he defines as "slipshod" Japanese efforts. But in the final analysis Yamamoto offers little concrete data to demonstrate that the information the United States gleaned from the few Japanese POWs translated into effective US propaganda regarding Japan. See also Iriye, *Across the Pacific*, and *The Chinese and the Japanese*.

102. Drea, *In the Service of the Emperor*, p. xii
103. Gilmore, *You Can't Fight Tanks with Bayonets*, p. 7.
104. As quoted in ibid., p. 36.
105. Schrijvers, *The GI War against Japan*, p. 157.
106. As quoted in ibid., p. 208. For a discussion of Japanese POWs in the US, see Kramer, "Japanese Prisoners of War in America."
107. Carter, *Mission to Yenan*, p. 11. John K. Emmerson, in *The Japanese Thread*, p. 180, says that Davies intimated that Emmerson should go to Yenan to talk to the Japanese POWs and investigate the source of the effective CCP propaganda.
108. Carter, *Mission to Yenan*, p. 65.
109. Beechert and Beechert, eds., *From Kona to Yenan*, pp. 176–177.
110. Kagawa and Maeda, *Hachirogun no nihonheitachi*, introduction, p. 5.
111. Carter, *Mission to Yenan*, p. 70.
112. Emmerson, *The Japanese Thread*, p. 221.
113. Fairbank, *Chinabound*, p. 293.
114. Yoneda, *Amerika jōhō heishi no nikki*, p. 67.
115. Ibid., p. 73.
116. Emmerson, *The Japanese Thread*, p. 166.
117. Yoneda, *Amerika jōhō heishi no nikki*, p. 74.
118. Yamagiwa, "Beisenji jōhōkyoku (OWI) no [Enan hōkoku]," p. 10. Emmerson talks about this in *The Japanese Thread*, pp. 196–197.
119. Yamagiwa, "Beisenji jōhōkyoku (OWI) no [Enan hōkoku]," p. 11.
120. Ibid., p. 14.
121. Ibid.
122. See Davies, *Dragon by the Tail*, for an on-the-ground look at US relations with prewar and wartime China.
123. Record Group 493, Entry 30339 (China Theater), Box 51, *Reports - Progress of PW (psychological warfare) April-Aug 1945* folder, Headquarters United States Forces, China Theater, Psychological Warfare Section, August 2, 1945. Report to the Commanding General China Theater. Located in the United States National Archives II, College Park, Maryland.
124. A fascinating record of Japan's use of Australian POWs for a wartime propaganda film in Indonesia is dissected and reproduced in part in the 1987 Film Australia produced documentary called *Prisoners of Propaganda*.

Chapter 6: Preparing for Defeat
1. Occupation-era American soldiers committed crimes throughout the occupation, and archives illuminate the extent to which SCAP censored US criminal activity in occupied Japan. See the series edited by Awaya and Nakazono, eds., *Haisen zengo no shakai jōsei*, vol. 7, *Shingun no fuhō*. For a full account of occupation-era criminal activities and a book that takes a viewpoint somewhat opposed to John Dower's academic study, see Whiting, *Tokyo Underworld*.
2. Dower, *War Without Mercy*, p. 302.

3. For details on the manner in which the war restructured and reorganized Japanese society, see Johnson, *MITI and the Japanese Miracle;* Gao, *Economic Ideology and Japanese Industrial Policy;* and Noguchi Yukio, *1940 nen taisei.*

4. Awaya, ed., *Haisen chokugo no seiji to shakai,* vol. 1, *Shiryō Nihon gendaishi* 2, p. 459. For more concerning postwar power matrices, see Haley, *Authority without Power.*

5. Whiting, *Tokyo Underworld,* p. 10.

6. Ibid., p. 14.

7. Kisaka, *Shōwa no rekishi,* vol. 7, *Taiheiyō sensō,* p. 391.

8. Service, "The Situation in China and Suggestions Regarding American Policy," p. 138. Italics in original. Service was primarily discussing the KMT's ability to withstand the Japanese assault.

9. Kisaka, *Shōwa no rekishi,* vol. 7, *Taiheiyō sensō,* p. 322.

10. The Japanese titles were *Machi no koe* and *Shūhō yoron hōkoku.*

11. The police used the expression *kakugo shite kita,* which implies a kind of "we knew it might eventually come to this" idea.

12. Ikō, ed., *Taiheiyō sensōki naimushō chian taisaku jōhō,* vol. 2, p. 152. Document marked top secret, Keihokyoku, "Saipantō zenin senshi ni taisuru kyōdo minshin no dōkō," August 1, 1944. Kawashima, *Jūgo.*

13. Ogino, ed., *Tokkō keisatsu kankei shiryō shūsei,* vol. 30, p. 435. All of these rumors come from the same report, *Shisō junpō,* dainigō, April 20, 1944, section 1, "Saikin ni okeru ryūgen higo no keikō."

14. Ibid., p. 435.

15. Ibid.

16. Ibid.

17. For more, see Awaya, *Shōwa no seitō.* In English and with a slightly different take on the same situation, see Kinmonth, "The Mouse that Roared."

18. Awaya and Nakazono, eds., *Sensō makki no minshin dōkō,* vol. 1, *Haisen zengo no shakai jōsei,* pp. 1–11.

19. Ibid., p. 48. See the April 1944 document "Toshi ni okeru shakai fuan no onshō o miserarure shogenshō ni tsuite, naimushō, hoanbu."

20. Ibid., p. 54. See the April 1944 document.

21. Ibid., p. 69. See the April 22, 1944, document "Saikin ni okeru shojōsei, daigoka, keishichō jōhōka."

22. Coox, "Needless Fear," p. 415; and Feifer, *Tennozan.* Soon after the end of the war, a full military analysis raised the troop estimates to 735,000 massed in Kyushu.

23. For more on *tonarigumi,* see Aldous, *The Police in Occupation Japan,* pp. 36–40.

24. Tokyo Daikūshū Sensaishi Henshūiinkai, ed., *Tokyo daikūshū sensaishi, daigokan,* vol. 5, *Tōkyō kūshū o kiroku suru kai,* p. 115. The document is an example of one of the *kairanban* (a newsletter passed from house to house) from the Nakano section in western Tokyo, from July 12, 1945. The title of the *kairanban* is "Seni kōyō taikaisai ni tsuite."

25. Ibid., p. 255. See the January 30, 1945, document, Kakugi ryōkai, "Daitōasen no gendankai ni sokuō suru yoron shidō hōshin."

26. Ibid., pp. 300, 310–311. Taken from the September 1944 reprint of the Naikaku jōhōkyoku daiichibu shūhōka, daijūnigō, "Shūhō yoron hōkoku." This September issue marked the Shūhō yoron hōkoku's first year of publication. The magazine divided information and letters received into different categories to show how the population felt and to analyze public concerns.

27. Ibid., p. 347. The pulse of the people was taken by censoring mail, see March 1945, taken from a Tsūshinin tsūshinkantokukyoku report.

28. Ibid., p. 348.

29. Ibid., p. 364. Conditions from June to August 1945, as described in Home Ministry Metropolitan Police, Peace Preservation Section Reports.

30. Ibid., pp. 385–387. Document from Special Higher Police report on Koreans residing in Japan, "Zainichi chōsenjin ni miru minshin no dōkō," August 1945.

31. Awaya and Nakazono, eds., Sensō makki no minshin dōkō, vol. 1, Haisen zengo no shakai jōsei, pp. 350–352. From the June 21, 1945, document "Kōden hōdōtai secchi yōryō ni kansuru ken." This archive is a part of a larger report focusing on having the Home Ministry work collaboratively with the Military Police in order to stabilize society. The larger report is Document 20, "Haisenteki wahei sakudō narabi ni gendōsha nado no shisatu torishimari ni kansuru ken (shōwa 20nen 6gatsu) kenpei shireibu."

32. Ibid., p. 354, the letter dated July 31, 1945.

33. Ibid., p. 370. From a police report, July 1945, "Keishichō yori mita shakai jōsei ippan."

34. Ibid., pp. 425–429. From a gōgai (newspaper extra report) on July 29, 1945, in the Special Higher Police magazine Shisō junpō.

35. Ogino, ed., Tokkō keisatsu kankei shiryō shūsei, vol. 30, p. 452. From the document in Shisō junpō, July 21, 1945, "Kūshū gekika ni tomonau minshin no dōkō."

36. Ibid., p. 469. Taken from the August 1, 1945, Special Higher Police directive "Minshin no dōkō haaku ni kansuru ken."

37. Awaya and Nakazono, eds., Haisen chokugo no minshin dōkō (Kihon shirei ippan), vol. 2, Haisen zengo no shakai jōsei, pp. 3–5. From the August 1945 document "Naimudaijin, keihokyokuchō jimu hikitsugi jikō."

38. Dower, Embracing Defeat, p. 45.

39. Ibid., p. 46.

40. Lori Watt discusses the issues and complexities of repatriation in "When Empire Comes Home."

41. Awaya and Nakazono, eds., Haisen chokugo no minshin dōkō (Kihon shirei ippan), vol. 2, Haisen zengo no shakai jōsei, pp. 188–200. From the report on the collected leaflets "Fuon bunsho hanpu gaiyō," Shōwa 20.

42. Kōdansha, ed., Haikyo kara no shuppatsu, shōwa 20nen–21nen, vol. 7, Shōwa niman nichi no zenkiroku, p. 135.

43. Awaya and Nakazono, eds., Haisen chokugo no minshin dōkō (Kihon shirei

ippan), vol. 2, *Haisen zengo no shakai jōsei,* p. 37. From the August 1945 Tokubetsu kōtōka document "Tsūchōtei."

44. Ibid., p. 316. From the September 1, 1945, document "Kakushu zassantei."

45. Ibid., p. 78. See the document "Kōtō keisatsu kunjibo."

46. Takami was a proletarian writer before the war. He engaged in Dadaism during the 1920s, and later worked for Columbia Records. After 1940 he was drafted as a writer for the war and went to Burma. He continued writing after the war. Since Takami was a prewar Marxist, who switched allegiance to support the government in its wartime aims, his works reflect this changeover.

47. Takami, *Takami Jun nikki,* vol. 5, p. 6.

48. Ibid., p. 15.

49. Awaya and Nakazono, eds., *Haisen chokugo no minshin dōkō (Kihon shirei ippan),* vol. 2, *Haisen zengo no shakai jōsei,* p. 40. See the document for August 27, 1945, a notification to the head of police of Chiba prefecture concerning "Rengōgun no shogū nado ni kansuru ken."

50. Ibid., pp. 43–47. The quote is from page 47, from the Special Higher Police report on October 2, 1945, entitled, "Beikokujin kishitsu no samazamasō." Italics mine.

51. Ibid., pp. 214–215. From the August 15, 1945, document "Yamaguchiken keisatsu jōhō, hachigatsu ikō kugatsu hatsuka made."

52. Awaya and Kawashima, eds., *Haisenji zenkoku chian jōhō,* p. 30. Unfortunately, Kawashima does not provide the exact date of the broadcast, but we can assume it was August 15th or 16th because Suzuki handed the Prime Ministry to Higashikuni Naruhiko on August 17, 1945.

53. Takami, *Takami Jun nikki,* vol. 5, p. 53. On August 21, 1945, Takami quotes the newspaper *Yomiuri hōchi,* which stated that the war was lost essentially because the enemy had greater scientific and technological advancement. The paper stated the government now had a duty to promote these ideals of science and technology.

54. Awaya and Kawashima, eds., *Haisenji zenkoku chian jōhō,* pp. 90–91. Taken from "Kikan gunjin no gendō ni kansuru ken (dai ippō)," September 9, 1945.

55. Ibid., p. 92.

56. Ibid., pp. 114–115. Taken from an August 22, 1945, report, Naimushō keihoka, hoanbuchō, "Rengōgun shinjū ni saishi minshin antei ni kansuru ken."

57. Ibid., pp.116–117. From a questionnaire entitled "Gaikoku guntai shinchū chīki jūmin ni taisuru kairanban dentan montō."

58. Ibid., p. 233. Taken from the October 1, 1945, report filed on the scene, Keishi sōkan Saka Nobuyuki (kanbō shuji) kanjōhō dai 712 gō, Shōwa nijūnen jūgatsu tsuitachi, memo to naimu daijin Yamazaki Iwao, Gifuken chiji [futsū yō shisatsu hito no dōsei ni kansuru ken].

59. For fuller coverage of these ideas in English, see Burkman, ed. *The Occupation of Japan: Educational and Social Reform.* A second collection of essays, also edited by Burkman, is called *The Occupation of Japan: The International Context.*

60. Record Group 493 (China Theater), Entry 30340, Box 54, Intelligence - PW

Annex 6, G-2 Periodic Dept. Folder. Located in the United States National Archives II, College Park, Maryland.

61. Ibid.

62. Ariyama, *Senryōki mediashi kenkyū*, p. 57.

63. Ibid., p. 238.

64. Ibid., p. 242.

65. The term *chōsa* is often translated as "investigation," but this bureau dealt more with surveying public opinion and polling.

66. Kawashima, "Sengo seron chōsa jishi," p. 56.

67. *Asahi shimbun* (Tokyo edition), August 31, 1945.

68. Kawashima, "Sengo seron chōsa jishi," p. 55.

69. The numbers tell the extent of the mobilization. The army alone still operated 169 regular divisions, 4 tank divisions, and 15 airborne divisions, for a total mobilized manpower topping 5.5 million. Of that number, 2.4 million remained on the main island of Honshū and 3.1 million were abroad in various locations. The navy had already lost the majority of its ships, and most of its personnel had been shifted to the army. Nonetheless, Japan still managed to mobilize 1.3 million men for its domestic forces and 400,000 for forces abroad.

70. Fujiwara Akira, *Nihon gunjishi, gekan, sengohen*, pp. 5–7.

71. Bamford, *Body of Secrets*, pp. 11–12.

72. Fujiwara Akira, *Nihon gunjishi, gekan, sengohen*, pp. 16–17.

73. Morris-Suzuki, "Ethnic Engineering," p. 502. Morris-Suzuki suggests that public opinion polls were of interest to both the Japanese and the United States as a means of manipulating the public during the occupation.

74. Koyama, "Sensō to kokusai kankō senden."

75. Nanba, *Uchiteshi yamamu taiheiyō sensō to kōkoku no gijutsushatachi*, p. 200.

76. Morris-Suzuki, "Ethnic Engineering," p. 515.

77. Ibid.

78. "Senji hōsō senden," *Hōsō* (December 1942): 4–12.

79. Nanba, *Uchiteshi yamamu taiheiyō sensō to kōkoku no gijutsushatachi*, p. 203.

80. Record Group 331, (SCAP files), Box 5871, Yoneyama Keizo Folder. United States National Archives II, College Park, Maryland.

81. For Yokomizo's own view of his career, see Yokomizo, *Shōwashi henrin*.

82. GHQ disbanded the Special Higher Police in October 1945, but their role at the start of the occupation was key.

Conclusion

Epigraph: Ota was coordinator of the massive, last-ditch attempt to rid Okinawa of Americans. His words are quoted in Nakashi, "Okinawa senron," p. 298.

1. Nihon no Firipin Senryōki ni kansuru Shiryō Chōsa Fōramu, eds., *Nihon no Firipin senryō*, p. 504.

2. Specifically, the works of John Dower, Sheldon Garon, Chalmers Johnson,

Richard Samuels ("Rich Nation, Strong Army"), Bai Gao, and Sharon Minichiello (*Japan's Competing Modernities*) focus on the economic and social continuities of transwar Japan.

3. Wakakuwa, *Sensō ga tsukuru joseizō*, p. 253.

4. Aldous, *The Police in Occupation Japan*, p. 46.

5. Field, *In the Realm of a Dying Emperor;* Buruma, *The Wages of Guilt.*

6. Akazawa and Awaya, eds., *Ishihara Hiroichirō kankei monjo*, vol. 1., *Kaisōroku,* p. 196. For a similar understanding of French wartime propaganda's relation to postwar France, see Rousso, *Le Syndrome de Vichy.*

7. See Matsuo, *Chūgokujin sensō higaisha to sengo hoshō,* for full details on this case and a concise overview of Chinese legal complaints against Japan for wartime actions.

8. "Kokunai keihatsu senden," 1949, vol. 5, [Kokunai keihatsu senden] Kōbun-ruishū dai 74hen, dai5kan, shōwa 24, (2A-28-2rui 3317), located in the Kokuritsu Kobunshokan.

9. Katō, *Rikugun Nakano gakkō no zenbō*, p. 98.

10. The hazy relations between wartime and postwar Japan make excellent scenarios for contemporary fictional films. A 2002 Korean/Japanese production called *Killing Target* centers on a plot dealing with the mysterious 1973 kidnapping of Korean opposition leader Kim Dae Jung. The story hinges on wartime relations between Japanese and Korean leaders who attended military school together during the war. The film is fictional, but its plausibility and its attention to the positions of authority that military men continue to hold after the war in both countries render its message that much more convincing.

11. Taikai naimushōshi henshūiinkai, ed., *Naimushōshi,* vol. 4, p. 259.

Bibliography

Unless otherwise noted, all Japanese books are published in Tokyo. Japanese and Chinese names are cited last name first.

Akazawa Shirō. *Kindai nihon no shisō dōin to shūkyō tōsei.* Azekura shobō, 1985.

———. "Kyōka dōin seisaku no tenkai." In Kano Masanao and Yui Masanomi, eds., *Kindai nihon no tōgō to teikō,* Vol. 4. Nihon hyōronsha, 1982.

———. "Nihon fashizumu to taishū bunka." *Nihonshi kenkyū* 295 (March 1986): 32–44.

Akazawa Shirō and Awaya Kentarō, eds. *Ishihara Hiroichirō kankei monjo.* Vol. 1, *Kaisōroku.* Kashiwa shobō, 1994.

———. *Ishihara Hiroichirō kankei monjo.* Vol. 2, *Shiryōshū.* Kashiwa shobō, 1994.

Akazawa Shirō, Awaya Kentarō, and Yoshida Yutaka, eds. *Gendaishi to minshushugi.* Azuma shuppan, 1996.

Akazawa Shirō, Awaya Kentarō, et al., eds. *Nenpō nihon gendaishi, dai nana gō: Sensōka no senden to bunka.* Gendai shiryō shuppan, 2001.

Akazawa Shirō, Kitagawa Kenzō, and Yui Masanomi, eds. *Shiryō nihon gendaishi.* Vol. 12, *Taiseiyokusankai.* Ōtsuki shoten, 1984.

Akiyama Masami, ed. *Maboroshi no sensō manga no sekai.* Natsume shobō, 1998.

Aldous, Christopher. *The Police in Occupation Japan.* New York: Routledge, 1997.

Allen, Ernest, Jr. "Waiting for Tojo: The Pro-Japan Vigil of Black Missourians, 1932–1943." *Gateway Heritage* (1994): 16–33.

Allied Translator and Interpreter Section South West Pacific Area. Selected documents. Located in the National Diet Library, Kensei shiryō room, Tokyo, Japan.

Amō Eiji nikki shiryōshū kankōkai ed. *Amō Eiji nikki shiryōshū.* Amō Eiji nikki shiryōshū kankōkai, 1982.

Aoki Tamotsu, Kawamoto Saburō, Tsutsui Kiyotada, Mikuriya Takashi, and Yamaori Tetsuo, eds. *Sensō to guntai.* Vol. 10, *Kindai nihon bunkaron.* Iwanami shoten, 1999.

Arai Seiichirō. *Aru kōkokujin no nikki.* Dawiddo, 1972.

———. "Senden ippeisotsu no shuki." *Nihon senden bunka kyōkai* (October 1941).

Aramata Hiroshi. *Kessenka no yūtopia.* Bungei shunjū, 1996.

Argall, Phyllis. *My Life with the Enemy.* New York: Macmillan Company, 1944.

Ariyama Teruo. "Senji taisei to kokuminka." In Akazawa Shirō, Awaya Kentarō, et al., eds., *Nenpō nihon gendaishi, dai nana gō.* Vol. 7, *Sensōka no senden to bunka.* Gendai shiryō shuppan, 2001.

———. *Senryōki mediashi kenkyū.* Kashiwa shobō, 1996.

————. "Sōryokusen to gunbu media seisaku." In Tamotsu Aoki et al., eds., *Sensō to guntai*. Vol. 10, *Kindai nihon bunkaron*. Iwanami shoten, 1999.

Ariyama Teruo and Nishiyama Takesuke, eds. *Jōhōkyoku kankei shiryō dai yonkan: "Johokyoku senden tōsei kankei shiryō."* Kashiwa shobō, 2000.

Asahi shimbun (Tokyo edition). Selected articles.

Atkins, E. Taylor. *Blue Nippon*. Durham, NC: Duke University Press, 2001.

Awaya Kentarō, ed. *Haisen chokugo no seiji to shakai*. Vol. 1, *Shiryō nihon gendaishi 2*. Ōtsuki shuppan, 1980.

————. *Shōwa no seitō*. Shōgakukan, 1983.

Awaya Kentarō and Chatani Seiichi, eds. *Nicchū sensō taichūgoku jōhōsen shiryō, dai sankan (shōwa 14nen)*. Gendai shiryō shuppan, 2000.

Awaya Kentarō and Kawashima Takane, eds. *Haisenji zenkoku chian jōhō*. Nihon tosho sentā, 1994.

Awaya Kentarō and Nakazono Hiroshi, eds. *Sensō makki no minshin dōkō*. Vol. 1, *Haisen zengo no shakai jōsei*. Gendai shiryō shuppan, 1998.

————, eds. *Haisen chokugo no minshin dōkō (Kihon shirei ippan)*. Vol. 2, *Haisen zengo no shakai jōsei*. Gendai shiryō shuppan, 1998.

————, eds. *Haisen zengo no shakai jōsei*. Vol. 7, *Shingun no fuhō*. Gendai shiryō shuppan, 1998

Awaya Kentarō and Yoshida Yutaka, eds. *Kokusai kensatsu kyoku (IPS) jinmon chōsho*. Vol. 8. Nihon tosho sentā, 1993.

Azabu Shin. "Sensen imon yori kaerite." *Yūben* (July 1938): 302–306.

Ba Maw. *Breakthrough in Burma: Memoirs of a Revolution, 1939–1946*. New Haven: Yale University Press, 1968.

Bamford, James. *Body of Secrets*. New York: Anchor, 2002.

Barnhart, Michael A. *Japan Prepares for Total War: The Search for Economic Security, 1919–1941*. Ithaca, NY: Cornell University Press, 1987.

Barrett, David. *Dixie Mission: The United States Army Observer Group in Yenan*. Berkeley: Center for Chinese Studies, University of California, 1979.

Barrett, David, and Larry Shyu, eds. *Chinese Collaboration with Japan, 1932–1945: The Limits of Accommodation*. Stanford, CA: Stanford University Press, 2001.

Barshay, Andrew. *State and Intellectual in Imperial Japan*. Berkeley: University of California Press, 1988.

Baskett, Michael. "The Attractive Empire: Colonial Asia in Japanese Imperial Film Culture, 1931–1953." PhD dissertation, University of California, Los Angeles, 2000.

————. "Dying for a Laugh: Post-1945 Japanese Service Comedies." *Historical Journal of Film, Radio and Television* 23, 4 (October 2003): 291–310.

Beechert, Alice M., and Edward D. Beechert, eds. *From Kona to Yenan: The Political Memoirs of Koji Ariyoshi*. Honolulu: University of Hawaiʻi Press, 2000.

Benedict, Ruth. *The Chrysanthemum and the Sword*. Boston: Houghton Mifflin Company, 1946.

Benson, Carlton. "From Teahouse to Radio: Storytelling and the Commercialization of Culture in 1930s Shanghai." PhD dissertation, University of California, 1996.

Binfield, J. C., and John Stevenson, eds. *Sport, Culture and Politics*. Sheffield: Sheffield Academic Press, 1993.

Bix, Herbert P. *Hirohito and the Making of Modern Japan*. New York: Harper Collins Publishers, 2000.

Bōeichō Archives, Tokyo, Japan (Ministry of Defense Archives).

Bungei shunjū. Selected articles.

Burkman, Thomas W., ed. *The Occupation of Japan Educational and Social Reform*. Proceedings of a Symposium at Old Dominion University sponsored by the MacArthur Memorial Foundation Oct. 1980. Norfolk, VA: Gatling Printing and Publishing, 1982.

———. *The Occupation of Japan: The International Context*. Proceedings of a Symposium at Old Dominion University sponsored by the MacArthur Memorial Foundation. Norfolk, VA: Gatling Printing and Publishing, 1984.

Buruma, Ian. *Wages of Guilt: Memories of War in Germany and Japan*. New York: Farrar, Straus, Giroux, 1994.

Bytwerk, Randall L. "The Dolt Laughs: Satirical Publications under Hitler and Honecker." *Journalism Quarterly* 69, 4 (Winter 1992): 1029–1038.

Carter, Carolle. *Mission to Yenan: American Liaison with the Chinese Communists 1944–1947*. Lexington: University Press of Kentucky, 1997.

Cheng Jihua, ed., *Zhongguo dianying fazhanshi*. 2 volumes. Beijing: Zhongguo dianying chubanshe, 1980.

China at War. Selected articles.

Coble, Parks. *Facing Japan: Chinese Politics and Japanese Imperialism, 1931–1937*. Cambridge, MA: Council on East Asian Studies, Harvard University, 1991.

Collection of Propaganda Leaflets, World War II, Pacific Area, Philippines (N.P.), 1944–1945, Microfilm, New York Public Library, New York City.

Cook, Haruko Taya, and Theodore F. Cook. *Japan at War: An Oral History*. New York: The New Press, 1992.

Coox, Alvin. "Needless Fear: The Compromise of US Plans to Invade Japan in 1945." *The Journal of Military History* 64 (April 2000): 411–438.

Corbett, P. Scott. *Quiet Passages: The Exchange of Civilians between the United States and Japan during the Second World War*. Kent, OH: Kent State University Press, 1987.

Cull, Nicholas. *Selling War: The British Propaganda Campaign against American "Neutrality" in World War Two*. New York: Oxford University Press, 1995.

Cunningham, Stanley B. *The Idea of Propaganda: A Reconstruction*. London: Praeger, 2002.

Daihonei kaigun hōdōbu, ed. *Sangokai kaisen*. Bungei shunjūsha, 1942.

Daitōa kyōdō sengen. Dainippon yūbenkai kōdansha, 1944.

Daniels, Gordon. "Japanese Sport: From Heian Kyoto to Tokyo Olympiad." In J. C. Binfield and John Stevenson, eds., *Sport, Culture and Politics*. Sheffield: Sheffield Academic Press, 1993.

Davies, John Paton. *Dragon by the Tail*. New York: Norton, 1972.

Dezain shōshi henshūkai, ed. *Nihon dezain shōshi.* Dawiddo, 1970.

Don Brown Collection, Yokohama Kaikō Shiryōkan, Yokohama, Japan. Various publications.

Doob, Leonard William. *Propaganda: Its Psychology and Technique.* New York: H. Holt and Company, 1943.

———. *Public Opinion and Propaganda.* New York: H. Holt, 1948.

Douglas, Allen. *War, Memory, and the Politics of Humor 'The Canard Enchâiné' and World War I.* Berkeley: University of California Press, 2002.

Dower, John. *Embracing Defeat: Japan in the Wake of World War II.* New York: W. W. Norton and Co., 1999.

———. *Empire and Aftermath: Yoshida Shigeru and the Japanese Experience 1878–1954.* Cambridge, MA: Council on East Asian Studies, Harvard University, 1988.

———. *Japan in War and Peace.* New York: New Press, 1993.

———. *War without Mercy: Race and Power in the Pacific War.* New York: Pantheon Books, 1986.

Drea, Edward. *In the Service of the Emperor.* Lincoln: University of Nebraska Press, 1998.

Dunnigan, James F., and Albert A. Nofi. *The Pacific War Encyclopedia.* Vols. 1 and 2. New York: Facts on File, Inc., 1998.

Duus, Peter. *The Abacus and the Sword.* Berkeley: University of California Press, 1995.

Eastman, Lloyd E. *The Abortive Revolution: China under Nationalist Rule, 1927–1937.* Cambridge, MA: Harvard University Press, 1974.

———. *Seeds of Destruction.* Stanford, CA: Stanford University Press, 1984.

Eastman, Lloyd, and Jerome Ch'en, eds. *The Nationalist Era in China 1927–1949.* New York: Cambridge University Press, 1991.

Ellul, Jacques. *Propaganda: The Formation of Men's Attitudes.* Translated by Konrad Kellen and Jean Lerner. New York: Knopf, 1965.

Emmerson, John K. *The Japanese Thread: A Life in the U.S. Foreign Service.* New York: Holt, Rinehart and Winston, 1978.

Esherick, Joseph W., ed. *Lost Chance in China: The World War II Despatches of John S. Service.* New York: Random House, 1974.

Eskildsen, Robert. "Of Civilization and Savages: Mimetic Imperialism of Japan's 1874 Expedition to Taiwan." *American Historical Review* (April 2002): 388–418.

Fairbank, John King. *China Watch.* Cambridge, MA: Harvard University Press, 1987.

———. *Chinabound: A Fifty-year Memoir.* New York: Harper & Row, 1982.

Feifer, George. *Tennozan: The Battle of Okinawa and the Atomic Bomb.* New York: Ticknor and Fields, 1992.

Field, Norma. *In the Realm of a Dying Emperor.* New York: Random House, 1991.

Fitzgerald, John. *Awakening China: Politics, Culture, and Class in the Nationalist Revolution.* Stanford, CA: Stanford University Press, 1996.

———, ed. *The Nationalists and Chinese Society 1927–1937: A Symposium.* Melbourne: University of Melbourne, 1989.

Fletcher, William Miles. *The Search for a New Order: Intellectuals and Fascism in Prewar Japan.* Chapel Hill: University of North Carolina Press, 1982.
Fogel, Joshua A. *The Literature of Travel in the Japanese Rediscovery of China, 1862–1945.* Stanford, CA: Stanford University Press, 1996.
Fogel, Joshua A., ed. *The Nanjing Massacre in History and Historiography.* Berkeley: University of California Press, 2000.
FRONT. Selected articles.
Fujime Yuki. *Sei no rekishigaku: Kōshō seido, dataizai taisei kara baishun boshihō, yūsei hogohō taisei e.* Fuji shuppan, 1997.
Fujita, Frank. *Foo: A Japanese American Prisoner of the Rising Sun.* Denton: University of North Texas Press, 1993.
Fujiwara Akira. *Nihon gunjishi, gekan, sengohen.* Nihon hyōronsha, 1987.
———. *Nihonjinmin hansen dōmei shiryō, bekkan.* Kaji Wataru shiryō chōsa kankōkai, ed. Fuji shuppan, 1995.
———. "Nihon no chūgoku shinryaku to hansen dōmei." In *Nihonjinmin hansen dōmei shiryō, bekkan.* Kaji Wataru shiryō chōsa kankōkai, ed. Fuji shuppan, 1995.
Fujiwara Akira and Awaya Kentarō, eds. *Tettei kenshō shōwa tennō [dokuhakuroku].* Ōtsuki shoten, 1991.
Fujiwara Akira and Himeta Mitsuyoshi, eds. *Chūgoku ni okeru nihonjin no hansen katsudō.* Aoki shoten, 1999.
Fujiwara Iwaichi. *F. kikan: Japanese Army Intelligence Operations in Southeast Asia during World War II.* Translated by Akashi Yoji. Hong Kong: Heinemann Asia, 1983.
Fukuda Toshiyuki. *Sugata naki senpei: Nicchū rajio senshi.* Maruyama gakugei tosho, 1993.
Furuya Tetsuo, ed. *Nicchū sensōshi kenkyū.* Yoshikawakobunkan, 1984.
Gaiji keisatsuhō. Selected articles.
Gaikōshiryōkan, Tokyo, Japan (Diplomatic Record Office of the Ministry of Foreign Affairs). Selected reports.
Gakushūkenkyūsha, ed., *[Zusetsu] Shinkansen zenshi.* Gakushūkenkyūsha, 2003.
Gao, Bai. *Economic Ideology and Japanese Industrial Policy: Developmentalism from 1931 to 1965.* New York: Cambridge University Press, 1997.
Gao Yuan. "[Futatsu no kindai] no konseki." In Yoshimi Shunya, ed., *Senkyūhyaku sanjūnendai no media to shintai.* Seikyūsha, 2002.
———. "[Rakudo] o hashiru kankō basu." In Yoshimi Shunya, ed., *Iwanami kōza kindai nihon no bunkashi 6: Kakudai suru modanati.* Iwanami shoten, 2002.
Garon, Sheldon. *Molding Japanese Minds: The State in Everyday Life.* Princeton, NJ: Princeton University, 1997.
Gary, Brett. *Nervous Liberals: Propaganda Anxieties from World War I to the Cold War.* New York: Columbia University Press, 1999.
Gillin, Donald G., and Charles Etter. "Staying On: Japanese Soldiers and Civilians in China, 1945–1949." *Journal of Asian Studies* 42, 3 (1983): 497–518.
Gilmore, Allison. "'We have been reborn': Japanese Prisoners and the Allied Propa-

ganda War in the Southwest Pacific." *Pacific Historical Review* 64, 2 (1995): 195–215.

———. *You Can't Fight Tanks with Bayonets: Psychological Warfare against the Japanese Army in the Southwest Pacific.* Lincoln: University of Nebraska Press, 1998.

Gonda Yasunosuke. "Senjika ni okeru shimin goraku mondai." *Toshi mondai* (September 1940): 79–88.

———. "Shintaisei ni okeru iangoraku mondai." *Shakai jigyō kenkyū* (November 1940): 1–11.

Guo Moruo. *Kōnichisen kaisōroku.* Translated by Okasaki Tatsuo. Chūō kōronsha, 1959.

———. *Zhangshi xuanchuan gongzuo.* Chongqing: Qingnian shudian, 1938.

Hagi Shūgetsu. *Kasen no haha.* Fujokaisha, 1941.

Haley, John Owen. *Authority without Power: Law and the Japanese Paradox.* New York: Oxford University Press, 1991.

Harada Katsumasa, ed. *Daitōa jūkan tetsudō kankeishorui.* Fuji shuppan, 1988.

Hasegawa Nyozekan. "Senden no nihonteki seikaku." *Senden* (May 1942): 6–9.

Hasegawa Teru. *Arashi no naka no sasayaki.* Translated from Esperanto by Takasugi Ichirō. Shinhyōronsha, 1954.

Hata Ikuhiko. *Gun fashizumu undō shi.* Kawade shobōshinsha, 1962.

———. *Nihonjin horyo (Jō):* Hara shobō, 1998.

———. *Nicchū sensō shi.* Kawade shobōshinsha, 1961.

———, ed. *Nihon rikukaigun sōgōjiten.* Heibonsha, 1991.

———, ed. *Senzenki nihon kanryōsei no seido soshiki jinji.* Daigaku shuppankai, 1981.

Havens, Thomas R. H. *Valley of Darkness.* New York: W. W. Norton and Company, 1978.

Heiwa Hakubutsukan o Tsukuru Kai. *Kami no sensō dendan.* Emirusha, 1990.

Hicks, George L. *The Comfort Women.* St Leonards, NSW: Allen & Unwin, 1995.

High, Peter B. *Teikoku no ginmaku: Jūgonen sensō to nihon eiga.* Nagoya: Nagoya daigaku shuppankai, 1995.

Himeta Mitsuyoshi. "Sōron, nicchū sensō to kōnichi sensō no hazama." In Fujiwara Akira and Himeta Mitsuyoshi, eds., *Chūgoku ni okeru nihonjin no hansen katsudō.* Aoki shoten, 1999.

Hinode. Selected articles.

Hirakushi Takashi. *Daihonei hōdōbu.* Tosho shuppansha, 1980.

Hōdō gijutsu kenkyū (Media research technology). Selected articles.

Hōdō Gijutsu Kenkyūkei, ed. *Senden gijutsu.* Seikatsusha, 1943.

Holm, David. *Art and Ideology in Revolutionary China.* Oxford: Clarendon Press, 1991.

Honda Katsuichi. *Chūgoku no tabi.* Asahi shimbunsha, 1972.

———. *The Nanjing Massacre: A Japanese Journalist Confronts Japan's National Shame.* Frank Gibney, ed. Karen Sandness, trans. Armonk, NY: M.E. Sharpe, 1999.

Hori Eizō. *Daihonei sanbō no jōhōsenki.* Bungei shunjū, 1996.

Horton, Andrew, ed. *Inside Soviet Film Satire: Laughter with a Lash.* New York: Cambridge University Press, 1993.

Horton, Gerd. *Radio Goes to War: The Cultural Politics during World War II.* Berkeley: University of California Press, 2002.

Hoshi Tōru. "Wasureenu shichisanichi butai no kyōki." *Shūkan kinyōbi,* February 25, 2000: 48–51.

Hōsō. Selected articles.

Hu Lei. *Fulu riji.* Place Unknown: Quanmin chuban, 1938.

Ienaga Saburō. *The Pacific War, 1931–1945.* Translated by Frank Baldwin. New York: Random House, 1978.

Ikeda Norizane. *Puropaganda senshi.* Chūō kōronsha, 1981.

Ikō Toshiya, ed. *Taiheiyō sensōki naimushō chian taisaku jōhō.* Vol. 1. Series edited by Awaya Kentarō. Nihon tosho sentā, 1995.

Imai Seiichi. "1940 nen zengo no nihon no kōsen chūgoku ninshiki." *Chikaki ni arite* (November 1991): 23–30.

Imaizumi Takeji. "Jiyū no atarashisa." *Kōkokukai* (February 1940).

———. Papers of the Imaizumi Takeji collection, Ritsumeikan University, Kyoto, Japan.

Inaba Masao. *Gendaishi shiryō.* Vol. 37, *Daihonei.* Misuzu shobō, 1967.

Inoue Yūko. "Hōdō gijutsu kenkyūkai no [gijutsu] to sakuhin-senjika no aru kōkoku-jin gurūpu." *Mediashi kenkyū* (May 1998): 82–110.

Iritani, Toshio. *Group Psychology of the Japanese People in Wartime.* New York: Kegan Paul International, 1991.

———. *Nihonjin no shūdan shinri.* Shinchōsha, 1987.

Iriye, Akira. *Across the Pacific: An Inner History of American-East Asian Relations.* New York: Harcourt Brace Jovanovich, 1967.

———. *The Chinese and the Japanese: Essays in Political and Cultural Interactions.* Princeton, NJ: Princeton University Press, 1980.

———. *The Origins of the Second World War in Asia and the Pacific.* New York: Longman, 1987.

———. *Power and Culture: The Japanese-American War, 1941–1945.* Cambridge, MA: Harvard University Press, 1981.

Iriye, Akira, and Warren Cohen, eds. *American, Chinese, and Japanese Perspectives on Wartime Asia, 1931–1949.* Wilmington, DE: SR Books, 1990.

Ishida Ichimatsu and Kyōyama Wakamaru. *Warawashitai hōkokuki kōgun imon no tabi.* No publisher, 1938.

Ishikawa Hiroyoshi, ed. *Goraku no senzenshi.* Tokyo shoseki, 1981.

———, ed. *Yoka goraku kenkyū kiso bunkenshū.* Ōzorasha, 1990.

Ishizuka Hiromichi and Narita Ryūichi. *Tōkyōto no hyakunen.* Yamakawa shuppansha, 1986.

Ivens, Joris. *The Camera and I.* New York: International Publishers, 1974.

Iwai Yoshikazu. "Koyama Eizō no yoron kenkyūshi ni tsuite." *Meiji gakuin ronsō* (Shakaigaku Shakai Fukushigaku Kenkyū) (March 1997): 37–74.

Iwao Shibata. "Hasegawa Teru kenkyū." *Chiba kōgyō daigaku kenkyū hōkoku jinbunhen* 35 (1998): 107–115.

Jansen, Marius. *The Japanese and Sun Yat-Sen*. Cambridge, MA: Harvard University Press, 1954.

Japanese Devils. Riben Guizi Production Committee, 2001.

Japanese Ministry of Foreign Affairs. Division of Special Records. *Documents concerning the Allied Occupation of Japan*. Vol. 1, *Basic Documents*. 1949. Reprint Nihon tosho sentā, 1989.

Johnson, Chalmers. *An Instance of Treason: Ozaki Hotsumi and the Sorge Spy Ring*. Stanford, CA: Stanford University Press, 1964.

———. *MITI and the Japanese Miracle: The Growth of Industrial Policy, 1925–1975*. Stanford, CA: Stanford University Press, 1982.

Jowett, Garth S., and Victoria O'Donnell, *Propaganda and Persuasion*. Newbury Park, CA: Sage, 1986.

Junshi weiyuanhui zhengzhibu translation. *Shibing bixu zhi*. Translated into Chinese from Japanese. No publishing date. Located in KMT Central Party Headquarters Archives, Taipei, Taiwan.

Kagawa Hideo. *Hokushi senbukō*. Matsuyamashi: Matsuyama kōtō shōgyō gakkō shōkei kenkyūkai, 1941.

Kagawa Takashi and Maeda Mitsushige. *Hachirogun no nihonheitachi*. The Simul Press, 1984.

Kagayaku Butai. *Kagayaku*. 3 volumes. Fuji shuppan, 1988.

Kageyama Masao. *Marē kessen kamera senki*. Arusu, 1943.

Kaigai Hōsō Kenkyū Gurūpu, ed. *NHK senji kaigai hōsō*. Hara shobō, 1982.

Kaji Wataru. *Kotoba no dangan*. Chūō kōronsha, 1947.

Kajimoto Masato. "Online Documentary: The Nanjing Atrocities." MA thesis, University of Missouri School of Journalism, 2000. Site address: (http://www.missouri.edu/jschool/nanking).

Kanda Kōichi. *Shisōsen to senden*. No publisher, 1937.

Kankō. Selected articles.

Kano Masanao and Yui Masanomi. *Kindai nihon no tōgō to teikō*. Vol. 4. Nihon hyōronsha, 1982.

Kaplan, David E., and Alec Dubro. *Yakuza: The Explosive Account of Japan's Criminal Underworld*. Reading, MA: Addison-Wesley, 1986.

Karnow, Stanley. *In Our Image: America's Empire in the Philippines*. New York: Random House, 1989.

Kashiwagi Hiroshi. "Senji senden no modanizumu." *Geijutsuronchō* (December 1989).

———. *Shōzō no naka no kenryoku*. Heibonsha, 1987.

Katō Masao. *Rikugun nakano gakkō no zenbō*. Tendensha, 1998.

Katō Masuo. *The Lost War: A Japanese Reporter's Inside Story*. New York: Knopf, 1946.

Katō Yūzaburō. "Shin naikaku no shisei taikō to keisatsu no ninmu." *Keisatsu kyōkai zasshi* (March 1937).

Kawamura Minato. *Ikyō no shōwa bungaku*. Iwanami shinsho, 1990.

———. *Manshū hōkai-daitōa bungaku to sakkatachi*. Bungei shunjū, 1997.

———. *Manshūtetsudō maboroshi ryokō*. Bungei shunjū, 1998.

———. *Sakubun no naka no dainihon teikoku.* Iwanami shoten, 2000.

———. *Umi o watatta nihongo: Shokuminchi no [kokugo] no jikan.* Seidosha, 1994.

Kawano Hitoshi. "Gyokusai no shisō to hakuhei shōtotsu." In Aoki Tamotsu, et al., eds., *Sensō to guntai.* Vol. 10, *Kindai nihon bunkaron.* Iwanami shoten, 1999.

Kawashima Takane. *Jūgo: Ryūgen tōsho no "taiheiyō sensō."* Yomiuri shinbunsha, 1997.

———. "Sengo seron chōsa jishi: Senryōgun no jōhō seisaku to nihon seifu no chōsa kikan." *Mediashi kenkyū,* 2 (February 1995): 49–65.

Kawayase Fuhō. *Senbukō.* Sakkasha, 1940.

Keene, Donald. "The Barren Years: Japanese War Literature." *Monumenta Nipponica* 33, 1 (1978): 67–112.

———. *Emperor of Japan.* New York: Columbia University Press, 2002.

———. "Japanese Literature and Politics in the 1930s." *Journal of Japanese Studies* 2, 2 (1976): 225–248.

———. "Japanese Writers and the Greater East Asia War." *Journal of Asian Studies* 25, 2 (1964): 209–225.

Keisatsu shichō. Selected articles.

Keishichōshi Hensaniinkai. *Keishichōshi shōwazenhen.* Keishichōshi hensan iinkai, 1962.

Kido Nikki Kenkyūkai, ed. *Kido Kōchi kankei monjo.* Daigaku shuppankai, 1966.

Kinmonth, Earl H. "The Mouse That Roared: Saito Takao, Conservative Critic of Japan's 'Holy War' in China." *Journal of Japanese Studies* 25, 2 (Summer 1999): 331–360.

NIPPON. Selected articles.

Kisaka Junichirō. *Shōwa no rekishi.* Vol. 7, *Taiheiyō sensō.* Shōgakukan, 1989.

Kitagawa Kenzō. "Sensōka no sesō fūzoku to bunka." In Fujiwara Akira and Imai Sei-ichi, eds., *Jūgonen sensōshi.* Vol. 2. Aoki shoten, 1988.

Kitaoka Juitsu, ed. *Yūjō no hito Tsurumi Yūsuke sensei.* Kitaoka self-publishing, 1975.

Kitayama Setsurō. *Rajio Tokyo.* Vol. 3, *Haiboku e no michi.* Tahata shoten, 1988.

Kiyosawa Kiyoshi. *A Diary of Darkness.* Eugene Soviak, ed. Princeton: Princeton University Press, 1999.

KMT Central Party Headquarters Archives, Taipei, Taiwan. Selected documents and reports.

Koba Keiten. *Rikusentai senbuki.* Shimizu shobō, 1941.

Kobayashi Kiyoshi (Xiaolin Qing). *Zai zhongguo de tudi shang: Yi ge "Riben balu" de zishu.* Beijing: Jiefangjun chubanshe, 1985.

Kobayashi Yoshinori. *Shin gomanizumu sengen Special sensōron.* Gentōsha, 1998.

———. *Shin gomanizumu sengen Special sensōron (2).* Gentōsha, 2001.

———. *Shin gomanizumu sengen Special sensōron (3).* Gentōsha, 2003.

———. *Shin gomanizumu sengen Special Taiwanron.* Shōgakukan, 2000.

Kobayashi Yoshinori and Alice King (Jin Meili). *Nyūkoku kyohi [Taiwanron] wa naze yakaretaka.* Gentōsha, 2001.

Kōdansha, ed. *Haikyo kara no shuppatsu, shōwa 20 nen- 21 nen.* Vol. 7, *Shōwa niman nichi no zenkiroku.* Kōdansha, 1989.

Kojima Teiji. *Manzai sesōshi*. Mainichi shinbunsha, 1978.

———. *Rakugo sanbyakunen: Shōwa no kan*. Mainichi shinbunsha, 1966.

———, ed. *Taishū geinō shiryō shūsei*. Vol. 7, *Manzai*. Sanichi shobō, 1980.

Kokon tōzai hanashika shinshiroku. CD produced by the APP company, 2000.

Kokonteishinshō. *Binbō jiman*. Rippu shobō, 1969.

Kokuritsu Kobunshokan, Tokyo, Japan (Cabinet Archives). Numerous reports.

Kokuritsu Kokkai Toshokan, Kensei Shiryō shitsu, Tokyo, Japan. (National Diet Library, Kensei shiryō room.) Numerous reports.

Kokusai kankō. Various articles.

"Kokusaku manga." *Shashin shūhō*, January 31, 1940.

Komota Nobuo, et al, eds. *Shinpan nihon ryūkōkashi (chūkan)*. Shakai shisōsha, 1995.

Kōriyama Kazuo. *Kessen manzai sakura hinode kessakushū*. Seikyōsha, 1943.

Koronbia Gojūnenshi Henshūiinkai, ed. *Koronbia gojūnenshi*. Nihon koronbia, 1961.

Kōseishō Kenkyūbu Jinkō Minzokubu, eds., *Minzoku jinkō seisaku kenkyū shiryō: senjika ni okeru kōseishō kenkyūbu jinkō mondai minzokubu shiryō*. Kōseishō, 1942.

Koshizawa Akira. *Manshukoku no shuto keikaku*. Nihon keizai hyōronsha, 1988.

Koyama Eizō. *Daitōa sensō to chūgoku minshū no dōkō*. Minzoku kenkyūjō, 1944.

———. "Kankō seisaku to minzoku ninshiki." *Kokusai kankō* (October 1938): 10–15.

———. *Senden gijutsuron*. Koyoshoin, 1937.

———. *Senji sendenron*. Sanseidō, 1942

———. "Sensō to kokusai kankō senden." *Kokusai kankō* (January 1938): 8–13.

———. "Shōseiken no bunka senden seisaku." *Hōsō* (1939.4): 18–22.

Koyanagi Tsugukichi and Ishikawa Yasumasa. *Jūgun kameraman no sensō*. Shinchōsha, 1993.

Kramer, Arnold. "Japanese Prisoners of War in America." *Pacific Historical Review* 52, 1 (1983): 67–91.

Kurata Yoshihiro. *Meiji taishō no minshū goraku*. Iwanami shoten, 1980.

———. *Nihon rekōdo bunkashi*. Tokyo shoseki, 1975.

Kurata Yoshihiro and Fujinami Takayuki, eds. *Nihon geinō jinmei jiten*. Sanseidō, 1995.

Kushner, Barak. "Laughter as Materiel: The Mobilization of Comedy in Japan's Fifteen-Year War." *The International History Review* 26, no. 2 (June 2004): 300–330.

Kuwajima Setsurō. *Kahoku senki*. Tosho shuppansha, 1978.

Large, Stephen S. *Emperor Hirohito and Showa Japan: A Political Biography*. New York: Routledge, 1992.

Lasker, Bruno, and Agnes Roman. *Propaganda from China and Japan*. New York: Institute of Pacific Relations, 1938.

Laurie, Clayton. "The Ultimate Dilemma of Psychological Warfare in the Pacific: Enemies Who Don't Surrender, and GIs Who Don't Take Prisoners." *War & Society* (May 1996): 99–120.

Lebra, Joyce C. *Japanese-trained Armies in Southeast Asia*. Singapore: Heinemann Educational Books, 1977.

———. *Jungle Alliance: Japan and the Indian National Army*. Singapore: Asia Pacific Press, 1971.

Levine, Steven I. *Anvil of Victory: The Communist Revolution in Manchuria, 1945–1948.* New York: Columbia University Press, 1987.

Levine, Steven I., and James Hsiung, eds. *China's Bitter Victory: The War with Japan 1937–45.* New York: M.E. Sharpe, 1992.

Li, Lincoln. *The Japanese Army in North China 1937–1941.* New York: Oxford University Press, 1975.

Liao Tiren. "Duidi xuanchuan gongzuo zhi jianshi." *Balujun junzheng zazhi* (March 1942): 16–21.

Life. Selected articles.

Linhart, Sepp, and Sabine Fruhstuck, eds. *The Culture of Japan as Seen through Its Leisure.* Albany, NY: State University of New York Press, 1998.

Lone, Stewart. *Japan's First Modern War: Army and Society in the Conflict with China, 1894–95.* New York: St. Martin's Press, 1994.

Mabuchi Itsuo. *Hōdō sensō.* Kaizōsha, 1941.

Machida Keiji. *Aru gunjin no shihi.* Fuyo shuppansha, 1978.

———. *Tatakau bunka butai.* Hara shobō, 1967.

Maema Takanori. *Dangan ressha maboroshi no tōkyōhatsu pekin iki chōtokkyū.* Jitsugyō no nihonsha, 1994.

Mainichi shimbun (Tokyo edition). Selected articles.

Manshū nippōsha, ed. *Jikyoku oyobi hainichi posutā shashinchō.* Dalian, Manchukuo: Manshū Nippōsha, 1931.

Matsuhara Eiji. "Nōmin to kokumin engeki." *Kokumin engeki* (April 1941): 128–138.

Matsumoto Naoji. *Daihonei haken no kishatachi.* Katsura shobō, 1993.

Matsuo Shōichi. *Chūgokujin sensō higaisha to sengo hoshō.* Iwanami Booklet No. 466. Iwanami shoten, 1998.

Matsuura Sōzō. *Senchū senryōka no masukomi.* Ōtsuki shoten, 1984.

———. *Tennō to masukomi.* Aoki shoten, 1975.

Meserve, Walter, and Ruth Meserve. "From Teahouse to Loudspeaker: The Popular Entertainer in the People's Republic of China." *Journal of Popular Culture* 13, 1 (1979): 131–140.

Messinger, Gary S. *British Propaganda and the State in the First World War.* New York: Manchester University Press, 1992.

Mikami Isao. "Nandaka omoshiroin desu yo, kaisha no naka ga." In Tagawa Seiichi, Imaizumi Takeji, and Okada Kazuo, eds., *FRONT (Fukkokuban) Kaisetsu III.* Heibonsha, 1990.

Mikuni Ichirō. *Senchū yōgoshū.* Iwanami shinsho, 1985.

Minami Hiroshi, ed. *Kindai shomin seikatsushi.* Vol. 8, Yūgi, Goraku. Sanichi shobō, 1984.

———. *Shakai ishiki to rekishi ishiki.* Keisō shobō, 2004.

———, ed. *Showa bunka, 1925–1945.* Keisō shobō, 1987.

Minichiello, Sharon A., ed. *Japan's Competing Modernities: Issues in Culture and Democracy 1900–1930.* Honolulu: University of Hawai'i Press 1998.

Mitchell, Richard H. *Janus-faced Justice: Political Criminals in Imperial Japan.* Honolulu: University of Hawai'i Press, 1992.

———. *Thought Control in Prewar Japan.* Ithaca, NY: Cornell University, 1976.

Miura Shigeji. "Koyama Eizō no kōhō ikōru PR seisaku ni tsuite." *Meiji gakuin ronsō* (Shakaigaku Shakai Fukushigaku Kenkyū) (March 1996): 47–79.

Miyako shimbun. Selected articles.

Morioka, Heinz, and Miyoko Sasaki. *Rakugo: The Popular Narrative Art of Japan.* Cambridge, MA: Council on East Asian Studies, Harvard University, 1990.

Morris-Suzuki, Tessa. "Ethnic Engineering: Scientific Racism and Public Opinion Surveys in Midcentury Japan." *Positions* 8, 2 (Fall 2000): 499–529.

Muneo Matsuji. *Shisōsen.* Rikugeisha, 1942.

Murakami Yasuo. "Posutā haifu ni kansuru chōsa." *Senbu geppō* (May 1941): 67–72.

Nagahama Isao. *Kokumin seishin sōdōin no shisō to kōzō senjika minshu kyōka no kenkyū.* Akashi shoten, 1987.

Nagasaka Keiichi. "New Information Chief Amau." *Contemporary Japan* (July 1943): 838–844.

Naikaku Jōhōbu. *Shisōsen kōshūkai kōgi sokki, daiichigō.* Publisher unknown, 1938.

———. *Shisōsen tenrankai kiroku zukan.* Naikaku jōhōbu, 1938.

Naimushō Keihokyoku. *Shuppan keisatsu gaikan (fukkokuban): Dai 3 kan.* 1934, 1935. Reprinted Fuji shuppan, 1988.

Naimushōshi Kenkyūkai, ed. *Naimushō to kokumin.* Bunken shuppan, 1998.

Naiseishi Kenkyūkai, ed. *Arai Zentarō shi danwa sokkiroku, naiseishi kenkyūshiryō.* Naiseishi kenkyūkai, 1983.

———, ed. *Yokomizo Mitsuteru shi danwa sokkiroku (ge), naiseishi kenkyūshiryō.* Naiseishi kenkyūkai, 1963.

Nakajima Kenzō. "Kokumin goraku no shiten." *Kaizō* (December 1941).

Nakano Minoru. "Senbuhan kara." *Bungei shunjū* (January 1938): 320–325.

Nakashi Yōhachirō. "Okinawa senron." In Kano Masanao and Yui Masanomi, *Kindai nihon no tōgō to teikō,* Vol. 4. Nihon hyōronsha, 1982.

Nanba Kōji. *Uchiteshi yamamu taiheiyō sensō to kōkoku no gijutsushatachi.* Kōdansha, 1998.

National Diet Library, Tokyo. Selected material.

Newman, Joseph. *Goodbye Japan.* New York: L.B. Fischer, 1942.

NHK. *Rekishi e no shōtai, shōwahen.* Vol. 23. NHK, 1982.

Nihon no Firipin Senryōki ni kansuru Shiryō Chōsa Fōramu, eds. *Nihon no Firipin senryō: Intabyū kiroku.* Ryūkei shoten, 1994.

Nishioka Kaori. *Hōdōsensen kara mita "Nicchū sensō."* Fuyō shobō, 1999.

Noguchi Yukio. *1940 nen taisei: Saraba senji keizai.* Tokyo keizai shinposha, 1995.

Norgren, Christiana. "Abortion before Birth Control: The Politics of Reproduction in Postwar Japan." PhD dissertation, Columbia University, 1998.

Nornes, Mark. *Japanese Documentary Film: The Meiji Era through Hiroshima.* Minneapolis: University of Minnesota Press, 2003.

Nornes, Mark, and Yukio Fukushima, eds. *Media Wars Then and Now: Yamagata International Documentary Film Festival 1991*. Sōjinsha, 1991.

Nornes, Mark, and Yukio Fukushima, eds. *The Japan/America Film Wars*. Chur, Switzerland: Harwood Academic Publishers, 1994.

Nosaka Sanzō. *Nosaka Sanzō senshū (senjihen)*. Nihon kyōsantō chūōiinkai shuppanbu, 1962.

Ogawa Chikagorō. *Ryūkōka to sesō*. Nihon keisatsu shinbunsha, 1941.

Ogino Fujio, ed. *Gaiji geppō (fukkokuban) kaisetsu*. Vol I. Fuji shuppan, 1994.

———, ed. *Tokkō keisatsu kankei shiryō kaisetsu*. Fuji shuppan, 1995.

———, ed. *Tokkō keisatsu kankei shiryō shūsei*. Vols. 19, 20. Fuji shuppan, 1993.

———, ed. *Tokkō keisatsu kankei shiryō shūsei*. Vol. 30. Fuji shuppan, 1994.

Ohnuki-Thierney, Emiko. *Kamikaze, Cherry Blossoms and Nationalisms*. Chicago, IL: University of Chicago Press, 2002.

Ōoka Shōhei. *Taken Captive: A Japanese POW's Story*. Translated by Wayne P. Lammers. New York: John Wiley & Sons, 1996.

Okamoto, Rei. "Pictorial Propaganda in Japanese Comic Art, 1941–1945: Images of the Self and the Other in Newspaper Strips, Single-panel Cartoons, and Cartoon Leaflets." PhD dissertation, Temple University, 1999.

Okamoto, Shumpei. *Impressions of the Front: Woodcuts of the Sino-Japanese War, 1894–95*. Philadelphia: Philadelphia Museum of Art, 1983.

Osaka Mainichi Company. *Japan Today and Tomorrow: America and Japan in Amity and Trade*. Osaka, 1938.

Ōtani Tadashi. *Kindai nihon no taigai senden*. Kenbun shuppan, 1994.

———. "'Shinbun sōjū' kara 'taigai senden' e: Meiji taishō no gaimushō tai chūgoku senden katsudō no hensa." *Mediashi kenkyū* 5 (November 1996): 71–97.

Ōtani Tadashi and Hara Keiichi. *Nisshin sensō no shakaishi: [Bunmei sensō] to minshū*. Osaka: Fōramu, 1994.

Ouchi Takeo. "Kanminzoku to senden." *Senbu geppō* (September 1943).

Ōwarai hyakkajiten, Shōwa 12nen–20nen senran no naka no warai. CD. King Records, 1999.

Ozaki Shirō. *Bungaku butai*. Shinchōsha, 1939.

———. "Nihon no PK Butai (1)." *Kaizō* (May 1953): 214–219.

Ōzarasha Publishing Company, ed. *Senjika hyōgoshu*. Ōzarasha, 2000.

Paxton, Robert O. *Vichy France: Old Guard and New Order, 1940–1944*. New York: Knopf, 1972.

Purdy, Roger. "The Ears and Voice of the Nation: The Domei News Agency and Japan's News Network, 1936–1945." PhD dissertation, University of California, 1987.

Rentscheler, Eric. *The Ministry of Illusion: Nazi Cinema and Its Afterlife*. Cambridge, MA: Harvard University Press, 1996.

Robertson, Jennifer Ellen. *Takarazuka: Sexual Politics and Popular Culture in Modern Japan*. Berkeley: University of California Press, 1998.

Rosenfeld, David M. *Unhappy Soldier: Hino Ashihei and Japanese World War II Literature*. Lanham, MD: Lexington Books, 2002.

Rossingnol, Dominique. *Histoire de la propagande en France de 1940 a 1944.* Paris: Presses Universitaires de France, 1991.

Rousso, Henry. *Le Syndrome de Vichy: 1944–1985.* Paris: Seuil, 1987.

Rubin, Jay. *Injurious to Public Morals.* Seattle: University of Washington Press, 1984.

Ryū Ketsu. *Kankan saiban.* Chūkō shinsho, 2000.

Sakai Torakichi. *Marē senki.* Asahi shinbusha, 1942.

Sakuramoto Tomio. *Bunkajintachi no daitōa sensō PK butai ga yuku.* Aoki shoten, 1993.

Samuels, Richard J. *"Rich Nation, Strong Army": National Security and Ideology in Japan's Technological Transformation.* Ithaca, NY: Cornell University Press, 1994.

Sano, Peter. *One Thousand Days in Siberia: The Odyssey of a Japanese-American POW.* Lincoln: University of Nebraska, 1997.

Sanyūteikinba. "Hokushi kenbutsu." *Kingu* (September 1937).

Satō Masaharu. "Senjika nihon no senden kenkyū." *Mediashi kenkyū* (1996): 98–114.

Satō Masaharu and Barak Kushner. "'Negro Propaganda Operations': Japan's Short-wave Radio Broadcasts for World War II Black Americans." *Historical Journal of Film, Radio and Television* 19, 1 (1999): 5–26.

Satō Tadao. "Kusa no ne no gunkokushugi." In Aoki Tamotsu, et al., eds., *Sensō to guntai.* Vol. 10, *Kindai nihon bunkaron.* Iwanami shoten, 1999.

Satō Takumi, "The System of Total War and the Discursive Space of the Thought War," In Yasushi Yamanouchi, et al., eds, *Total War and "Modernization."* Ithaca, NY: Cornell University Press, 1998.

Sawada Shinnojō. *Sugata naki tatakai.* Kibundo shobō, 1944.

Sawada Takaharu. *Warai o tsukuru: Kamigata geinō warai no hōsōshi.* Nihon hōsō-shuppan kyōkai, 2002.

Schrijvers, Peter. *The GI War Against Japan: American Soldiers in Asia and the Pacific during World War II.* New York: Palgrave Macmillan, 2002.

Selden, Mark. *China in Revolution: The Yenan Way Revisited.* Armonk, NY: M.E. Sharpe, 1995.

Senji kōtsūhen. *Nihon kokuyū tetsudōhan nihon rikuun shiryō.* Vol. 3, *Nihon rikuun jūnenshi.* Tsukiji shokan, 1993.

Sensō no omote to ura. CD. Teichiku Company, 1995.

Senzen no jōhō kikō yōran. Vol. 20. Reprinted in the *Genron tōsei bunken shiryō shūsei.* Nihon tosho sentā, 1992.

Service, John. "The Situation in China and Suggestions Regarding American Policy." In Joseph W. Esherick, ed. *Lost Chance in China: The World War II Despatches of John S. Service.* New York: Random House, 1974.

Shi Gang. *Shokuminchi shihai to nihongo (zōhoban).* Sangensha, 2003.

Shakai Mondai Shiryō Kenkyūkai, ed. *Shina jihen ni okeru shinagun no bōryaku senden bunsho.* Tōyōbunkasha, 1977.

Shibusawa Hideo. *Kōgun imon.* Tōhō shoten, 1944.

Shibuya Shigemitsu. *Showa kōkoku shōgenshi.* Senden kaigi, 1978.

Shigeta Tadayasu. *Fūzoku keisatsu no riron to jissai.* Nankōsha, 1934.

Shillony, Ben-Ami. *Politics and Culture in Wartime Japan*. Oxford: Clarendon Press, 1981.

Shimada Atsushi and Tsuganesawa Toshihiro, eds. *Puresuaruto*. Kashiwa shobō, 1996.

Shimazaki Akemi. *Senbuhan*. No publisher, 1940.

Shimizu Katsuyoshi, ed. *Shōwa senzenki nihon no kōshū eiseishi*. Fuji shuppan, 1991.

Shimokawa Koshi. *Showa seisōshi*. Daisanshokan, 1992.

Shina Hakengun Hōdōbu, ed. *Shidan*. Shanghai: Taihei shuppan, 1943.

Shisō geppō. Selected articles.

Shisō junpō. Selected articles.

Shūhō. Selected articles.

Shūkan asahi. Selected articles.

Shuppan keisatsuhō. Selected articles.

Shulte-Sasse, Linda. *Entertaining the Third Reich: Illusions of Wholeness in Nazi Cinema*. Durham, NC: Duke University Press, 1996.

Sledge, E. B. *With the Old Breed at Peleliu and Okinawa*. Annapolis, MD: Naval Institute Press, 1996.

Smedley, Agnes. *China Fights Back: An American Woman with the Eighth Route Army*. New York: The Vanguard Press, 1938.

Snow, Edgar. *Red Star over China*. New York: Random House, 1938.

Stites, Richard. *Russian Popular Culture: Entertainment and Society since 1900*. New York: Cambridge University Press, 1992.

Storry, Richard. *The Double Patriots: A Study of Japanese Nationalism*. London: Chatto and Windus, 1957.

Suzuki Yūko. *Feminizumu to sensō*. Marujusha, 1987.

Swinton, Elizabeth de Sabato. *In Battle's Light: Woodblock Prints of Japan's Early Modern Wars*. Worcester, MA: Worcester Art Musuem, 1991.

Tabi. Selected graphics.

Tagawa Seiichi. *Sensō no gurafizumu kaisō no [FRONT]*. Heibonsha, 1988.

———. "Taigai sendenshi [Front] no kiroku." In Tagawa Seiichi, Imaizumi Takeji, and Okada Kazuo, eds. *FRONT (Fukkokuban) Kaisetsu I*. Heibonsha, 1990.

Tagawa Seiichi, Imaizumi Takeji, and Okada Kazuo, eds. *FRONT (Fukkokuban) Kaisetsu II*. Heibonsha, 1990.

Taikaikai naimushōshi henshū iinkai, ed. *Naimushōshi*. 4 volumes. Taikaikai, 1971.

Taiwan. Ministry of Justice, Bureau of Investigation Archives, Taipei, Taiwan. Selected documents.

Taiseiyokusankai, ed. *Taiseiyokusankai jissen yōkō no kihon kaisetsu*. Taiseiyokusankai sendenbu, 1941.

Taiseiyokusankai Chōsakai. *Yokusan seijikai shiryō: Kokumin seikatsu kankei*. Taiseiyokusankai, 1943.

Takada Kazuo. *Biruma minzoku kaihōroku*. Shinshōsetsusha, 1944.

Takami Jun. *Takami Jun nikki*. 8 volumes. Keisō shobō, 1965.

Takagi Noritsune and Fukuda Kizō. "Nihon fashizumu keiseiki no masu media tōsei (2)." *Shisō* (November 1961): 80–97.

Takahashi Genichi. "Kōtō senden o jūshi seyo." *Senbu geppō* (December 1940): 2–7.

Takaoka Yasunori. "Haisenchokugo no bunka jōkyō to bunka undō." In Akazawa Shirō, Awaya Kentarō, and Yoshida Yutaka, eds., *Gendaishi to minshushugi*. Azumashuppan, 1996.

Takenouchi Shizuo, ed. *Dai niki gendai manga*. Vol. 11. Chikuma shobō, 1970.

Takasaki Ryūji. *Pen to sensō*. Seikō shobō, 1976.

———. *Senjika no jānārizumu*. Shin nihon shuppansha, 1987.

———. *Zasshi media no sensō sekinin*. Daisan bunmeisha, 1995.

Takeyama Akiko. "Media ibento toshiteno nyūsu eiga." In Tsuganesawa Toshihiro and Ariyama Teruo, eds., *Senjiki nihon no media ibento*. Sekai shisōsha, 1998.

———. *Sensō to hōsō*. Shakai shisōsha, 1994.

Tamamatsu Wakana. *Wakana Ichirō kessaku manzaishū*. Kinreisha, 1940.

Tan Luo Fei. *Kangzhan shiqi de Guo Moruo*. Chengdu: Sichuan daxue chubanshe, 1985.

Tanaka, Toshiyuki. *Hidden Horrors: Japanese War Crimes in World War II*. Boulder, CO: Westview Press, 1996.

Tanimoto Shigeki. "Posutā no kōkateki sakusei to sono riyō." *Senbu geppō* (October 1942): 41–49.

Taylor, Philip M. *British Propaganda in the 20th Century: Selling Democracy*. Edinburgh: Edinburgh University Press, 1999.

Teruoka Yoshitō. "Jikyoku to yūmoa." *Hōsō* (December 1938): 19–21.

Tipton, Elise. *The Japanese Police State: The Tokkō in Interwar Japan*. Honolulu: University of Hawai'i Press, 1990.

Tokkō geppō. Selected articles.

Tokyo Daikūshū Sensaishi Henshūiinkai, eds. *Tokyo daikūshū sensaishi, daigokan*. Vol. 5. Tokyo kūshū o kirokusuru kai, 1974.

Tokyo Shisei Chōsakai Shisei Senmon Toshokan, Tokyo, Japan (Tokyo Institute for Municipal Research Special Library).

Tomioka Taeko. *Manzai sakusha Akita Minoru*. Chikuma shobō, 1986.

Tonoshita Tatsuya. "Ongaku ni yoru kokumin kyōka dōin." *Ritsumeikan daigaku jinbun kagaku kenkyū kiyō* 73 (February 1999): 81–104.

Toshi mondai. Selected articles.

Towle, Philip, Margaret Kosuge, and Yoichi Kibata. *Japanese Prisoners of War*. New York: Hambledon and London, 2000.

Tozaki Tetsu, et al. "Sensō to rekōdo." *Rekōdo bunka* (October 1943).

Tsuganesawa Toshihiro. "'Puresuaruto' ni miru senjiki dezainā no kenkyū (jō)." *Nikkei kōkoku kenkyūjōhō* 189 (Feb/March 2000): 2–6.

Tsuganesawa Toshihiro and Ariyama Teruo, eds. *Senjiki nihon no media ibento*. Sekai shisōsha, 1998.

Tsuganesawa Toshihiro and Satō Takumi, eds. *Naikaku jōhōbu jōhōsenden kenkyūshiryō, dai 8 kan*. Vol. 8. Kashiwa shobō, 1994.

Tsuneishi Shigetsugu. *Shinri sakusen no kaisō*. Tosen shuppan, 1978.

Tsurumi Yūsuke. "Dainihon no kōryū ni tsuite kokumin ni utau." *Kingu* (March 1938).

———. "Taibei kankō senden dashin." *Kokusai kankō* (October 1939): 20–23.

Uchida Kazuyuki, "Jūkei kokumin seifu no kōnichi seiji senden seisaku to nihonjin hansen undō." *Chūgoku kenkyū geppō* (October 1998): 1–16.

Uchida Kazuyuki and Mizutani Naoko. "Jūkei kokumin seifu to nihonjin horyo seisaku." In Fujiwara Akira and Himeta Mitsuyoshi, eds., *Chūgoku ni okeru nihonjin no hansen katsudō*. Aoki shoten, 1999.

Uchikawa Yoshimi, ed. *Gendaishi shiryō*. Vol. 40, *Masu media tōsei*, 1. Misuzu shobō, 1973.

———, ed. *Gendaishi shiryō*. Vol. 41, *Masu media tōsei*, 2. Misuzu shobō, 1975.

Uchikawa Yoshimi and Kōuchi Saburō. "Nihon fashizumu keiseiki no masu media tōsei (1)." *Shisō* (July 1961): 23–40.

United States Strategic Bombing Survey. *The Effects of Strategic Bombing on Japanese Morale*. Washington DC: Government Printing Office, 1947.

United States National Archives II, College Park, Maryland. Selected files.

United States State Department. Confidential US State Department Central Files (microfilm). Selected files.

Valliant, Robert B. "The Selling of Japan: Japanese Manipulation of Western Opinion, 1900–1905." *Monumenta Nipponica* 29, no. 4 (1974): 415–438.

Wakakuwa Midori. *Sensō ga tsukuru joseizō*. Chikuma shobō, 1995.

Waseda kōkokugaku kenkyū. Selected articles.

Watanabe Shoichi and Kobayashi Yoshinori. *Aikoku tairon*. PHP Kenkyūjo, 2002.

Watt, Lori. "When Empire Comes Home: Repatriation in Postwar Japan, 1945–1958." PhD dissertation, Columbia University, 2002.

Weisenfeld, Gennifer. "Touring Japan-as-Museum: *Nippon* and Other Japanese Imperialist Travelogues." *Positions* 8, 3 (2000): 747–793.

Welch, David. *Propaganda and the German Cinema, 1933–1945*. Revised edition. New York: St. Martin's Press, 2001.

———. *The Third Reich: Politics and Propaganda*. New York: Routledge, 1993.

Wenhuan gongyingshe. *Kangzhan jianguo shouce*. 1940. Microfilm reproduced by the Center for Chinese Research Materials, Washington, DC.

Whiting, Robert. *Tokyo Underworld*. New York: Vintage, 2000.

Williams, Frederick Vincent. *Behind the News in China*. New York: Nelson Hughes Company, 1938.

Wu, Odoric. "Communist Sources for Localizing the Study of the Sino-Japanese War." In David Barrett and Larry Shyu, eds., *Chinese Collaboration with Japan, 1932–1945: The Limits of Accommodation*. Stanford: Stanford University Press, 2001.

Xiao Xiaoqin and Zhong Xingjin, eds. *Kangri zhanzheng wenhuashi (1937–1945)*. Beijing: Zhonggong dangshi chubanshe, 1992.

Yamachi Yukio. *Kokumin goraku engei dokuhon*. Asahi shobō, 1942.

Yamagiwa Akira. "Beisenji jōhōkyoku (OWI) no [Enan hōkoku]." *Kokusai seikei ronshū* (March 2000): 1–19.

Yamaguchi Takeshi. *Aishū no manshū eiga*. Santen shobō, 2000.

Yamamoto Akira. "Senji senden bira no ideorogī (1)." *Tenbō* (January 1978): 88–103.

————. "Senji senden bira no ideorogī (2)." *Tenbō* (February 1978): 108–123.

Yamamoto Hirofumi, ed., *Technological Innovation and the Development of Transportation in Japan*. United Nations University Press, 1993.

Yamamoto Taketoshi. *Nihonhei horyo wa nani o shabetta ka*. Bungei shunjū, 2001.

Yamana Ayao. "Futatabi nihon senden gijutsuka kyōkaikumiai no igi o nobete kakui no sanka kyōryoku o motome to kuni shidōteki jōsō shokei ni uttau." *Senden* (January 1942): 94–96.

————. *Taikenteki dezainshi*. Dawiddosha, 1976.

Yamana Ayao, Imaizumi Takeji, and Arai Seiichirō, eds. *Sensō to senden gijutsusha: Hōdō gijutsu kenkyūkai no kiroku*. Dawiddosha, 1978.

Yamashita Keitarō. *Nakiwarai gojūnen (Yanagiya Kingorō no denki)*. Ōzorasha, 1998.

Yanagita Kunio "Berurin Tōkyō orinpikku mahi." *Shisō no kagaku* (September, 1964).

Yasui Sankichi. "Kōnichi sensō jiki kaihōku ni okeru nihonjin no hansen undō." *Chikaki ni arite* (March 1983): 37–48.

Yazawa Kan. *Sensō to ryūkōka*. Shakaishisōsha, 1995.

Yershov, Peter. *Comedy in the Soviet Theater*. New York: Praeger, 1956.

Yokohama Kaikō Shiryōkan, Yokohama, Japan. Selected archives.

Yokomizo Mitsuteru. *Showashi henrin*. Keizai ōraisha, 1974.

Yoneda Karl. *Amerika jōhō heishi no nikki*. PMC, 1989.

Yoneyama Keizō. *Shisō tōsō to senden*. Meguro shoten, 1943.

Yoshida Saburō. "Bunkasen no kiso." *Tōabunkaken* (July 1942): 6–18.

Yoshida Yutaka and Yoshimi Yoshiaki, eds. *Shiryō nihon gendaishi 10, Nicchū sensōki no kokumin sōdō 1*. Ōtsuki shoten, 1984.

Yoshihisa Tak Matsusaka. *The Making of Japanese Manchuria, 1904–1932*. Cambridge, MA : Harvard University Asia Center, 2001.

Yoshimi Shunya, ed. *Senkyūhyaku sanjūnendai no media to shintai*. Seikyūsha, 2002.

————, ed. *Iwanami kōza kindai nihon no bunkashi 6, kakudai suru modanati*. Iwanami shoten, 2002.

Yoshimi Yoshiaki. *Comfort Women: Sexual Slavery in the Japanese Military during World War II*. Translated by Suzanne O'Brien. New York: Columbia University Press, 2000.

————. *Kusa no ne no fashizumu*. Tokyo daigaku shuppankai, 1986.

Yoshimoto Shashi Hensan. *Yoshimoto hachijūnen no ayumi*. Osaka: Yoshimoto kōgyō kabushiki kaisha, 1992.

Young, Louise. *Japan's Total Empire: Manchuria and the Culture of Wartime Imperialism*. Berkeley: University of California Press, 1998.

Yui Daizaburō and Kosuge Nobuko. *Rengōkoku horyo gyakutai to sensō sekinin, Iwanami Bookuletto #321*. Iwanami Shoten, 1993.

Yui Masanomi. "Joron: Sōdōin taisei no kakuritsu to hōkai." In Kano Masanao and Yui Masanomi, eds., *Kindai nihon no tōgō to teikō*, Vol. 4. Nihon hyōronsha, 1982.

Index

About the Author

Barak Kushner received his PhD from Princeton University. He taught Japanese and Chinese history in the Department of History at Davidson College in North Carolina. Currently, he lives and works in Washington DC.